Growing Toward Peace

The sun is peace
and the heart is love.
Together it is beautiful
like a flower.

—Art and poem
by Justin Kauffmann, age 9

Growing Toward Peace

Stories from teachers and parents
about real children learning to live peacefully

Kathryn Aschliman

Coordinating Editor

HERALD PRESS
Scottdale, Pennsylvania
Waterloo, Ontario

Library of Congress Cataloging-in-Publication Data
Growing toward peace : stories from teachers and parents about real children
learning to live peacefully / [edited by] Kathryn Aschliman.
   p.   cm.
   Includes bibliographical references.
   ISBN 0-8361-3602-0
   1. Peace of mind in children—Religious aspects—Christianity. 2. Peace of
mind in children. 3. Peace of mind in children—Case studies. 4. Children—
Religious life. 5. Learning, Psychology of.
   I. Aschliman, Kathryn.
   BV4908.5.G76   1993
   241'.697—dc20   93-18505
                                                                                                            CIP

The paper used in this publication is recycled and meets the minimum re-
quirements of American National Standard for Information Sciences—
Permanence of Paper for Printed Library Materials, ANSI Z39.48-1984.

Scripture is quoted by permission of the publishers, with all rights reserved:
KJV, *Holy Bible, King James Version; The Inspired Letters,* by Frank C. Laubach,
Nelson; LB, *The Living Bible* © 1971, owned by assignment by Illinois Regional
Bank N.A. (as trustee), Tyndale House Publishers, Inc.; NASB, *The New
American Standard Bible,* © The Lockman Foundation 1960, 1962, 1963, 1968,
1971, 1972, 1973, 1975; NEB, *The New English Bible,* © The Delegates of the
Oxford University Press and the Syndics of the Cambridge University Press
1961, 1970; NIV, *Holy Bible, New International Version®,* copyright © 1973, 1978,
1984 by International Bible Society, Zondervan Publishing House; NRSV,
New Revised Standard Version Bible, copyright 1989 by the Division of Christian
Education of the National Council of the Churches of Christ in the USA; TEV,
Good News Bible—Old Testament copyright © American Bible Society 1967,
New Testament copyright © American Bible Society 1966, 1971, 1976.

GROWING TOWARD PEACE
Copyright © 1993 by Herald Press, Scottdale, Pa. 15683
   Published simultaneously in Canada by Herald Press,
   Waterloo, Ont. N2L 6H7. All rights reserved
Library of Congress Catalog Number: 93-18505
International Standard Book Number: 0-8361-3602-0
Printed in the United States of America
Book design by Gwen M. Stamm/Cover art by Justin Kauffmann

02 01 00 99 98 97 96 95 94 93 10 9 8 7 6 5 4 3 2 1

To Dr. Mary Royer,
who for almost half a century
in her elementary education courses at Goshen College
and her relationships with students,
helped many persons
share the gospel of peace
with children
throughout the world

Contents

Foreword

THE PURSE-SNATCHER is in prison. He could be sentenced up to seven years, according to the latest news, but Eileen Egan, almost 80, says she has forgiven him and is attempting to help him turn his life around. Miss Egan, a friend and biographer of Mother Teresa, says, "I feel compassion for all people who live by violence or act in violence. . . . For me, people who hurt others are the most tragic."

How did this woman get to be that way? Where did she learn peace? How did Mother Teresa become a healer of bodies and souls? How can our children turn away from violence and become peaceful members of society, active reconcilers?

The good news is that peace can be learned. The first step is peace with God. Without personal inner peace, nobody will go far in peacemaking; the vertical comes before the horizontal— which is not to say that peacemaking by unbelievers is of no value. It is.

Once we are reconciled to God, our learning of peacemaking begins. Paul wrote to the Corinthians, "All this is from God, who reconciled us to himself through Christ, and has given us the ministry of reconciliation" (2 Cor. 5:18, NRSV). The Lorraine Avenue Mennonite church in Wichita, Kansas, offers such training in a School for Peace, an annual event for the past fifteen years. Learning takes place in The Lion and the Lamb Peace Arts Center at Bluffton (Ohio) College, dedicated to exploring and teaching nonviolence and conflict resolution to children from preschool through high school. Learning happened in India when Mennonite Central Committee sponsored schoolchildren to participate with stories, poems, pictures, and songs in celebrating the International Year of Peace (1986), as reflected in the book *My Vision.*

Then there is Mary Royer, who inspired her students at Goshen (Ind.) College to be peacemakers. Now eighty-five, she has the joy of seeing how some of them have taken her words, example, and inspiration to all parts of the world. That's what this book is all about—stories gathered by the editor, Kathryn Aschliman, from Mary's former students wherever they happen to be today.

From strife-ridden Ireland, one writes, "I think so often of the spirit in which Mary Royer taught her classes, and I wish she were here." Seeds were sown in that Goshen classroom, and they sprouted and grew. Now these former students have themselves become sowers of the seeds of peace in homes and schools, in businesses and many professions, in word and in deed.

Library shelves are filled with books about children, and even in our modest private library we have at least 100 books on peace. But where are the books that bring together these two components, children and peace, in one volume? There are a few, but not enough. Here is a volume to help fill that gap.

Peace must begin with the children if we are going to make significant headway in creating a more peaceful world. We received in the mail a beautiful display of ten of the most famous swords ever made. We wish we could say that the caption of this attractively repulsive poster were not true: "For over 2,000 years the destiny of the world was determined by the sword." To turn that around, we simply must help our children grow toward peace.

And it can be done. The beginning is in the home. If the home atmosphere is peaceful and warm and loving, if there is forgiveness and encouragement, children will learn peace by osmosis. They will absorb it with their Wheaties.

On November 11 our thirteen-year-old granddaughter,

Deborah Scott, was in a class where the teacher asked his students to write a poem entitled "Veterans." Aware of the school's patriotic stance (with Desert Storm enthusiastically applauded), she nevertheless had the courage to write this poem:

War is a horrible, gory thing,
Full of blood and hate.
And those who have survived it
Have all been changed to date.

For often they saw no glory,
Instead, a mangled friend,
Or a dying person beg for help,
Then no longer suffer—'twas the end.

Those who have survived a war,
And been in these conditions,
Are called heroic veterans—
They've been in stressful positions.

I respect their own decisions
Of whether to fight or not;
And even though I don't agree,
They are entitled to their thought.

Some who have come out of war,
Have had a change of heart;
After seeing those dire tragedies
They vow no more in war take part.

Still others think that war is needed,
And that's just fine with me;
I just don't see how it could be
That killing makes us free.

The bottom line is really quite simple:
I don't believe in war and fight—
But I still honor those brave veterans
For doing what they believed was right.

When children are encouraged to be peacemakers in home and church, they want action, not long lectures. They want handles, some concrete project for them to start doing something for peace—like the tips found all through this book.

Yet there is a thin line that parents and teachers must recognize between peacemaking as a method and peacemaking as a motive. We instill in children's sensitive hearts and minds the hope for a better and more peaceful tomorrow, and we encourage them to dream of a world without violence. At the same time, we need to take care not to step over that thin line and give them the impression that universal peace can be attained quickly or by human action alone. That could be tragically disappointing.

Success stories, such as abound in this book, have their place. Yet the truth must also be told: many peace efforts go unrewarded. In the end there is the cross. We have a sure hope of resurrection and of God's new heaven and new earth, in which death will be no more. Now on the way of peace, there often is suffering, but with God's grace to keep going.

It is crucial that children understand the difference between method and motive. When nonviolence is merely one of many methods of resolving conflict, if it doesn't work, it will be rejected in favor of a different method. When, however, nonviolence is a motive, a deep conviction that peace is the will of God, that Jesus Christ taught and lived the way of peace, and that his followers must also be peaceful—then the soil is prepared for costly discipleship.

The joy and reward of peacemakers is to know that we are blessed and that we are sons and daughters of God (Matt. 5:9).

—*Peter and Elfrieda Dyck*

Preface

A CHILDREN'S choir sang earnestly:

> Let there be peace on earth,
> And let it begin with me.

How do children grow toward peace—that wholeness, harmony, justice, well-being, and hope through faith in Jesus Christ? Peace can "begin with me" as each one is empowered by God's Spirit to live the good news of the Prince of Peace.

The essence of peace is love. From the moment of conception, we begin to grow in our understanding of peace which is rooted in love. As we experience love, we respond with love, and that brings peace within and between others near at hand and far away. Children grow toward peace as they live with persons who reflect the love of Christ.

Helping children grow toward peace requires much prayer, wisdom, and patience. This book records examples of peace development gathered from Professor Mary Royer's Goshen College elementary education alumni scattered across the United States and around the world. These accounts come from homes, schools both public and private, and church communities in rural and urban settings. Nine chapters by Goshen College alumni incorporate anecdotes like pieces of a patchwork quilt, whose beauty stems from pieced-together, personalized materials. To emphasize the developmental nature of growth toward peace, we identify the child's age or grade in each story.

Parents will find support in this book for assisting children in the primary laboratory for peace development, the home and family setting. Teachers in Sunday school, church school, and public school will find stimulation and encouragement throughout this volume to facilitate growth toward peace in their classroom settings. Other adults interested in peace and children will want to join in finding ways children can be nurtured in their peace development.

Peace on earth is continual growth within each individual toward the wholeness fully attained upon joining the Prince of Peace in eternity. In the meantime, we keep growing toward peace through his power and presence.

—Kathryn Aschliman
Professor of Education
Goshen College

Inner Personal Relations

PEACE in the world begins with peace in individual persons. Everlasting peace comes through acquaintance with the Prince of Peace. Children grow toward peace as they live with persons who practice and interpret the spirit of Christ. If we want to help children develop inner peace, we need to use much prayer, wisdom, and time. Children grow toward peace as they are in contact with nurturing, attentive, friendly adults in responsive, caregiving relationships.

PEACE

Peace is a calm feeling inside,
Like a light touch of a paintbrush
Or a gurgling stream flowing on its
course to the sea.

Peace is a quiet countryside
Where there are no blaring radios
No cars with honking horns,
Just you and the big sky.

—*Tim Shenk, age 10*

1. Where Is Peace Born?

Rhoda Trost Derstine

GROWING toward peace begins in the family circle. The family is a special place to celebrate the tenderness, triumphs, challenges, and pain of a shared life. Many precious firsts occur there—first smile, first step, first word. These moments bond members together in delight and struggle.

In the family, a child needs to feel cherished as a person regardless of performance or competence. We can never provide the "perfect" family life for our children. Yet we can put a conscious priority on enabling growth in the love, understanding, and respect which constitute peace living.

As a mother of three, I find my greatest challenge. Christina, Adam, and Nathan offer me daily motivation to seek peaceful, life-giving ways within myself, with them, and with our surrounding community. As an educator and Sunday school teacher, I am committed to structure environments and guide children's interactions to grow in respect for self and others.

A mother of young children found a simple way of sharing her love with two children at the same time.

> When nursing our second-born daughter, I got into the habit of reading a book to our firstborn, avoiding a lot of tears and obnoxious behavior brought on by jealousy. Years later our firstborn

wrote to me saying she was using the same technique with her
two sons.
—*Marian Brendle Hostetler, Kalona, Iowa. Ages 1 month and 19 months*

How Does Jesus' Life Show Us
How to Treat Our Children?

We remember the respect and love Jesus had for children as we
consider shaping their attitudes and personalities. Jesus' respect and compassion for people of all ages are basic to peace
living and are the standards for our interactions with children.
As we care for our children with an understanding of their perspectives and needs, we strive to do unto them as we would like
them to do unto others.

Because of the small bedrooms in our apartment, Leah and Jessica needed to sleep in the same bed. For many nights there was
crying, fighting, and laughing an hour or more after they had
been put to bed. Two-year-old Jessica seemed to be the one the
most stimulated by the situation. Rocking her to sleep before putting her in bed would have been a good solution, but I had a ten-
month-old baby who also needed my attention at that time, and
my husband was not home at the children's bedtime. Instead, I
started putting Jessica to bed in our bedroom and then carrying
her to her bed after she went to sleep. From then on the girls went
to sleep peacefully.
—*Elizabeth Miller Broaddus, Terre Haute, Indiana. Ages 2 and 5*

Who can provide respect and compassion when parents
need to find substitute care for their young children? Carefully
screened home daycare can provide warmth, attention to individual schedules, and interaction with relatively few other children and adults in a familiar home setting.

As a caregiver for several young children, I try to be open and
honest about where parents are going and when they can be expected to return to make the separation from parent as bearable
as possible. I speak about parents as often as there is an occasion
throughout the day, exclaiming about the snowy-white diapers

Mommy sent, whose parents sent the apples or sand or Christmas wreath or whatever.

To show I respect the children as individuals, I let them know that I believe they are capable of choosing something to do (or not to do if they prefer watching or resting).

To check my effectiveness in meeting the needs of the children, I watch for that look of concentration and contentment exhibited by children at peace with themselves and their surroundings.

—*Lenora Dietzel Sempira, Goshen, Indiana. Age 3 and under*

A significant part of the adult responsibility in preparing children to be peacemakers is to nurture their love for Jesus.

Jesus knew that young children were not old enough to understand many of the words he spoke; so he gave them what they could understand and what they needed most of all—his love. He took them in his arms and loved them. Jesus' love, sympathy, help, and forgiveness become increasingly real to children as they experience these Christlike qualities in their parents' relationships with each other and with them.

At home and in Sunday school, Phyllis heard the beautiful stories of Jesus which stirred her heart with the warmth of his love. Jesus was so real to her that she spoke often of him. One day while playing with Bobby, who had no Christian teaching, Phyllis said, "Jesus loves you."

Bobby replied, "But I don't like him."

"Well," said Phyllis, "that doesn't matter. He loves you anyway."

As you read stories of Jesus reverently, prayerfully, and joyously, children will feel that Jesus loves them as dearly as he loved the people in the Bible stories. The way you read the stories affects children's attitudes toward Jesus. They can feel that Jesus is really important to you, and will eagerly respond to the loving Friend of their parents.[1]

The purpose of early Bible story books is to give children impressions of Jesus as a dear and loving friend. Bible story books adapted for two- to four-year-olds,[2] three- to five-year-olds,[3] four- to nine-year-olds,[4] and nine-year-olds and up[5]—these all carry the good news story of peace.

How Does the World Look Through Children's Eyes?

For children to be at peace, they must feel accepted and adequate. Adults must view the world from the perspective of children to know how to nourish positive feelings.

Childhood is a time when fantasy and reality are difficult to separate. Young children believe their thoughts can actually become reality. As far as a child is concerned, the scary creature seen on television really could be in the closet.

It is important to understand the reality of children's fears. Children feel what they feel, not what they *ought* to feel, and these feelings are translated into action—jumping, sobbing, withdrawing, or giggling. Children need the patient responses of understanding adults to avoid being overwhelmed by the intensity and immediacy of their own feelings.

Kenneth had never gone to Sunday school or visited away from home. In this one-room school, he had two older sisters, one in grade four and one in grade six. The family originally lived in Kentucky. He was extremely timid, always keeping his arm over his eyes. I knew Kenneth would never learn to read if he didn't look. He did enjoy music and heartily joined in the singing, his eyes still covered. I praised him for his singing, touched him, and showed him I loved him.

One day after about five weeks, I saw him peeping out under his arm during reading class. James, the other boy in the first grade class, couldn't read what was on the chart. Suddenly Kenneth read the story loudly and correctly. The whole school smiled and exclaimed at how good it was. From then on he was an eager learner.

I had Kenneth again in my fourth-grade class. He was well adjusted and the star in a children's operetta.

—*Minnie Sutter, Kouts, Indiana. Grade 1*

We always encouraged our children to be aware of their feelings and verbally express them. "Tell me in words" was repeated over and over. These quotes of our son show his awareness of his feelings from thirty-one months to five and one-half years of age.

Thirty-one months: When we mentioned that the babysitter was coming that evening, Jeff said, "I might cry."

Three years, seven months: "When I get fussy again, I'll read these books."

Four and one-half years: "I'm worried what would happen if you and Daddy got hurt."

Five and one-half years: "Mommy, I have a secret." Three minutes later, "It's a bad secret." Three minutes later, "Do you want to know my secret? I almost got hit by a car coming home from kindergarten." Jeff wore a cap with a face mask that day due to the cold weather and crossed at Eighth Street with some friends rather than coming and crossing alone at Ninth Street. He explained that the driver put on his brakes, making a loud noise, but didn't hit him.

After exposing his secret, Jeff cried for five minutes. Five hours later as we passed the hospital, he said, "I'm sure glad I'm not there."

Five and one-half years: Jeff and a friend were having differences of opinions. Jeff came home from kindergarten very angry. After walking in the door, he announced he was going to go to the friend's house and talk about it. He did, alone. When he came back, he felt much better.

—*Ruthann Brilhart Peachey, Goshen, Indiana*
Ages 31 months to 5 1/2 years

Children have a budding sense of justice which is keenly aware of fair play. Initially this may be primarily self-protective, but it can expand to include friends and eventually enemies, too. I am often inspired to see children resolve conflicts in their own way and quickly continue the activity at hand. A child's forgiveness is genuine. The offense is forgotten, and no grudge is borne.

Two children, a brother and sister, were visiting in our home one summer. While their parents were packing suitcases preparing to leave, the brother teased his sister, and she began to cry. I decided the incident probably occurred because they needed something to do while they were waiting, so I proceeded to "make peace" by comforting the little girl, and then I invited them both to sit down, one on each side of me, while I read a story.

I read *The Elephant Who Couldn't Forget*[6] to them. I wasn't sure they grasped the full meaning of Grandma Elephant's comment that "some things aren't worth remembering." However, they en-

joyed the story and empathized with Baby Elephant when his brother threw mud over him. After we talked about the story and how we all have times when we need to forget and go ahead with important things, I told these two children they could have the book and take it home with them. Later their mother wrote a note thanking me. Her comment was, "And what a good story it is!"
—*Margaret Kauffman Sutter, Mount Prospect, Illinois. Ages 2 and 6*

What Are Children Like?

Children's perceptions are simple, yet in the midst of a complex and often violent world. This sets the stage for the joys and dilemmas of growing toward peace.

Children are a bundle of paradoxes. They are at once delightful and frustrating, forgiving and ruthless, honest and scheming, meticulous and careless, amazing and alarming, tender and merciless, creative and destructive.

Young children approach life from their hearts first. They absorb love from our smiles, hugs, and eager affirmation. They absorb attitudes from our responses and decisions. They begin understanding in the intuitive, emotional realm.

When our daughter was in second grade, the psychologist tested her. He later reported to us one of the questions he asked her: "If you had one wish, what would it be?" Her answer: "That all the weeds would be flowers!" I have thought of that many times. Was she thinking of her father's constant battle against weeds in his garden? Or was she thinking of it in terms of good and evil? Probably she meant it literally. Whatever her thinking, it was an unusually unselfish wish for a young child.
—*Twila Hostetler Nafziger, Wadsworth, Ohio. Age 8*

When our nine-year-old son received a new ball glove in his birthday month, he came home from town and excitedly called up the steps, "Mom, look what I got to catch your kisses!"
—*Frederick E. Meyer, Rittman, Ohio. Age 9*

The world of children is bounded by the five senses. Time is one-dimensional—the present. Children have no time clock to punch, no reason to hurry the activity of the moment. Patience and future goals, such as things that will happen "in a minute" or "next week," are difficult for them to understand.

Two-year-old Jessica could not wait for her turn, as reported from before the days of mandatory car seats:

> In our everyday family life, I try to be aware of any problems that occur regularly and then discover some way to eliminate the problem.
>
> For example, when I took the children for a ride in the car, I had been letting our two oldest children, Nathan and Leah, take turns sitting in the front seat. Before long, two-year-old Jessica noticed what was going on and asked to sit in the front. I agreed and let her take turns with her brother and sister.
>
> However, I soon learned that Jessica did not understand about taking turns, and a fight developed every time we got in the car. The change that worked for us was to go back to having Nathan, Leah, and Jessica sit in the back seat. Now they seem satisfied that everything is fair; we can get into the car without tension.
> —*Elizabeth Miller Broaddus, Terre Haute, Indiana. Ages 2, 5, and 7*

Children's acute observational powers make them particularly sensitive to contradictions between word and deed. They trust actions rather than words. If I complain about having to go to someone's house, then exclaim upon arrival how glad I am to be there, my daughter is sure to ask me what I really mean.

Being observant, children are also aware of differences and will usually mention them. This can be awkward if the difference concerns a specific personal characteristic such as someone's nose. These differences usually have no value judgment attached to them until children see older friends and adults evaluating and criticizing. A big or long nose is neither bad nor good.

An accepting attitude is certainly a childlike virtue to be encouraged in situations where feelings of vulnerability run high.

> First grade offered Becky, our adopted Korean daughter, the challenges most first graders have, plus a few more. One evening I announced that it was time to cut her bangs. I had been announcing that for several weeks, but Becky always had some reason why her hair shouldn't be cut right then. On this particular evening, I

insisted, and when I was finishing the trimming Becky quietly said, "Now they'll really call me 'Chinese Eyes.' "

Becky's comment took me by surprise, and my first impulse was to find out who was doing the name-calling and see to it that it happened no more. But deep inside I knew that was the wrong approach. Instead, I had to think of a way to help Becky realize that even though her eyes were different from those of anyone in school, her eyes were still beautiful and shouldn't be hidden with bangs.

So I lifted her off the step stool where she had been sitting to get her hair cut, and we went to the big mirror in the living room. We looked at our eyes, and I asked her what she noticed. She noticed mine were blue and hers were brown. And then she noticed they were shaped differently. She was surprised when I told her the children in China had eyes like hers. As we continued to look, I asked how our eyes were the same, and she guessed it—we could both see. I explained that some children had probably never heard of Korea, and so they thought she had Chinese eyes.

I may have oversimplified Becky's problem, but she left for school a happy girl the next morning with no ill feeling toward the name callers because they "probably didn't understand." Anyway, she had beautiful eyes, too, like the children in faraway China.

—*Marjorie Yoder Waybill, Scottdale, Pennsylvania. Age 6*

Young children are literalists and expect every word to be accurate. The *Amelia Bedelia* books[7] are useful for discovering the multiple meanings of many words and phrases. Many children echo Amelia Bedelia's exasperated cry, "Why did she get so upset? I just did what she said." I recall telling my three-year-old Christina to keep her eyes peeled for a person we were to meet. She sincerely wondered if peeling her eyeballs would improve her vision.

In the 1960's, before desegregation, our eleven- and nine-year-olds found the two buildings which said Men and Women. Each one had a door marked "White" and a door marked "Colored." They thought they would see some of the new, colored bathroom fixtures. When they came out, Alta asked Greg, "Was yours colored?"

"No," he said, "mine was white like usual."

"So was mine," said Alta, still puzzled.
—*Winifred Erb Paul, Myrtle Beach, North Carolina. Ages 11 and 9*

Children's responses create what to an adult might be humorous situations but also reveal the earnestness with which they are trying to make sense out of the adult world.

> Our three-year-old foster son had been told that his other mother and father, whom he didn't remember, were Spanish, and so he was Spanish. He had experienced playing with Hispanic children at migrant camps. One day he asked me, "Mom, are you Spanish or are you ticklish?"
> —*Neva Miller Beck, Archbold, Ohio. Age 3*

How Does a Healthy Self-Concept Within a Child Lay the Foundation for Growth Toward Peace?

Self-concept is the way the child thinks about self. It is a collage of images and feelings which are being formed by relationships with people and interactions with the environment.

> We adopted Nate when he was six years old. He was born in Vietnam; his mother was Vietnamese-French, and his father was an American serviceman. Nate came over to America at age four and was legally adopted by a family, but was put up for adoption again as the family was unable to make the necessary adjustment.
> When Nate was fourteen and in junior high, we received glowing reports from his teachers at conference time. I was amazed at Nate's ability to transcend his early years of disruption and rejection. In sharing the good reports with Nate, I asked him, "Nate, what makes you such a good kid?" He responded without hesitation, "Because I have good parents." It was an unexpected reply as well as humbling.
> Later I was confiding with my friend Lucy, "I am so aware of my many mistakes as a parent. I do not know what I offered that enabled Nate to take root and grow."
> Lucy responded, "Oh, I can think of lots of things you did that helped Nate know that he is loved. Like the time you painted freckles on Baby Jesus that were just like Nate's freckles."
> I had purchased a large Christmas nativity set at an after-

Christmas sale and then set it aside to paint later. That fall after the children were again enrolled in school, I dug out the box containing the nativity set and began my project by selecting one of the characters. My first choice was Baby Jesus.

The baby Jesus was exquisitely formed by the sculptor who designed the mold, and I thought of Nate, also a beautiful child designed by the greatest Creator and Artist of all eternity. I thought about Nate's freckles, placed on his nose and cheeks in such an artistic design, with that one freckle placed so delicately upon his left upper lip. I had often teased Nate, saying that I was sure an angel did the final touching up on him, putting those freckles in just the right spots with a paint brush.

It was only natural that our Baby Jesus would have freckles (Jewish or not) in just the same spots as Nate. Our Baby Jesus has one special freckle on his upper left lip, and that makes him unique to our family just as Nate is unique and special.

—*Marian L. Kauffman Miller, Manson, Iowa. Age 9*

For the child, self-concept functions as a road map providing internal guidance for responses and decisions. When children have healthy, positive self-concepts, there will be a greater potential for sensitivity and compassion for self and others at the traffic jams and roadblocks of conflicts. They have greater potential for accepting differences and for being willing to risk for the sake of others.

In our son Jeremy's kindergarten was Jake, who had suffered severe burns on his scalp a year or two before. Most of the left side of his head was red and bald. The handsome blond hair covering the remainder of Jake's scalp could simply not hide the repulsive scar.

Many of the children avoided playing with Jake, though he was less self-conscious than an older child would be with a similar disfiguration. One day Jake overheard one girl say to another, "Don't play with him. He's ugly!"

At this point Jeremy intervened. "Don't talk like that. It hurts people's feelings."

Having delivered the rebuke, Jeremy took it upon himself to befriend Jake for the rest of the day.

—*Donna Yordy Grove, Tampa, Florida. Kindergarten*

Individuals with healthy self-concepts are likely to perceive other people in positive ways. Such perspective lays the foundation for peace.

A positive self-concept facilitates the learning process and is essential to becoming a person who loves and cares. This loving and caring attitude is an important link in the chain of peaceful behavior. Through this process, one teaches children to grow toward peace. This was my philosophical premise when I first began my work with children as a teacher and/or a father. Dr. Mary Royer, along with my own parents, planted the seeds for this approach to teaching.

One of my fourth-grade students had a real struggle being herself. Her brother was in the fourth grade the year before. He was an outstanding student academically, socially, and in almost all aspects. He was the teacher's dream. The sister was not the ideal student her brother was. Even though she tried, she could not satisfy the teachers like her brother did.

Regardless who the individual may be, there are things which can be recognized positively. This little girl's handwriting was quite good—much better than her brother's; so I began giving her positive comments on her papers about her nice handwriting. This led to other recognitions. During a parent-teacher conference, her mother indicated that no time in her daughter's school life did teachers give this girl positive strokes such as her brother often received.

Stroke by stroke and day by day, the girl began to develop inner peace and an attitude of love. Over a period of time, a noticeable change developed in her behavior. She eventually transmitted love and inner peace to others. Through positive interaction with me and her peers within the classroom, these qualities were strengthened, expanded, and continued to grow.

As this girl's self-image improved through receiving positive recognition, the love inside of her began to emerge. If there was danger of ridicule, she would retreat within her closed self. Only when the climate was safe would she risk exposing her inner qualities. It requires ample time to nurture this type of growth.
—*N. Emerson Miller, Wooster, Ohio. Grade 4*

Self-concept provides a frame of reference for a child's behavior and response to the world around. Out of each child's concept of self, the child judges whether to tackle a new skill area or find an excuse to avoid it, whether to befriend the new kid or join in the taunts. The consequences of these adventures, the success or failure in accomplishment, the approval or disapproval of peers and adults—these and many other factors will further shape self-concept.

> "I'm not good at anything."
> "I don't understand."
> "I give up. I'll never learn the multiplication tables."
> Statements such as these from a group of thirty-six sixth graders during my student teaching semester made me search for ways to spark a feeling of self-worth in each individual student. This was especially important as twelve of these youngsters had already repeated a grade and looked upon themselves as failures.
> After discussing how each person is different and that everyone is good at something, I wrote a short description of each child, pointing out some unique aspect he or she possessed. The day I read these to the normally restless, talkative class, not a sound could be heard. They strained their ears to hear something good being said about them.
> "When we are running relay races, whom do we want on our team? Why, Steve, of course. He can outrun a rabbit."
> "When we fall down and scratch a knee, Susan is the one always there helping us up and comforting us in our pain. A great nurse she could become."
> In the days that followed, the children asked to hear these words again and again. To learn to love, a child must feel loved and worthwhile.
> —*Robert Duane Lehman, Goshen, Indiana. Ages 11 and 12*

Actually, there is more than one self-concept operating within a child. Which one dominates depends on the immediate situation or role the child is in. The same child can be daughter, sister, friend, oldest, or first in line. Each of these roles brings out a differing quality which colors the self-image. Given the immediate role and situation, the self-image of the moment could be capable, unloving, kind, responsible, or self-conscious, and this affects behavior.

What Fosters a Positive, Healthy Self-Concept?

It is widely accepted that there is rapid and significant development of self-concept in the first months and years of life. Certain basic self-understandings are formed earliest and lie closest to the center of the personality. Research shows that these are most resistant to change. Right from the beginning, each child needs a warm, responsive climate where basic material needs for food, shelter, and clothing are met in order to thrive physically and emotionally.

As newborns, babies quickly know whether their messages are being heard. They develop notions of who they are in response to the behavior of significant adults around them. "If I coo or cry and someone responds, I must be worthwhile."

Loving, consistent care builds trust and fosters hope in the world around. "What begins as hope in the individual infant is in its mature form faith, a sense of superior certainty not essentially dependent on evidence or reason."[8] These initial months of being at others' mercy for survival greatly influence a child's developing feelings of security and worth.

Parents convey acceptance by stroking, cuddling, and holding little ones. Even as children grow older, physical contact remains a significant way to communicate caring.

> On a summer day, Erik, our three-year-old neighbor, accidentally locked himself in and his mother out of the house. As his mother drove off to get help, I heard Erik crying. I went over to be near him. As I talked to him through the screen door, he began to calm down.
>
> Several days later he knocked at my back door, saying, "Come sit with me." So I went with him to the front steps of his home where I had sat talking to him through the screen door until his mother returned with his dad.
>
> There were other times we sat together. I used these opportunities to read Bible stories to him. My husband and I gave him Bible story books for birthday and Christmas gifts.
> —*Loretta Zehr Simmons, Elkhart, Indiana. Age 3*

> Tuong was a little Vietnamese boy who came to my room in the childcare center just as he was turning three years old. His cousin,

in the older room, said they were "boat people." Tuong was as frightened as any child I've ever seen. For at least one week, he cried constantly, all day long. Everything was new to him—the language, the food, the teachers, the children, and the routines. We first tried to establish a sense of trust by holding him, hugging him, rocking him, and continually talking to him.

When he trusted us, then we could begin teaching him with a lot of love. We taught him to do little things at first—go to the bathroom by himself, sit through a circle time on his own mat, eat just one bite of food. . . .

As time passed, Tuong responded beautifully. He smiled, he laughed, he said words, he ate all the food on his tray, he ran and played with the other children, he hugged us back, and he brought things from home that he was proud of.

Tuong was a new little boy. He belonged, he felt accepted, he felt important, and most of all he felt loved.

—*Linda Harshbarger Heiser, Goshen, Indiana. Age 3*

Since children operate from the heart, they are tuned into touch, voice tones, and attitudes of caregivers. These things are internalized. Long before their language can accurately define such relationships, feelings about self and other people have developed. As children mature, they need to learn that people care for them and that they are still lovable even if their needs are not immediately met.

During the month of September, my nursery school staff and I center our curriculum around self and feelings. We assure the children from day one that each of them is very special and is a friend of ours.

In the first week of school, the children enjoy playing a game which involves a construction paper house taped to a mirror. Each child takes a turn peeking into the mirror house but keeps what he or she saw a secret. After everyone has had a turn, we ask the question, "What special person did you see in the house (mirror)?" The secret is told.

Singing songs, reading books and poems, and doing art projects about self and one's feelings help to reinforce the idea that each child is a special person whom we are delighted to have as a nursery school friend.

—*Sarah Roth Smucker, Lusby, Maryland. Ages 3 and 4*

When our sons were eight and ten years of age, Kelly, an eight-year-old hearing-impaired foster son, came to live with us. Kelly was developmentally delayed and needed to practice many basic social skills.

Our children were active participants in the decision to invite Kelly to live with us, but our youngest son experienced a difficult period of adjustment. One evening, as everyone was ready to say good-night, he pulled me down to his bed and asked, "When there are three children to love, do you love each of them less than when there are only two children?" I assured him that I still loved him as much as I always had, and together we would learn to love Kelly.

Kelly is now sixteen years of age. Our family has experienced the growth of love one for another.

—Marie Kanagy Stevanus, Amarillo, Texas. Age 8

A caring, respectful home atmosphere is foundational to developing security and nurturing peaceful attitudes in children. We cannot control all the events of our children's lives, but we can seek to create a positive balance on the ledger sheet of upbuilding experiences which will nourish an acceptance and esteem of self.

Cheryl was in my transitional first-grade class, having had kindergarten twice but still not being ready to concentrate on first-grade work. She would come to school pouting and stay that way until about 10:00 a.m. I finally found out she was mad at her mother, who she thought loved only the baby. I explained that the baby was helpless, but Cheryl could do things to help mother and the baby.

I had Cheryl's mother come in for a conference. She told me Cheryl was an illegitimate child. They had lived with Cheryl's grandmother, who showered lots of attention upon Cheryl. Cheryl's mother later married and had her own home and a second child. She didn't realize Cheryl was feeling "unloved" since the baby came.

Cheryl's mother resolved to give Cheryl more time and love. She also permitted her to do things for the baby and herself. She made special efforts to give her praise and encouragement.

Almost immediately one could see Cheryl's self-esteem raised in school. She became cheerful and interested in school work.

The school had assumed it would take three years for the children in this class to complete the first two years of work. But by the end of the second year, Cheryl was placed in an advanced third grade. (This was before we had the government title programs and special education teachers.) I found that with kindness and understanding, children can make progress in any classroom.
—*Minnie Sutter, South Bend, Indiana. Age 7*

How Does Self-Esteem Relate to Self-Concept?

Self-esteem is dependent on the perception children have of themselves. For example, if I perceive myself as friendly, behave in a friendly way and have good friends, I am affirmed.

In my third-grade classroom, one would find a bulletin board that is a little unusual. Each child's name appears on the board, with a little hook beneath it. To the left of the bulletin board is mounted a potpourri of laminated construction paper keys. Each key bears a goal statement, such as "I will work well with others" or "I will write everything in cursive."

Students place the keys of their choice under their names before school each day. We often discuss choice of goals—hoping that children will learn realistic goal-setting and honest evaluation. They work toward completion of their goals. The keys are available at all times, so students can encourage each other with their goals. Before leaving in the afternoon, the students tell me if they feel they have reached their goals.
—*Nancy Ryan Nussbaum, Kayenta, Arizona. Grade 3*

When a child's self-concept is frequently challenged, it must be defended or modified. As in Nancy's class process, a realistic self-perception can open up choices for growth and further development. This can also cause fluctuation in self-esteem. Self-esteem is not acquired once and for all. It is something that must be continually nurtured. A teacher shared an example of how he nurtured self-esteem in his classroom.

Darla was a tall, ten-year-old girl. Her biological background was Spanish. She had dark hair and dark olive skin. She was intelligent and able. Her academic progress was excellent. She was quite sensitive, emotional, and at times self-deprecating. One day she was very upset. Someone had derided her, calling her a "nigger." Counseling with her, I pointed out her qualities, her abilities, attractiveness, and her parents' love for her. Then I asked her, "Who has the problem, you or your accusers?" She had thought she had the problem, but now she began to see that the problem really belonged to those who were deriding her.

—*Ivan I. Miller, Elkhart, Indiana. Grade 4*

Parents, teachers and other significant adults have an important role in assessing how children are evaluating themselves in light of the challenges, accomplishments, and emotional factors of their lives, and in providing opportunities to build confidence.

Cedric could hardly wait for me to finish the Bible story; his mind was already racing ahead to the next activity—playing out the story. He could identify with the characters and play the speaking parts without self-consciousness.

Once after we had acted out the story, Cedric noticed that the quiet boys played only passive or subtle roles. "Arne and Orlin aren't very good at acting out the story," he observed.

"You are really good at playing out the story," I told him. "But Arne and Orlin are really good at listening so they know the story very well."

"I'm kind of good at both." This came from Scott, who was looking at me for agreement.

"Yes, you are," I nodded. "You and Clark are quite good at both listening to the story and playing it out."

As the bell signaled the end of the class, each of the five boys left feeling pleased with himself, yet respecting the other's uniqueness.

—*Kathryn Gregory Yoder, Surrey, North Dakota. Ages 4 and 5*

Victims of low self-esteem are likely to respond negatively to others in similar life situations, to belittle someone lower in the pecking order to bolster their own morale. Feeling insecure can prevent them from showing tolerance of others in need. With guidance, however, these areas of insufficiency can become bonds to others. With thoughtful interpretation, weakness becomes strength as it leads to greater empathetic understanding.

> Because of being behind in mastery of skills, Gary bolstered his ego kicks by clowning. Fortunately, he did have a sense of humor.
> One morning when he asked for a turn to role play with the classroom puppet, I said, "Gary, I want to give you a turn. I know you can do a good job. However, I'm afraid you'll goof off and cause a commotion, and that makes me uncomfortable."
> He looked surprised, and so did the other children. They weren't often asked to consider their teacher's feelings.
> He said, "Really?"
> "Yes, really. That's the way it is with me."
> "Okay. I'll be serious and do a good job."
> And he did.
>
> —*Thelma Miller Groff, Goshen, Indiana. Grade 4*

While success is important, failure can be a useful part of the learning process, too. A child's self-correcting skills need to develop. We do children no service when we point out all their mistakes or try to prevent them. Confidence develops as children learn to experience failure, accept and evaluate it, and compensate for error in the next attempt.

Book characters can become vicarious friends to help children identify with circumstances and emotions of failure. These new "friendships" help children gain valuable insights to sharpen their own self-understanding.

> I used *Kelly's Creek*[9] with my third-grade son, Chris. He has reading disabilities because of minimal brain dysfunction and feels keenly the slighting comments of peers.
> The story concerns nine-year-old Kelly O'Brien, who can't ride a bike, catch a football, or even write his own name because of a learning disability. His parents and teacher think he is not trying, and the pupils at school laugh at him. Philip, a marine biology student, discovers how much Kelly knows about the fascinating creatures in the tidal marsh, and he helps Kelly take an important step in conquering his problems.
> Chris' reaction to the book was wonderful! The evening I began to read it, I was only going to cover one chapter. Chris asked for more, and I eventually read the entire book. Afterward we dis-

cussed the story, and Chris said, "I guess you *can* have learning disabilities and still make it." Needless to say, that book will be under our tree at Christmas!

—*Cheryl Morin Stratton, Goshen, Indiana. Grade 3*

To respect and accept other people, children must first esteem themselves and believe they are capable, worthwhile people who are loved. To become peacemakers, they must first be at peace with themselves.

In my forty years in the public school system, the last few years were in the home-instruction program. My home-teaching experience brought me into nearly two hundred different homes, observing many kinds of home situations.

Larry was fourteen years old, on drugs, and suspended from school because he was uncontrollable. I shall never forget the first home visit. Mother came to the door. Larry was standing farther back in the living room. He looked me over critically. I was scared; Larry was scared, and, I think, a bit angry. He hated school, and now school was coming to him. We sat at the kitchen table. I never mentioned school. Larry's dog was with him, so we talked about his dog and other pets in general.

Home instruction required each teacher to spend one hour a day with each student. When I arrived the next morning, I was surprised and pleased to see that Larry had his pencil and paper with him at the kitchen table. I hadn't asked him to have any materials ready. I'm not sure why he projected himself even that much unless it was because the day before he didn't hear the teacher yell at him. I'm sure that happened at home and at school quite often.

I told Larry I had brought a set of books about the experiences of a race car driver. He was eager to see the books and leafed through one. Taking turns, we read the first chapter. I did my best to make Larry feel like a worthwhile person. In fact, wherever possible I recognized and praised him. I told him I was glad he thought of having a pencil and paper ready. He appeared surprised at any such statements, for he seldom heard anyone offer him much encouragement.

Larry worked hard the three months I was with him. He began to show an interest in passing the competency test, a required exam for graduating from eighth grade. I left homework, and he regularly had every detail worked out. I always told him that he was making good progress. Larry began to set goals for himself. He began to think that, after all, he was worth something.

One Friday Larry said, "Mrs. Schrock, when you leave, I'm going with my family to Hemet for the weekend."

I said, "If you plan to be gone, I won't assign any homework. You won't have time to work on it. Just have a good time."

Larry said, "Yes, Mrs. Schrock, I'll have time for my homework. I'll do it."

I made the assignment, thinking by Monday morning the lessons would be unfinished. Monday morning came, the homework was finished, and again I could praise Larry for a job well done. He was so pleased with himself.

Larry passed the competency test with some modifications. The school gave me a "social diploma" for Larry. I stopped at the dime store, bought a frame for the diploma, had it gift wrapped, and gave the framed diploma to Larry the last day we were together. He was thrilled; he just beamed. He had completed the year; this was a milestone.

In a home-teaching situation, one develops a close relationship with the student. I tried to keep in touch afterward with as many students as I could. I especially wanted to be in contact with Larry. I learned through the school that Larry, with his family, moved to Hemet, but I was unable to learn his address.

I shall always remember Larry and pray that he has found the Source of Strength for his troubled life. I certainly hope I was able to bring him a sense of peace and a sense of being an important person.

—*A. Joy Hooley Schrock, Ontario, California. Age 14*

How Does Self-discipline Build Self-Esteem?

Grown-ups foster growth in self-esteem and self-trust by allowing children to do things by themselves. We are preparing our children for independence and interdependence, to be able to make responsible life-shaping decisions. It takes practice to become responsible.

Children should be trusted to do things for themselves even before they are capable of doing so consistently. Because taking initiative may be risky and self-esteem may be in jeopardy, it is important to assure children of our faith in them as they try. For the adult, this implies the patience to wait. Anything worth doing will take time to learn. Children desire to be useful, to be contributors.

> Eight-year-old Jeff was an average, quiet student who was getting lost in the shuffle. One day I asked the class what time the sun came up in the morning. No one knew. So I asked Jeff if he could look in the newspaper where it is recorded.
>
> The next morning Jeff brought the clipping of sunrise and sunset times. He started a chart to record each day's times, watching the progression. Jeff rarely forgot to bring in the newspaper clipping. Each morning he came to school with a purpose. He felt he had a unique contribution to make.
>
> *—Bob Keener, Goshen, Indiana. Age 8*

Becoming competent and capable requires self-discipline. In providing structure and encouraging self-discipline, we are models of authority for our children. Parents are the first image of God's authority children have. To guide in the spirit of Jesus is to serve and protect, allowing steady progress toward greater responsibility and freedom to choose.

> Children can't make their own rules, and no child is happy without them. The great need of the young is for authority that protects them against the consequences of their own primitive passions and their lack of experience, that provides them with guides for everyday behavior, and that builds some solid ground they can stand on for the future. . . . This is authority that protects the young. It is not the kind that people battle and resent. Children can get mad for the moment, but that doesn't weigh heavily against the security of protection. It is rather sad that the word authority more often than not brings to people an association of something unpleasant, something to be escaped or outgrown. . . . No one knows better than children how much they need the authority that protects, that sets the outer limits of behavior with known and prescribed consequences.[10]

The loving exercise of authority and the gentle guidance of discipline—these free children from the inner turmoil of shouldering responsibilities and making decisions beyond their capabilities. They let children be children.

Discipline is providing direction, a framework within which children can develop and mature. Offering limits initiates movement toward self-discipline. In nurturing healthy self-concepts in children, it often seems like a fine line to distinguish between needed limits and structure, and freedom to make decisions and try ideas.

Extremes in either direction, overindulgence or overcontrol, represent dangers. Overcontrolled children may become mistrustful of themselves and fearful of reaching out and exploring their environment. Overindulged children may become dependent children who never get quite enough to be satisfied.

What Does Behavior Reveal About Self-Understanding?

Before offering guidance, it is important to listen to what is implied and acted out as well as what is said. This requires real sensitivity. Children's behavior may be viewed as language. "It's a way children have of telling what's on their mind, what is important, and what is bothering them."[11] Learning to understand this language may mean overlooking overt actions to see the motivating forces.

Especially with negative behavior, it is helpful to remember that some self-understanding is perhaps being acted out. We should respond to the self-understanding as well as to the behavior. When one child knocks down another child's block house, the offending behavior is inappropriate and must be discouraged.

But what is the message? How is the offending child perceiving the world and self? Does this child want to interact but merely lacks social skills? Is self-esteem so low that any attention, even negative, is desired? Or could it be a frustrated response to failure? Peaceful reconciliation in such a situation requires respect for the feelings of both parties and offers a real opportunity to model consideration of the needs of others. A climate of acceptance encourages the children to understand each other.

Because of an argument in the car between my five and one-half-year-old daughter and her five-year-old friend, the friend decided my daughter could not attend her birthday party, which was to be in four days. My daughter had earlier been invited. She retaliated by saying she didn't want to come to her friend's old party.

Arriving at the friend's house, the two were not communicating, only pouting. I told them both they would have to make a decision about the party since they would not be seeing each other before it. The friend walked to her house, turned around, and said, "I guess I'll let her come." My daughter replied, "I might, and I might not." I made no comment.

Later that afternoon while playing with her Bristle Blocks, my daughter announced, "I'll go to Mary's party." They had a great time together at the party. I gave them each the opportunity to make a decision and to let them work it out themselves.

—*Sarah Roth Smucker, Lusby, Maryland. Age 5 to 5 1/2*

It is useful to discriminate between limits that offer security and limits that say "you're not capable" or "I don't trust you." To perceive themselves as capable, children must have the flexibility to make decisions and act independently. Limits provide the necessary models and parameters for this exploration.

In the 1700 block of Frances Avenue, we had twenty-one children from ages one month to thirteen years old. This was not counting the high school and college-age people. There were three households with older people and two empty houses. Sometimes children from other blocks and friends of children came to our area. Therefore, we had a high concentration of young children. To add to this, there were about fifteen dogs, cats and rabbits, not to mention the litter of kittens born last spring.

We decided we needed to make a few rules. Our yard and most other neighbors' yards were small. We shared a driveway which seemed to be a good meeting place or thoroughfare for Big Wheels and bikes. Overall, the children related well, but conflict did arise and adult attention was needed. However, our yard and neighbors' yards were not respected as private property. Children would walk through the yard, litter, and play on the jungle gym and in the sandbox anytime of the day. Since our privacy was being invaded, we said that children needed to ask Bob or me to play in our backyard. In addition to the limits we set, we also wanted to see other adults involved with the children in a positive way.

About the same time we made this rule, I was teaching a course on *Parenting for Peace and Justice*.[12] Through this class we thought of several activities to do. At our weekly family meeting, we made a Shalom Box. One of the ideas was to have an organized Summertime Fun activity with the neighborhood children each week for about one and one-half to two hours.

Each family was to plan two Summertime Fun occasions. If the date assigned did not suit, the family was responsible for exchanging with someone else. In case of rain, another day was chosen. At least two or three adults were involved with the activities. It was a time when children and adults could interact and have fun. A simple snack was served. We worked with the children on cleaning up paper after the snacks so yards were not littered. The children looked forward to these times together and were excited when the Funtime was at their house.

Some of the activities included parades with decorated bikes and Big Wheels and music instruments, birthday parties, a field trip to McDonald's restaurant, a picnic at the park, swimming, and scavenger and treasure hunts. On other days, we painted ceramic magnetic Snoopys, watched the magic of microwave cupcakes, made sundaes, decorated bottles with tissue paper, made macaroni bracelets and necklaces, and made and decorated gingerbread cookies.

The activities generated positive feelings and goodwill among the children and adults in the neighborhood. This helped the children feel positive about the limits that were set, and they respected them.

One of the highlights of this project was to see the excitement of a foster boy (who was initially shy and would not talk) as he delivered a note and said, "Funtime is at my house tonight." Then he bounded off to deliver the other notes.

—*Mary L. Yoder Birkey, Elkhart, Indiana. Intergenerational*

In providing direction, and especially in setting limits and consequences, parents serve their children significantly by being consistent. Being pragmatists, children will try to find a way to get what they want. Sometimes this means playing Mom and Dad off against each other. Giving in to these situations is not a gain of affection, but a loss of security. For children, witnessing parental unity is a security comparable to knowing all four walls of the house are intact.

In the parent-child relationship, respect makes possible the transmission of values. Respect is built when children know they are cherished not just for who they are becoming and what they can do, but simply because they are. The basic meaning of love is experienced by the littlest one in *The Way Mothers Are.*[13] We speak of children being gifts to us rather than being our possessions, and this frees us to participate in their developmental process without seeking to control it.

> I have seen too many students nervous or cheating because they were working for grades to meet mother's and father's approval. I want to encourage my children to do their best, knowing that anyone can have problems. My children are to work for self-improvement, not grades. Their self-worth is more important than my role as a proud parent.
> —*Ardyth Hostetler Steckly, Houston, Texas. Ages 8 to 10*

Genuine parental acceptance leaves the door open for adolescents to consider and evaluate their parents' value system.

> Who starts a fight? Is it the person who taunts another? Is it the person who hits first? Or is it the person who hits back? We taught our children that a fight began when they hit back. We taught them to consider the alternatives available to them. When someone began to chase them, they had options other than to run. We consistently challenged them to talk with the aggressor, to try to resolve the conflict.
> On one occasion, two years of taunting, chasing, and petty stealing were finally ended when the aggressor said, "Let's shake hands and be friends." When our oldest son reached out his hand, the other boy punched him. Our son said, "I'd like to be your friend," thus ending the continual harassment. While they did not develop a close friendship, they did hold mutual respect for each other.
> —*Marie Kanagy Stevanus, Amarillo, Texas. Ages 8 to 10*

Children will not be locked into a rebellious pattern as they assert their own personhood and individuality if they have experienced acceptance by their parents. It is easier to consider the values of someone whom you respect and whom you know respects you. Children move from showing respect because it is required, to offering respect because of the valuable relationship.

Parents need support to create an affirming atmosphere for a child's development. Because of the delights and demands, child rearing lends itself to the extended family. For many children, this extension may not be a biological family, but church or support group "family," including teachers.

> Our daughter, Glenna, taught school at the army base in Savannah, Georgia. . . . She has often told of her almost daily consultations with Dr. Royer during her undergraduate practice teaching while at Goshen. We marvel at the interest Dr. Royer had in all her students and the time it must have taken. We wish there were some effective way we could convey to her the marvelous influence and personality change she unselfishly wrought in our shy, timid little teacher. . . . Eloise (my wife of 37 years and the loving mother of our three) and I are fortunate to have been deeply touched by the serenity and grace of Dr. Royer. We attribute what success we may claim in nurturing our children to her perceptive influence. We wish she could see our grandchildren. Much of what we hold dear we see developing in these wonderful souls, and we are so grateful.
> —*Gerald B. Miller, River Vale, New Jersey. College*

As we are surrounded by people with similar commitments and vision, we gain perspective, strength, and added abilities. The nurturing environment provides children with a sense of belonging to something larger than their family and acts as a bridge to the world community.

What Communicates Affirmation to Children?

The simple presence of caring adults, available and ready to listen, conveys a sense of worthiness to children of all ages.

A quiet time is set aside once a week in my third-grade classroom for the students to write in journals which they may or may not wish to share. As trust is established, real gut feelings are expressed. I often do write responses to dilemmas if the journal has been laid on my desk.

—*Irma Ebersole Bowman, Akron, Pennsylvania. Grade 3*

All the students are in my room because of learning difficulties. I look for at least one good thing to compliment them on as they do their work. I also use some kind of physical contact, such as a pat on the head or shoulders. I make it a practice to greet all students by name every morning and tell them good-bye when they leave my room. . . . And I try to ask questions about any school or family activities they have earlier shared with me.

—*Faye Newcomer Litwiller, Wakarusa, Indiana*
Grades 1 to 5, Special Education

What is more significant to persons than their own names? Simply greeting children by name sends a clear message that they are noteworthy. Additional ways adults have made a conscious effort to recognize the importance of names follow.

I succeeded in finding books with the children's names in print. Some children had entire books written with their names; other names were found among the pages or as the author/illustrator's name. It took me about two months to find books for everyone. I had to find one child's name in an encyclopedia under rivers. All the searching was worth it to see the children carrying "their" books around. They did not hesitate to show exactly where their names were printed or to even "read" the books using their own interpretation.

—*Ann Klink Herendeen, Goshen, Indiana. Kindergarten*

In our class newspaper, each child's name was mentioned monthly in many cases. The children were so proud that they asked for extra copies to send to distant relatives.

—*Elsie Eash Sutter, Goshen, Indiana. Grade 4*

Following are some examples of how grown-ups have discovered personal ways to communicate affection and affirmation.

I have After-School Tea with each pupil during the first six weeks of school. During this hour together, the pupil has my full attention as we drink lemonade or chocolate milk. Many secrets are shared after I show them my family picture and talk about my personal likes and hobbies.

—*Elsie Eash Sutter, Goshen, Indiana. Grade 4*

Home visits are appropriate at various times: illness, absence from class, birthdays, shyness, a new brother or sister, the beginning of a new school or Sunday school year.

We establish a climate of mutual respect through visiting pupils in their homes. We can teach with a greater sense of purpose, and our words will be more relevant to the lives of our students. A teacher must be a friend first of all.

Through a home visit I understood why Sharon was so nervous and unsure of herself in class. She came from an unstable home in which family members shouted at her and each other. "All I wish is to help my mother and father live in peace," Sharon told me. "They are always fighting, and I get sick when they fight. There is no place to go where it is quiet."

There wasn't much I could do to correct the situation in the home, but at least I understood and could try to make Sunday school a pleasant and relaxing experience for her.[14]

—*Geraldine Gross Harder, Scottdale, Pennsylvania. Age 7*

Affirmation is a legitimate need we never outgrow and a message we need to keep hearing. It is a primary way parents and teachers encourage feelings of worth. One good idea is to develop a list of positive phrases ready to be used on short notice. Compare Edward Reichbach's two lists[15] as you develop your own:

Phrases That Encourage	Phrases That Discourage
You can do it.	You usually make
Don't worry. Do the best	mistakes.
you can.	I doubt if you can do it.
Thank you for helping.	That was good, but you
You are doing great.	messed up at the end.
You are doing much	I don't think you can
better.	finish that.

Keep trying.
That's hard, but you can
  do it.
Let's see if we can finish
  it together.
	Why didn't you think
	  before you started?
	How can you be so dumb?
	How can you be so
	  clumsy?
	That will never work.
	It's too hard. Let me do it
	  for you.

Five teachers of primary through fourth grades suggested variations on the idea of giving each student special recognition for one week. Children assumed special responsibilities as line leader, doorkeeper, or message-bearer to the office and other teachers, or assisted the teacher in similar ways by doing things for others.

Last year we instituted the Student of the Week. All the children in the room wrote positive statements about the selected student. These were placed on the bulletin board beside the child's name. Then the child took pictures of favorite friends and activities with the school Polaroid camera. These were put on the bulletin board also. The items were removed on Friday and placed in a scrapbook for the child to keep. A party was held in honor of the child.
—*Bonnie Sommers Ratzlaff and Vernon P. Ratzlaff,*
Tuba City, Arizona. Primary

In my classroom, we write the special person's name on the board, and classmates suggest adjectives for each letter of the person's first name, such as *J*oyful, *O*utstanding, *H*onest, *N*eat. This is then put on a large chart and placed at a special place in the room where all can see it. At the end of the week, a booklet is made for the child. Each class member makes a page with this at the top: "I wish for you. . . ." A picture is made to go with the wish. The first page is a copy of the name with the adjectives. This is stapled to the child's self-portrait (placed all year in the classroom) and serves as a reminder of the feelings the class has.
—*Ethel Henry Rush, Doylestown, Pennsylvania. Grade 2*

In my third-grade classroom I have a Student of the Week board. Each week, as close to their birthdays as possible, children display self-portraits and family pictures, hobbies, awards, or other items special to them. On a cardboard apple (covered with contact paper to wipe off easily), they write their favorite foods; on a cat they write their favorite pets; and on a book shape, they write their favorite book. They also write short paragraphs describing their families.

—*Ruthann Brilhart Peachey, Middlebury, Indiana. Grade 3*

My fourth-grade group contained a diversity of social classes, and there was a definite need to make each child aware, no matter the race or social class, that each was someone unique. To work at accomplishing this, I made a poster entitled YOU ARE SPECIAL with a slit at the bottom to insert a name of one of the students.

Being the special person entitled the student to be my special helper. The special person of the week also had an opportunity to tell about their family, hobbies, and favorite things, with pictures and examples as visual aids. Then the other children had the privilege of asking questions. The most common question was "What's your favorite. . . ?" I realized the children find a commonness in the sharing of favorites.

I feel all of them gained more of an understanding of their personal self-worth and the importance of respecting the uniqueness of others.

—*Geneva Hershberger, Hazard, Kentucky. Grade 4*

How Can Children Help Each Other Grow Toward Peace?

Children can encourage each other. In a competitive society, it is important to create and capitalize on occasions of cooperation among children. The ability to work well with others is a skill we need to emphasize at all ages. One way to facilitate this is to structure activities at home and school where children work together toward a goal.

In early spring the students in our intermediate school like to play softball during the recesses. Mary, in my class of sixth graders, had some physical and social problems. She was the only girl in the family and had only one brother, approximately six years older. She had not had the opportunity to participate in family games and sports as most of the rest of the class did. She was cross-eyed and poorly coordinated.

Many children made fun of Mary and did not want to have her on their team. She could not hit the ball. Some laughed at the way she held her bat. However, some of them sympathized with her and complained about those who belittled her.

One day the ball-playing problem became so serious that I had to take steps. Some complained openly about Mary making outs in the game and being a poor fielder. A few girls said that the boys were unfair because they had said Mary could no longer play.

Later, in the classroom, we had an open discussion. "Do you realize that Mary has had no opportunity to really play ball? She has no one to practice with at home. They have no close neighbors either. What do you think we should do about this? During recess, should Mary play some other games, and play with someone else?" (Pause; no answer.) "Is there someone in our class who can show her some things that would help her improve in playing ball? What should she change?" I asked. We waited a little while.

Finally, a boy who was well-liked and respected for his sportsmanship and ability said that he would like to show her how to hold her bat, how to use it, and how to stand. He was not a bold person but a good and respected player. Then others in the group suggested ways that any fielder might improve.

Approximately two weeks later, two of the girls excitedly came into the room after recess and told me how well Mary was playing. Everyone was so happy.

—*M. Irene Slaubaugh, Montgomery, Indiana. Ages 11 to 12*

Adequate instruction and practice are prerequisites to mastery. Children are eager to please, but they cannot do so unless the expectations are clear. If children do not know the rules of the game, they are bound to feel inferior. It is like that sinking feeling a child has when surveying the playground activities the first day at a new school.

Developing competence and experiencing success are powerful builders of self-confidence and self-esteem. It is hard to feel good about yourself if you do not know how to interact with others well.

The father of this family was out of work and drunk much of the time. The mother was a battered, lonely, frightened woman. The child in my classroom was the third son in this violent home. He too was battered, frightened, shy, without any contact with books or writing materials before entering school. Most of his first year of school was spent under the chair or on the floor.

At the beginning of second grade, he had a meager speaking vocabulary and almost no reading vocabulary. He was assigned to me along with about a dozen other low achievers. I sensed that he was not really low mentally, but educationally and socially deprived. He did not have the skill of making or being a friend among classmates. He carried the proverbial chip on his shoulder and was constantly getting into fights.

Besides giving him the educational help he needed, starting where he was, to give him confidence, I paired him with another boy. We created situations for them to work and play together in the classroom and on the playground. I spent as much time as possible reading to them and talking with them. I wanted them to share with each other and with me.

It took all year, but this boy became a loving and confident person, willing to accept, share, and express love. He was able to accept a physical touch on the shoulder without jumping when I touched him. The final expression was a story he wrote about a little mouse and his mother. He put it into book form (with my help) and illustrated it. I then had him read it on tape and play it for the class, showing the book page by page. He was so pleased! So were we all. He was a different person and had progressed so much in one school year.

—*Shirley Holaway Troyer, Elkhart, Indiana. Grade 2*

Older children reading to or instructing younger children provide occasions for the older children to receive affirmation of their competence and for the younger one to receive quality attention.

After seeing the film on Ezra Jack Keats, my student teacher, Ruth Weldy, said she would like to let our fourth-grade children try his style of marbelized painting demonstrated in the movie. We invited Laura Lamb's first graders to join us as they had also enjoyed the Keats movie. We grouped each fourth grader with one or two first graders, and each group chose two or three acrylic colors for their design. Working with the "big kids" was a special treat for the first graders. Thus a favorite author-illustrator helped our children learn to interrelate with respect across age lines.

—*Berdene Boshart, Goshen, Indiana. Grades 1 and 4*

Children can encourage each other to grow toward peace as they learn to express positive comments to others.

There are bound to be times when students seem to be getting on each other's nerves a little more than usual. As children get edgy, the caring atmosphere of the classroom tends to disintegrate! Often I have relied on this simple exercise to bind us back together in a positive and meaningful way:

I ask my students to form a circle with their chairs. I take a large ball of yarn and hold on to the end of the string. I then throw the ball to someone in the circle while holding the end of the string. (We are "bound" together by the string.) I share something I appreciate about the one who caught the ball. That person holds part of the string and throws the ball to someone else, affirming that person. This process continues until time or string run out; the compliments never run out!

At the end, there is a huge spider web to untangle and a cohesive group of smiling children who feel both loved and loving!

—*Nancy Ryan Nussbaum, Kayenta, Arizona*
Grade 3 through high school

How Do Psychological Understandings Fit into a Faith Perspective on Peacemaking?

The challenge of preparing children to be peacemakers is a great one. Complexities of child development and its tremendous influence on adult development add to the mystery of nurture. But this is a creative mystery we must own. God's activity in our lives can make our future more than the sum of our past experiences. God's gracious love can give us self-esteem in spite of varying circumstances of life such as a birth defect, disease, loss of a parent, or natural disasters.

Children can cope with devastating situations, if they have the support and direction of God's love through us to help them deal with profound limitations, fear, or hopelessness.

Robert Coles, a Harvard psychiatrist, was mystified by the faith of six-year-old Ruby Bridges. Every morning and afternoon, accompanied by federal marshals, Ruby prayed as she walked through the mobs of people who protested her attendance at a white school. She kept on praying and quoting from the Bible when schools were desegregated a year later.[16]

We cannot respond despairingly or apathetically to the personal, corporate, national, and international violence surrounding us. We can affirm our faith in Jesus, the Prince of Peace, and his enormous love for all the members of his global family. It is the respectful, hopeful, reconciling, generous, people-affirming compassion of Jesus that I want to share with my children and the children I teach.

Psychological understandings can serve us as we stand with children and each other through the sunshine and the clouds of life. As we build homes, schools, and churches which are havens of genuine acceptance and encouragement, we are helping to lay the foundations of peace.

> As we sought names for our children, we discovered that a large number of boy's names are warlike, or have a significance connoting violent conflict. We wanted to select names which would influence our children positively. We finally chose Justin Kasimir and Nadia Esther.
> *Justin* means "one who is just," and *Kasimir* means "peace." The significance of our son's name is, therefore, "just one of peace." *Nadia* means "hope" and *Esther* means "star," therefore naming her "star of hope." Both *Nadia* and *Kasimir* are words which we discovered from others' observation and experience. These names came from Arabic and Slavic traditions.
> —*Maribeth Shank Shank, Sarasota, Florida. Prenatal*

In exploring the relationship between positive self-concept and peacemaking, one biblical idea kept recurring for me. "We love because he first loved us" (1 John 4:19, NIV). This has become a foundational principle for me in seeking to understand how to nurture the potential for peace in children.

We cherish life because our life was cherished. We care for others because we have been cared for. We trust others because we have been trusted. We accept others because we have been accepted. And so the hope for peace becomes truly possible.

The way Dr. Mary Royer modeled love and peace had a profound influence upon me as a beginning teacher. Her skill in presenting truth with a spiritual perspective was unique. Here is one story to show how following her example of extending love and peace to students helped me help them.

When I began teaching, we were encouraged each Monday morning to conduct an opening devotional with Bible reading. At the beginning of the school year, about fifteen of the forty-five students had the practice of attending church. It was evident many of them needed more than academic training, so I often encouraged students to attend church. A number of times a carload of boys were invited to our farm home for the night. One night the boys and I slept in the haymow, talking into the night.

Ralph, an eighth-grade boy from a large family of Dutch immigrants, had manifested tendencies toward vandalism (laying nails for the school principal's tires). He was one student who did not attend church. One day he told me, "I think youse is good enough you wouldn't need to go to church."

I replied, "Ralph, I need to go to church to stay decent."

It was gratifying to see changes for the good in many of the students' lives. Ralph went through high school, became a star basketball player, and eventually president of an industrial company.

Years later a former classmate of Ralph's wrote to inform me that Ralph was dying from cancer. Forty years had passed since I had last seen Ralph, so I was determined to visit him.

After driving 300 miles, we entered the lane leading past stately trees, beautiful flowers, a spacious lawn, and an inviting fish pond to a large well-kept home. Ralph had made it financially. "Has Ralph made it spiritually?" I asked myself.

After visiting for a short time, Ralph apparently sensed my concern. "Yes, I am a Christian. I am prepared to die. Both of my daughters are attending Mount Union, a Methodist college. The older daughter is planning to marry a young man who is studying for the Christian ministry," concluded Ralph.

Ralph is now gone, but he had proved to be a good husband and a loving father who was able to point his family in the right direction. Yes, Ralph had made it.

—*John Steiner, Elsworth, Ohio. Grade 8*

If we would see
peace
flowering
in the world
tomorrow,
we must plant
the seeds of love
today.

17

2. How Can Children Live Confidently in Spite of Fear and Hostility?

S. L. Yoder

ON a flight from Shanghai to Tokyo, our Japan Airlines plane landed briefly in Nagasaki. Coming in low over the city, I was struck by the sight of the glistening new office buildings, the clean wide boulevards, and the late afternoon traffic moving at a snail's pace. I pressed my face hard against the window to get a closer look at the now-peaceful city nestled in the mountains on Kyushu Island in southern Japan.

Racing through my mind was the thought of radioactive clouds hanging heavily over this ancient shipbuilding city of half a million people, a coastal town where Christianity got its foothold in Japan. One August day in 1945, the second atomic bomb in three days was dropped, killing nearly 40,000 men, women, and children. The A-bomb, the ultimate weapon, was a device to end all wars.

I well remember that summer day of the bombing. I was in my fourth year in Civilian Public Service, working in a mental hospital in lower New York State. Four years as a conscientious objector in a mental hospital gave me much time for reflection on war and peace. From my boyhood among the bearded-wheat fields of a Kansas Amish community, I had been taught that war was wrong, that human life was sacred. To take the life of another violated the teachings of Jesus. The day after Japanese planes attacked Pearl Harbor, I was inducted into an alternative service program with assignments that ranged from fighting forest fires in the High Sierras in California to mental hospital work as far east as Rhode Island.

Thus I was working at Poughkeepsie State Hospital when the news of the A-bombs drifted through the wards. There was an air of glee, rejoicing, and hope among the people that this would end World War II. Little did they know then that new bombs, a thousand times more powerful than those dropped on Hiroshima and Nagasaki, would be stockpiled, ready to deploy at the press of a button, to glide through space responding to sophisticated guidance systems, and strike with pinpoint accuracy.

Later the ravages of war became real to me during my two years with Mennonite Central Committee in Holland and Germany. Moving in on the heels of the occupation forces, our relief-work team came face-to-face with destruction and suffering. People who were enemies in battle now found much in common when the guns were silent.

Now the superpowers list enough nuclear bombs in their arsenals to wipe out every man, woman, and child on this earth several times over. As Martin Luther King, Jr., said, "Over the bleached bones and jumbled residue of numerous civilizations are written the words: Too late. . . . We still have a choice today: nonviolent coexistence or violent co-annihilation." [1]

What Effect Does the Nuclear Threat Have on Children?

The threat of nuclear war with all its potential devastation makes grown men cry. It makes children cry, too. Life-threatening calamities such as the pandemic Black Plague in fourteenth-century Europe and Asia; and the flu, polio, and AIDS epidemics in twentieth-century America—these brought fear and panic to many communities. Our world has never been free of major catastrophes. In fact, fear of nuclear war is not new.

> In the early sixties when our daughter Miriam was in kindergarten or first grade, she was crying one night at bedtime, unable to sleep. I asked what was wrong. She sobbed, "I'm afraid the Russians are going to drop an atomic bomb and kill us." I took her into our Goerz Hall living room. I put my arms around her and rocked her. We talked about how God loves and takes care of us. And God loves Russians too. After a long silence, she said, "I think somewhere in Russia a mother is holding a girl just my age, and a father is reading the newspaper."
> —*Elaine Sommers Rich, Newton, Kansas. Age 6*

In the early sixties, we heard the wailing counterculture lyrics of Bob Dylan and Pete Seeger in such pop music as "Where Have All the Flowers Gone?" and "A Hard Rain's A-Gonna Fall." They were expressing fears that many tried to suppress. The voices that express those same fears of destruction and waste, of apocalypse and a dead planet, are recurring in an increasing number. Evidence is growing constantly that children have more and more fear and anxiety as they become increasingly aware of the nuclear threat. Children are frightened by the world they have inherited, frightened by the world adults have created for them.

While many adults, with their highly developed defense mechanisms, tend to rationalize and even defend the need for high-powered sophisticated weaponry, there are children and youth who live in greater fear. Children's fears of a holocaust are particularly evidenced in large industrial cities where major populations reside. Many concerned and sensitive boys and girls experience a kind of morbid anxiety about the future. The nine-year-old who mused, "I want to know about nuclear war because when we all get blown up, I want to know why,"[2] causes us to reflect on our responsibilities.

The doom and gloom syndrome of the eighties and nineties is contrastingly different from the mood found in children several decades earlier. During the Korean War, I was teaching in a large public school in a city of 35,000. War games in free play after school were common scenes along our street. Combat art showed up in every classroom as students doodled in lax moments during the day. Store shelves were stocked with war toys, while bumper stickers and billboards were constantly screaming, "Better Dead than Red." Our country was in a fighting mood, and those feelings spilled over into the nation's classrooms.

In the early days of our International School, when I was the only teacher, I invited parents in to talk to the children once a week. They shared a devotional or some other type of cultural or inspirational story.

One parent, a missionary friend, chose to tell an experience he had while serving in the American army. Mr. S. was sent to Okinawa. He told the children his feelings of pride and bravery, and he said, "I knew just what I was going to do when I met my first 'Jap,' the enemy." I felt sad as I saw the children's excited and eager attention to the outcome of this story.

Mr. S. continued his story. "One day I went out for a walk without my gun. As I rounded the curve at the top of a small hill, I met my first Japanese. He also was unarmed, and we stood looking at each other. As I was wondering what to do, the Japanese soldier knelt down in the path in front of me and drew the design of a cross in the dust. I, too, knelt and drew a cross. We were not enemies—we were brothers! We couldn't speak each other's language, but the symbol of the cross gave each of us a message. We each bowed and turned back in the path to the way we had come."

The children were happy with this story, even though it ended differently from what they expected. We often referred to this story of Mr. S.'s as we interacted with our many friends in Japan who weren't "Japs" or enemies, but friends who learned, played, and did many things just like we did. Or was it that we did things just like they did?

—*Arletta Selzer Becker, Sapporo, Hokkaido, Japan. Grades 1-6*

How Does the Evening News Affect Children's Feelings?

Television brought war into the family living room. Children witnessed the horrors of destruction only hours after the actual happening. The turn of events in Vietnam and the revelation of gory suffering stories began to grip the conscience of many peace-loving Americans. A decade later programs such as *Catch 22* and *"M*A*S*H"* were tolerated by patriotic citizens.

Posters began to appear saying, "War is unhealthy for children and other living things." *Weekly Readers* distributed in elementary current events classes began to carry page fillers such as this note from a twelve-year-old Vietnamese boy: "One friend of mine went to the village to get rice for his mother and father. He crossed the field and the airplanes saw him and shot and killed him so you couldn't even see his body. It was scattered all over the field." [3] The Persian Gulf War accentuated such experiences as television sets in the classroom monitored the effectiveness of "smart" warheads on missiles or the direct hits through the front door of munition depots. These bits of news from the war front elicited serious discussions in many classrooms and had a significant impact on the youths of America; some went on to become active in peace efforts.

In March of 1991, out of an extreme sense of frustration, an idea grew that proved to be memorable for me and my second-grade students. As a public school teacher during the time of the Gulf War, I felt the urgency to somehow respond to what the majority of my students were hearing about the war outside of school. It was unsettling to hear seven- and eight-year-olds repeat derogatory phrases about persons they knew virtually nothing about on the other side of the globe.

I was excited when I came across *The Great Shalom* by Peter Dyck. It was written to the children's level of understanding and used language which immediately caught their attention. Having heard daily of Operation Desert Shield and Operation Desert Storm, they were now hearing about Operation Feathers, Operation Topple and Sting, and Operation Stink. We were able to talk openly of aggression without pointing fingers, as they watched how animals worked through their responses toward acts of aggression. The farmer who planned to destroy the animals' forest home was met with responses that covered the full spectrum from Badger who said, "He is our enemy now and will always be our enemy," to Rabbit who announced, "Hate is like that. Once you start hating, you can't stop. Before you know it, your whole life is filled with hate."

It was the children's idea to write letters to Peter Dyck. They summarized their feelings about the book and talked to him about their favorite parts. They even told him how they would have changed the outcome. Responses ranged from "You shouldn't have let the baby bunny die," to "I loved every single part," and "It's the best chapter book I've ever read." Kendra asked, "When is the video coming out?"

Imagine our delight when the author not only responded to our letters, but he also included a rough-draft manuscript of another book he was writing.

Dear Boys and Girls:

What a pleasant surprise that was to receive all your wonderful letters. I enjoyed reading every one of them. You really must have paid attention when your teacher read *The Great Shalom*. I can tell from your letters.

For some days I wondered how I could thank you and your teacher for writing to me. Just to write and say "Thanks" didn't seem quite enough. If I weren't so far away, I'd come and tell you some other stories. But I can't do that.

Then I had an idea: I would make a copy of *Shalom at Last* and send it to you. My grandchildren, for whom I write these stories, told me that the first story wasn't quite finished, and there wasn't really peace (shalom) in the end. The animals were only dreaming about making peace with the farmer.

So I wrote another story, part two, a *sequel*, and called it *Shalom at Last*. I hope you enjoy it.

And since you were so kind to let me know what you thought of my first story, I wonder whether you would also let me know what you think about this one. Your teacher will explain what I mean.

Thank you again for writing. I am sharing your letters with the Herald Press in Scottdale. They are the people who printed the book. (If you want to learn some new words: I am the writer of these stories and am called the *author*; Herald Press prints the books and is called the *publisher;* David Garber looks over what I have written to make sure there are no mistakes, and he is called the *editor.* And you are helping me improve the story and are called *advisers.*)

I love you,

—Phyllis Schrock Hostetler, Lyons, Ohio. Grade 2

Children of different ages ask probing questions concerning the threat of nuclear war. Many children are confused about the dangers headlined in their local newspaper or by the frightening images that flash across their television screens. At each age of development, children respond to danger and fear in ways typical of that age group. Parents and teachers should respond to questions on nuclear dangers and the threat of war in ways most natural to the child and thereby help youngsters deal effectively with such frightening ideas.

I gave my sixth graders the assignment of writing a poem in the cinquain style. They could choose any subject. Jeremy responded with this illustrated poem.[4]

When asked about his poem, Jeremy said, "I'm not sure why I did it. I was just reading in the newspaper. I thought it was really dumb that people were fighting to bring peace."

—Marge Pletcher, Goshen, Indiana. Grade 6

War
By Jeremy Garber
Grade 6, Parkside
Conflict
Soldiers fighting
Mothers cry for children
Fighting, wounding, killing, dying
For peace.

Parents have the privilege and responsibility to edit information. Sometimes the topic is too frightening for the child. It is best to protect young children from too much talk about war and nuclear danger. Adult discussions and TV programs on the nuclear threat and missile capability are best presented when the younger people are otherwise occupied. A child shielded from the more dramatic and overly exciting situations is less likely to experience crippling fears and nightmares at a time when the developing personality should be occupied with more pleasant aspects of childhood.

How Then Do We Speak to the Children?

Parents can make preprimary children feel wonderfully secure through their love and concern for them. The responsible and creative acts of early parenting become important foundations for building a more peaceful world. Children who experience love and security in their early years have a definite advantage in dealing with the ominous threats and fears of their world. Bill Drake of Weimar, California, advises, "We must help our children develop an inner strength before exposing them to harsh adult realities that would weaken them and lessen their ability to face and deal with these realities at a later time." [5]

Young children see their parents as all powerful, and basically trust them as protectors from every fear and danger. This carries over into the area of threats of war, which at this age are comparable to fears of getting lost in a crowd or of monsters under the bed. Included in the nuclear fear is the fear of losing parents as expressed by one child who asked, "Mommy, where will you be when the bomb drops? 'Cos I want to be with you," [6] and by a five-year-old who concluded a bedtime conversation about nuclear war with his father by asking, "Daddy, will you always be my daddy?" [7] Parental responsibility in dealing with childhood fears becomes particularly heavy at this age.

The younger the children are, the more they depend on parents for reassurance. Such reassurance comes through acknowledging the child's fear and moving beyond it with a brief explanation. Reasoning alone seldom comforts a young child. Sometimes the best reassurance is to comfort children with a good bedtime story, an extra snack, a night light, and knowledge that mother and father are not far away. Just being there brings needed comfort to most youngsters.

Young children tend to see everything, including the threat of war, through the actions and speech of their parents. Similar composure is learned from parents who remain calm and confident during a storm.

A young child's fear of storms is often learned from adults. If you excitedly call your child in from play and express anxiety about the wind and the lightning, he will share your apprehension. When thunder is loud, lightning sharp, or wind strong, if you remain poised, your child is not likely to develop fear of storms. Quietly tell him that the bright lightning is electricity in the sky like the electricity in your lamps and that it heats the air and causes the big thunder noise. Tell him that the blowing wind helps to bring the rain clouds. As you watch the lightning and listen to the thunder and the wind, say this rhyme with your child. He will enjoy doing the motions as you do them:

"See the lightning! Sparkle-flash!" (Make zigzag motion with the fingers.)

"Hear the thunder! Rumble-crash!" (Clap hands.)

"Listen to the wind! Wheeeeeeee!" (Whisper into cupped hands.)

"Rain is falling for you and me." (Raise hands and move fingers downward.)

When your child hears about houses destroyed and people hurt by storms, he may question like four-year-old Donnie, "Why do people get killed?" Explain that although storms sometimes hurt people and destroy buildings, they usually bring rain. Assure the child that God loves us during a storm as well as at all other times; that as long as we live in this world, God will care for us here; and when we go to heaven, he will care for us there; so no matter what happens, God always loves and cares for us. Rather than leading your child to expect immunity from danger, share with him the sense of security which you feel in God's undergirding love in all experiences. When you live confidently, cheerfully, and courageously, your child will begin to share your faith in God expressed in Psalm 56:3 (KJV), "What time I am afraid, I will trust in thee."[8]

Parents can learn how to help their children deal with nuclear fears from parent support groups organized through the church or through community, social, and professional organizations.

One group of parents formed Parenting in a Nuclear Age. They developed guidelines for parents who desire to protect children from debilitating feelings of fear and hopelessness. This group suggests parents expose *young* children to nature's pleasures and wonders. Children love to lie in the grass and watch trees move in the wind. They become fascinated by following a colony of ants in a sidewalk crack. Learning the names of birds, flowers, and trees brings an appreciation for the natural world and creates a positive attitude and respect for life.[9] These and other related family activities bring a greater understanding of God's creation and a feeling for the sacredness of life. This focus develops a desire to preserve life.

When children reach *primary age* (six-eight years old), teachers and other adults in the child's life become increasingly influential and share with parents in helping children cope with their fears. Sibylle Escalona[10] cites sources of fearfulness in children of this age. First, in school and on the street, they learn that they must rely more and more on themselves. Second, there are fewer things parents can do for them. Children worry about schoolwork, about not being able to do all that is required.

These children also have a growing understanding of the world beyond the family. Is it any wonder that they feel threatened by the idea that the world is so big that any one small person can feel lost and of no account? When the outside world appears out of control, their sense of danger is heightened.

Six- to eight-year-olds place enormous faith in knowing exactly what lies ahead of them and what they will be expected to do. Ability to predict what will happen fails when it comes to the nuclear threat or to the experience of war itself. We do not know all the answers. Children feel helpless just because they do not know what to expect.

A study by Beardslee and Mack is illustrative. They found that 40 percent of the elementary and high school children they interviewed said they were aware of nuclear developments before age twelve. Additionally, the majority of them expressed feelings of terror and powerlessness. Because they doubted

whether they would grow up, they had a "live for now" attitude.[11]

Boys and girls need simple and undramatic answers that give
positive reassurance that adults are working toward control of
nuclear bombs. Help them see that most people want peace.
Help them understand that what they do and say in school and
on the playground to promote friendship and goodwill is promoting peace. Children need to feel some ownership in the total peace efforts.[12]

Young children who are burdened with fear often base their
fright on misunderstandings. For instance, children can be confused about the difference between testing and actual bombing.
Their nightmares and dreams of war can be softened by the
comforting explanation of a parent.

> At the time of Pearl Harbor—December 1941—my husband, Len,
> our three children, and I were in Rangoon, Burma, where we had
> been on missionary assignment. The war moved quickly toward
> our city, and Len was appointed chief air-raid warden for our
> area. He was seldom home after dark, and I was often alone with
> our three small children. Every day we grew more fearful as we
> watched trenches being hastily dug around us.
>
> One evening as the children and I huddled together during the
> nightly blackout, five-year-old Kathy inched close to me.
> "Mommy, will we be killed tonight?"
>
> I groped for an answer that would reassure, but still be truthful.
> Finally I blurted out, "Let's see what Jesus says."
>
> We closed our eyes tight, and after a long silence, Kathy said, "I
> just know that since we prayed, Jesus won't let the bombs fall on
> us."
>
> My heart sank. People in Europe's smoldering cities had
> prayed, too. But Winnie, an old and wise six, said, "No, Kathy, Je-
> sus won't always take away the bombs. But he does take away the
> 'fraidness."
>
> It was the answer I was seeking. And it's been the answer I've
> needed again and again in all the years since—when I am
> frightened.[13]

While it is best to "cool" nuclear war talk with primary-age
children, *middle childhood* (nine- to twelve-year-olds) is a time

when youngsters have lots of information and want more. Issues on peace and justice and who is guilty in human relationships are frequent topics of discussion at home and in school. Children ask the difficult questions of middle-years. They see the global dimension of the nuclear threat. They begin to understand that people of other nations feel the same fears and have similar concerns for the human family. As their empathy grows, children feel deeply the horrors of war, the depth of violence, and the pity of hunger and poverty. They begin to weigh such actions and conditions with a new sense of morality and justice.

Patricia Fellers, an elementary teacher in Portland, Oregon, has been active in peace education since 1976. She outlines a five-point definition of peace education that includes (1) creating a positive self-image, (2) building a spirit of community, (3) developing an awareness of world problems, (4) guiding a recognition of global plurality and independence, and (5) action.[14]

Fellers and other teachers say a simple point in peace education is to give the student a home base in the midst of increasing terror of war and depression among young people, and to assure them of God's love for them. "We need to show them that there's hope and that there are things we can do," she said. "As Christians, we need to tell them that no matter what happens, God loves them. At the same time, they should know that we are stewards and we have a responsibility to try to change things."[15]

In contrast to the foregoing discussion, Robert Coles discovered that children of upper-middle class liberal parents are afraid of nuclear war, but children of poor families are not. He suggests they feel more threatened by immediate hunger and the daily turmoil of life than by the possibility of nuclear attack.[16]

How Much Fear Can Children Take?

Yes, fear and anxiety in children are common, and undue fear and high anxiety are harmful to children and adults alike. Children fear many things—family breakups, unemployment, poor grades in school, being rejected by their peer group, as well as nuclear war. High unemployment, constant moving, and the absence of solid family roots also bring fears and anxieties to countless children.

Another worry faced by children is fear of strangers. Among the games and books now available to children is a new breed designed to alert them to the potential dangers in their environment, primarily kidnapping and sexual abuse. Parents and teachers should be aware, however, that children under seven probably see games primarily as fun, not as learning tools. They thus become anxious but really do not understand what they are anxious about. Additionally, we know that most sexual abuse is committed by family, friends, or relatives of children—not strangers. Missing-child reports filed are mostly runaways and children of divorce abducted by the parent not receiving custody. Only a tiny fraction of the cases involve kidnapping by strangers.

> If parents keep child-safety issues in perspective, talking calmly and carefully about such problems, children can learn caution without being unduly frightened. . . . "Kids really should enjoy their childhood," says [psychologist Lee] Salk. "They should be given the opportunity to explore and satisfy their curiosity. We should be focused on nurturing that." [17]

Family or community conditions can also trigger feelings of insecurity, doubt, and unwantedness. Like all of us, children sometimes suffer from feelings of isolation. It is wonderful not to feel alone, to have parents and teachers who reach out to help overcome loneliness and low self-esteem. Sometimes a simple comment, a word of encouragement, will reassure children that they are loved and that someone cares—thus alleviating the worst of all fears—being unwanted.

> One morning Misty brought me a note from her mother which said, "Mrs. Schertz, Misty gets sick at the thought of school." My response was to talk to Misty.
> "Misty, you don't like school?" I inquired.

"No, it makes me sick. I can't wait till I'm sixteen and can be a drop-out."

"Do you have friends in school?" I asked.

"Nobody likes me," Misty replied.

"Michele [who sits next to Misty in class] is a kind girl. I'm sure she'd like to play with you. Let's ask her," I suggested.

"I asked Misty to play with me but she won't," Michele replied. But she tried again. "Misty, let's play pretend school at recess. You can play, too." In the same breath Michele asked, "Mrs. Schertz, may we play school?"

"Yes, I'll help you find a box and some books, paper, and pencils to put in it. Then you may take it outdoors at recess and play school."

What a joy to see fifteen to twenty boys and girls play school in a corner of the overcrowded playground. That box is carried out every recess with such joy and satisfaction.

Misty now likes school at recess.

—*Agnes Classen Schertz, Goshen, Indiana. Grade 3*

The class had been dismissed for recess. While walking out to the playground, Linda made a point of walking beside me. As her teacher, I was particularly interested in what she might have to say. At a certain pause in our stroll, Linda asked, "What do you do when your parents don't care for you anymore?"

"How do you know they don't care for you?" I asked.

"Well, last night they were both arguing and fighting," she replied.

"And where were you at that time?"

"I was in Dad's trailer with my ear against the screen in the open window," Linda answered.

"Do your parents have separate trailers?" I probed.

"Yes, they are side by side."

I gasped and breathed a prayer. What do I say to one of my pupils who fears she is losing her parents? After a bit of thought, I said, "Linda, God loves you, I care for you, and when it comes right down to it, I think your parents love and care for you."

With that bit of reassurance, she said, "Oh, okay," and skipped away to join the others in play.

—*Dorwin Carrol Myers, Kokomo, Indiana. Grade 5*

When Gary moved from another school to ours and joined the fourth grade several weeks after the school year had started, he refused to do any work. He really didn't have the necessary skills, so I kept trying to help him catch up and master them. It was uphill, especially in math. So one math period when he was stalling, giving up, and getting angry, I asked him to come out into the hall so we could talk. We went to a window where it was more pleasant.

"Gary, you really don't like math."

"I sure don't. I hate it."

"I see."

"Yeah, I've hated it ever since second grade. I just couldn't get it!"

"You kept trying, but you couldn't understand."

"Uh-huh. And then whenever I'd just about begin to see how to do it, then I'd have to move. My mom moved to lots of places."

"That made it harder for you to keep up."

"Yeah." Gary started crying.

"You feel discouraged about it, Gary." I was quiet, saddened by his tears, but comfortable with them. Slowly they lessened.

The outcome of that conversation came several months later when, to my astonishment, Gary stayed in from recess on his own, working at his desk. At first, involved in further preparations, I didn't notice him. When I did, I said in surprise, "Why Gary, what are you working on?"

"I'm practicing spelling (long pause). I've got math licked now. Next is spelling!"

—*Thelma Miller Groff, Goshen, Indiana. Grade 4*

In our mission school, the children leave their homes and parents to come for many hundreds of miles by plane. They live in dorms with dorm parents. Because of this situation, the younger ones especially face times of loneliness and fearfulness. We as teachers and the dorm parents are aware of this and constantly work with the children so they will share these feelings with us. We work with them on the basis that God loves them; they have mothers and daddies who love them; we love them.

Many times in our talks about fears and loneliness, we encourage these young children to memorize Bible verses and choruses about God's love and care. When the hard times come—often at night in their beds—they can talk to God, using these verses and songs. Many have shared with me how this has helped them, and they can relax and go back to sleep.

We've also encouraged our own children to recall God's promises when they've faced new experiences. It helped them. We feel they are learning to face problems when young, providing them a solid base for facing difficulties as they grow up.

—*Jewel Miller Schlatter, Amazonas, Brazil. Grades 1-3*

How Do Fear and Anxieties Affect Children's Behavior and Ability to Learn?

Young minds are greatly affected by the peace-war mood of the country. War fears intensify children's uncertainties and spill over into relationships with peers, parents, and teachers. Such terrors bring on fears and anxieties not directly related to war but built on needs to feel wanted and secure.

Indeed, unless children are caught up in feelings of emotional safety and self-esteem at home and school, they cannot properly function at higher cognitive levels. Inner peace brings motivation and release for school learnings in times of stress of any sort. This is further illustrated in the classroom experiences of the following teachers:

> Bobby was four years old. When he came to nursery school, his face was sullen and expressionless; all his responses were negative. Except for his favorite word, "no," he refused to talk even though he had good verbal skills. He would kick the wall and bang his head against it. If any children interfered with him, he would hit them. Most of the time his head was down, pressed against his chest, and he shrank away from any touch.
>
> We worked to help Bobby verbalize his feelings. "I see you're angry, Bobby, but we need to find ways to talk and not hit." We tried to understand and help him feel understood. We talked with the other children in the class about some of the things Bobby was feeling, and we encouraged them to share with him. While at first they drew back in fear, never knowing when he was going to strike out at them, gradually they began to play with him and to offer friendship.
>
> Bobby began to claim them as friends and to change in other ways. His chin came up off his chest, and he began to smile and to

talk. He began to paint eagerly: this picture was for his father, and this picture was for his mother. As he came to talk to us teachers, he welcomed our hugs, no longer shrinking from us. He stopped banging his head and kicking the wall.

We planned a special unit for the class, highlighting the Native American culture of his father, who was invited to come to the class to share about his home and background. Bobby fairly beamed.

Unfortunately, this wasn't the end of a successful story. Once again Bobby arrived at school sullen and expressing negative behavior. During the hours at school, he became happy. We learned that Bobby's father had left home, and his mother was filing for divorce. This was a recurring pattern of their family life, which created many intense feelings in the home. In Bobby's case, it brought back his negative behaviors.

The teacher has great opportunities for peacemaking, for offering wholeness to young children. The difficulties faced are also great, and the teacher needs many allies if children like Bobby are to come to wholeness. Let us not become weary in well doing.

—Lucille Schultz Roth, Goshen, Indiana. Age 4

A six-year-old boy was tossed off his bicycle by a drunk driver. He was taken to a hospital 200 miles from home, with a severed spinal cord, bruised, and just barely realizing he had no control at all over his body. After a year, he came to us at Chandler Tripp School for Physically Handicapped.

He had never, in three years with us, said anything about the bad time between the accident and his arrival at Chandler Tripp School, until one day while I was reading *The Acorn People*[18] to the class. I omitted the first chapter and told the class why. In it the author had listed all the stereotypes he had of special children—how horrible to him the reality of this so-called camp, his desire to leave the school despite his need for the money earned by working there.

After we read the rest of the book, the class members were adamant—I must read the first chapter; they could take it. So I did. A hush fell. Then Chris told us a little of his struggles the year following the accident. Pat, the social worker, had sat with him, talked to him, held him by the bands of his halo (designed to hold his head straight while the vertebrae healed). She tried to keep him from breaking the halo, which he did twice, although it was very painful. Chris finally decided (at seven) that his head was all he had, so he'd better use it to learn.

Chris came to us avid to hear stories, wanting to read, needing to know everything—now. I never taught him to read; he taught himself, quickly, by rereading what I had just read to him. He needed no workbooks (although he could manipulate a pencil with his teeth); he did not need practice—just content. He went on to win the Special School's Readathon, and he taught three other boys in class how to read by reading to them and motivating them by his example. Chris was the brains of many an enterprise and is now in regular sixth grade near his home in the mountains.

—*Hope Stutsman Adams, San Jose, California. Ages 7-10*

When Fear and Frustration Lead to Hostility and Aggression, How Can We Help Children?

Fears often lead to frustration which causes aggressive behavior. Frustration in some children may also lead to submission and withdrawal, but many children respond with outbursts of anger to seek relief in a frustrating situation. Since the frustration-aggression connection seems plausible, adults might pause and reflect on the amount of frustration they present to children by their expectations and demands in the home and in school.

Since children frequently imitate adult behavior, teachers and parents should monitor their own behavior to see how much and what kinds of aggressive behavior their children have picked up and are imitating. Picture the parent who is paddling the child and saying, "How many times have I told you not to hit people?" Some adult behavior says "might makes right" or "win at all costs," or even infers that "the strong make the rules, and the weak must follow." Such actions give messages to the child that aggression is justified as a way to satisfy certain needs.

For almost a month our family had been living in an integrated neighborhood in Champaign, Illinois, where our voluntary service unit was located. It was a hot Saturday in August, and since we had a swim pass to Spalding Pool, Kevin decided to bike to the pool to swim for the afternoon. He chain-locked his bike to the bike stand. When he was ready to come home, his bike was gone.

Kevin came home crying to report his bike had been stolen. We listened to his story. Knowing of no other way to comfort him, we turned to God in prayer. I remember Kevin prayed that he would find the bike. I prayed that Kevin could accept whatever happened, and I also prayed for the person who took his bike.

On Sunday afternoon Kevin was teasing his younger brothers and sister while Daddy was trying to rest. I suggested that Kevin run around the block to take care of his pent-up feelings. Kevin was soon back, excitedly telling us that he had seen his bike in a yard at the end of our block. Clayton got up from his nap and went with Kevin to check out the bike. Sure enough, even though the front of the bike had already been repainted black, they could tell that it was Kevin's because it still had his Goshen license plate on the rear. No one was home. We didn't know what to do. Finally we called the police and told them about the bike. They picked up the bike and returned it to us.

We talked about how we would relate to the family that had taken the bike. They had a son and daughter in the local middle school. We decided Kevin would ride his bike as usual, and we would act as naturally as we could in our contacts with them.

We had several visits in the yard as we walked past their home and chatted about the rabbits in the hutch beside the alley. Several weeks later our family saw the son and daughter trying to carry a heavy doghouse. They crossed the busy intersection by our home. As they came by our house, Kevin and his brothers went to get our wagon and offered to help them move the doghouse to the yard. So, overlooking the bike incident, Kevin and his brothers helped them transport the doghouse up the street to their yard.

—*Ruth Geiser Steiner, Champaign, Illinois. Grade 3*

How Important Is Family Atmosphere?

Parental love and reassurance can allay childhood frustrations and give that protective closeness necessary for healthy personality development. Children raised in such an atmosphere can more readily cope with a world full of fear and violence. If parents and teachers enable children to control their anger, to avoid destruction, and to respect the rights of others, they will help fortify children against fear and violence. They may come to know that nations, like families, do better with reason and fairness than with blind anger.

Gordon, our sunny, happy child, began to arrive at the supper table each evening with complaints about the food and complaints about his older brother. After several evenings of his negative responses, we decided to place on the table a box which had been used for a mission project during Lent. We announced that sometimes complaints may be necessary, *but* that the complainer would have to put a nickel in the box for each grumble. The results? Only one nickel was placed in the box, and we had a much happier experience at the table. Sometimes, of course, it's important to find out more about the underlying cause.

Gordon and Brian, who are two years apart, often *did* have conflicts. They would get into verbal battle, and my direct intervention would result in one or the other claiming I had been unfair. Then I would often find that they could indeed solve their own problems successfully and fairly. I had them sit down together and take turns telling each other how they saw the problem. Soon I found that I only had to speak a few words to help make sure the picture was clear.

Problem-solving in this manner has helped them learn how to express their feelings honestly and openly.

—*Marilyn Frey Kay, Urbana, Illinois. Ages 8 and 10*

My daughter, Rachel, was experiencing Bible school for the first time. It was rather difficult for her. All her negative feelings seemed to come to a head midweek when she came home upset over an incident that occurred on a farm her class visited. She said that all the other kids got to hold the lamb and she didn't; she only got to pet it. She cried periodically the rest of the afternoon. Even a couple of days later when she'd think about the incident, she'd cry. Although I'd talked to her about it, I guess I'd excused her teachers and told her how hard it is for a teacher to keep track of so many children. She was not soothed. Finally I sat down, held her on my lap, and asked her to tell me all about it again. Then I asked how it made her feel. Well, the dam burst, and she said, "That made me angry!" After I said I understood that she was angry at the injustice, she was ready to forgive the oversight and forget about it.

—*Marilee Roggie Schoolcraft, Goshen, Indiana. Age 4*

For many years I taught in the inner-city where quarrels between children were frequent and there was little help at home. Both persons would always claim to be innocent and make bitter complaints about the other. One measure that usually settled the problem was to have them say five nice things about each other. By the time they had finished, they were laughing and were friends again.

—*Elsie C. Bechtel, Canton, Ohio. Grade 6*

How Then Do We Deal with Aggression?

Channeling aggressive behavior into positive action is not always easy when flare-ups occur. However, at some point in the children's development, it is desirable for the supportive adults to ponder ways to sublimate these feelings into nonaggressive activities in order to bring relief to their emotions. Generally, parents and teachers can improve their track records by minimizing situations which trigger frustration in children. They can help youngsters continually raise their frustration threshold. Respect for others and an awareness of how aggressive behavior affects others are the most important traits to foster if the goal is to keep unhealthy forms of aggression in check. The following experiences at different age levels illustrate positive ways to deal with aggression.

When children quarrel accompanied by tears and anger, it seems best to ask them to wait and discuss the situation later when they are calm. I say to the child, "You are very unhappy and upset right now. You may wash your face, come back to the classroom, or wait with the secretary until you feel better. Later I will let you tell me what happened, and we will talk about it."

Usually time melts the anger, the child sees the situation in proper perspective, and reconciliation results. Apologies and forgiveness are not forced, but individuals are encouraged to do something for each other or to play together if they appear to be reconciled.

This method did not work with one boy in my class who seemed to have a deep hatred for a classmate. We worked at improving relationships as occasions arose. I hope sometime hatred will be replaced by love.

—*Mary Zehr, Morton, Illinois. Grade 4*

Helping a child become aware of angry feelings enables the child to grow toward peace. As a daycare teacher, I often help children sort out what is feeling and what is action. This story of Tom and Bob illustrates how that sometimes occurs.

After Tom called him a "girl," four-year-old Bob threw an empty play dough container at Tom. The result was two bleeding gums and a bleeding lip. At my request, Bob stayed nearby and watched while I put the ice pack on Tom's wound.

Later, when Bob went outside, he played that he was in an airplane crash and snakes and sharks were getting him. Then he pretended to be put in jail by another child. A few minutes later as I helped him dig the quicksand hole he asked for, I said, "You still feel bad about Tom, don't you?" Quickly he shook his head, "No." So I quietly added, "Sometimes we do things we feel bad about, but that doesn't mean we're all-bad people." And I kept digging in the sand. Soon Bob was building a sand castle beside me and began to turn to play that was no longer self-punishing.

—*Carol Troyer-Shank, Goshen, Indiana. Age 4*

R., a twelve-year-old child in our school, was labeled emotional behavior disordered. R. simply blew his cool whenever he got upset. He would throw things on the floor, yell obscenities, and stomp out of the room. Of course, this type of behavior is not acceptable in any public school. I worked a lot with R., and by the end of the school year, I saw a vast improvement in his behavioral reaction to anger or stress.

I worked with R. in a calm, caring way. When the teacher would call on the intercom to say that R. was on the way to my office, I would go out to meet him as he stormed in. I always talked quietly and calmly and asked him to tell me what happened. If he yelled and screamed as he talked, I simply said, "I choose not to talk to you until you are in control and can talk without yelling." I would let him decide when he had enough control to discuss the problems rationally.

When he was ready to talk, we discussed the situation. I always acknowledged his feelings by saying, "You felt hurt when that happened," or "You felt angry." We then would discuss other ways that he could have reacted that would have been acceptable. He could have said, "That makes me feel angry." He could have walked away from the situation. He could have continued what he was doing. He could have talked to the teacher. He could have talked to me. . . .

I always told R. that if he ever felt so angry that he thought he would explode, I would give him permission to leave the situation and come to sit in my office until he got himself under control.

We went over the process above as many times as R. lost his temper. Gradually, he started showing up in my office to sit or to discuss a situation. He learned that he could control his temper if he wanted to. He began to realize that he was a *normal* person. I'm happy to say that today R. is staffed out of the emotional behavior program and is functioning as a normal student.

—*Kay Freyenberger Frunzi, Denver, Colorado. Grade 6*

Is Playing War Healthy?

Children see aggression everywhere. Quarreling and hitting become everyday activities in some backyards. Television programs often promote violence. Children's cartoons in their animated glory all too frequently impress violence and killing on young minds. Playing war seems to intrigue many youngsters.

A widely read psychologist suggested that it is healthy for little boys to play combat games with guns in order to develop identity with masculine models, and that such shooting does not involve emotional arousal. I thought of a six-year-old friend, an active and brilliant child whose father was shot to death. The boy brought his toy gun to his mother, saying, "I think I should throw this away." His mother responded, "It is only a toy, but if you feel that way, you may do so." And he did. Such a game was no longer casual fun. It was too close to real life.

—*Mary Royer, Goshen, Indiana. Age 6*

According to Turner's studies at the University of Utah, *Today's Child* reports, "Contrary to earlier beliefs that acting out violence in a play situation has a cathartic effect on children, research shows that, in fact, this type of play increases aggressive tendencies." [19] In the same issue reference is made to Berkowitz's study at the University of Wisconsin-Madison, which finds that playing with toy guns may have long-term effects, and that "youngsters' aggressive behaviors may get reinforced from others around them, thus encouraging the continuation of these behaviors." [20] Third-grade children who "were encouraged to verbally express their anger toward a child who had frustrated them ended up liking that child less than children did who were not permitted to express anger," as reported in a study in *The New York Times*.[21]

How Do Children Learn to Forgive?

When fears and frustrations turn into hostility or violence, children depend on us to help them restore peaceful feelings and relationships through forgiving one another. Our own examples are the strongest kind of teaching. Parenting and teaching demand much of us who serve as models, protectors, disciplinarians, and lovers.

> There were times at the end of a hectic day when I knew it was necessary for me to go to the children's rooms to ask for forgiveness for something I had done or said. I usually said something like, "I'm sorry I said . . . today. I must have been too tired. Will you please forgive me?" They were always ready to forgive.
>
> One evening after my eight-year-old daughter had given me a hard day, I found a note from her. At the top she had drawn a large lion with tears running down his cheeks. Below the lion she printed, "This is how I feel. I'm sorry for what I said to you. It just slipped out. Will you forgive me? If so, I'm up in my room." Forgiveness can happen anywhere, but for my eight-year-old, the bedroom where she often forgave me provided a safe place to accept forgiveness.
>
> —*Marjorie Yoder Waybill, Scottdale, Pennsylvania. Age 8*

> The phone rang just as I was getting dinner. I answered hurriedly, and a voice said, "Are you the Mrs. L. whose son delivers our

evening paper?" I replied that I was, and then she immediately went on to say that her husband had seen my son intentionally riding his bike through her newly planted flower beds. My immediate reaction was that this surely couldn't have been my son and that there must be some error. But I did assure her that we would discuss it with him.

Later that evening my husband and I sat down with our son and told him of our call. He promptly denied it. We wanted to believe him—we've always trusted and respected our children, and we told him this. We suggested waiting until the next day to talk with his customer. We promised that we would go with him. He then went on to bed. It wasn't long, however, until a tearful boy came to tell us he had not told the truth and to ask for forgiveness.

The experience was valuable for all of us as we received love and forgiveness from each other as well as the customer and above all from our heavenly Father. We were also prompted to look at the reasons for his behavior. We realized that too much structure immediately following a rigid day in the classroom was not the best for an active boy. We have continued this kind of open dialogue over the years, and it's made teenage years a rich time for all of our family.

—*Marjorie Schertz Liechty, Goshen, Indiana. Age 10*

When my husband and I have a disagreement, we have found that resolving some of our problems while the children observe is important. Both of our sons can sense when we are unhappy or in conflict. They need to see how two people who love each other very much can resolve the conflict. We hope that they will have a good model for forgiving their own spouses some day.

—*Marilyn Frey Kay, Urbana, Illinois. Age 11*

A word of caution to those who use certain currently popular disciplinary programs and techniques primarily as a ploy for power and a way to gain control of children. Authoritarian, dictatorial, demanding approaches have not proven successful. Love-oriented techniques coupled with strong parent-child relationships through firmness and fairness have much to offer. Growing toward peace does not just happen. To love and be loved, to teach and be taught, to forgive and receive forgiveness—such actions form a noble art that children and adults should learn together. *The Quarreling Book,*[22] *The Poppy Seeds,*[23] and *The Light at Tern Rock*[24] are examples of books with clear messages of love and forgiveness.

Jerome was very protective of his one sister, Ella. Jerome and Ella had always been taught to be respectful of teachers and students.

Amy's family included her mother and brother, Grandma and Grandpa, and four cousins.

I'm not sure who started it, but quietly, in the classroom, either Amy or Jerome made a remark about someone in the other family. Soon there was verbal combat, and before long another student was involved.

All three of them came to me on the playground. It was an emotional, mixed-up story I heard. I suggested that the three of them go, sit on the cement steps, stay there until they had solved the problem, and then report to me.

In a few minutes they were back, and Jerome spoke for all of them. "It's such a mess, and we've just decided to forget the whole thing," he said.

How forgiving they were! I never heard another word about the incident and, as far as I know, that truly was the end of it.

—*Fern Yoder Hostetler, Altoona, Pennsylvania. Grade 4*

School was difficult for Carolyn. She had a vision problem and had to wear heavy glasses to correct it. However, having to wear this type of glasses created a problem for her. Awkwardness involved her in many little accidents. Thus, quite often she came to school without wearing those heavy lenses and frames.

Carolyn's desk was placed near the front of the room where she could more easily see material on the chalkboard. In spite of this, her schoolwork began to show a downward trend. She needed much individual help to complete her assignments. I tried to encourage her as much as possible. I praised her on every achievement. I wrote little notes such as "Good work, Carolyn."

Occasionally I wrote a letter to her parents, telling them of her success that day in school. Carolyn could hardly wait to deliver such a letter. She somehow knew beforehand what it was all about.

The school year came to a close. Carolyn smiled and kissed me good-bye. I will never forget the tight hand grasp she gave me. It was like giving me her vote of confidence.

The years come and go. I have retired from teaching. Carolyn still keeps in touch. When her father passed away, she made a long-distance telephone call to relate the news. Likewise, upon the death of her mother, she called me. The detailed letters following both events were full of news concerning her life and family. She recalled memories of her days in the first grade.

She wrote, "When I look at my own children, I can thank God again that I had parents that cared enough to raise me right and to see that I had good Christian teachers. And you know, even with all that going for me, I still went wrong in several things and several ways, but God forgives, and thank God, you get another chance.

"But those early years are the ones I cherish the most. My first good Christian teachers laid the groundwork both in school and church for me to know the right and wrong way of raising my own children. That's why someday I would like my girls to meet you and get to know and love you as I do. Please don't stop telling the little ones about Jesus. It was some of those first stories that you told me which I am telling my girls today."

—*Pauline Yoder, Bellefontaine, Ohio. Grade 1*

VERDICT—NOT GUILTY!

I can't forget. It is January 14, 1971, the day before a school holiday is to be declared in honor of the birthday of Dr. Martin Luther King, Jr. We are instructed to observe this event with "appropriate exercises" in our classrooms.

So late afternoon finds the children and me having our own memorial service. We are reading a biography of Dr. King's life. The children interrupt with questions and opinions.

"Why couldn't black people sit where they wanted on a bus, or eat in a place they chose?"

"Why should a black lady be sent to jail for sitting in a bus and refusing to stand for a white person?"

"It's not fair!" "Those white laws are rotten!"

Some children are pounding on their desks; many faces have clouded up. From all over the room come shouts of "daw, daw."

What shall I say as a white to excuse past wrongdoings to an entire race? I search and grope for words to explain why to the children. I am speechless for a moment; it grows quiet, and all eyes turn to me. I can only mumble that some people have so much hate in their hearts. Someone says, "I think those people should be put in jail."

I stand, one white, before twenty-nine inquiring black faces, feeling the guilt of every hateful deed ever done by any white against a black. To be white is to be guilty. Never before have my children looked at me as a white teacher.

A dull hush has fallen over the classroom—some of the children are sitting with chin in hand, staring into space. Genel and Allyson beg to sing "We Shall Overcome" and come forward to lead it.

"We shall overcome. . . .

"Hand and hand together. . . .

"God is on our side. . . .

"We will walk in peace. . . ."

By now Jerome and Willie are clapping; Colin is tom-toming on his desk. Genel and Allyson are swaying up front, while Carleen, Yolanda, and Anitra, in a circle with hands clasped and crossed, are singing.

"Black and white together. . . ."

And it tears me up till it's not possible to hold tears back. I walk toward my desk, staying there half sobbing. The song ends. I finally turn to face the class, trying to explain what I feel—my despair at what their people have had to face, my hope that what they sang, "Black and white together," will become reality. Half the class is crying with me. The other children are busy fanning, wiping foreheads, and handing out Kleenex. Suddenly Sharon rushes up to me, puts her arms around me, and says, "But you're not one of them; you're one of us!" I am acquitted of my guilt! (But should I have been?)

Allyson now begs to sing "A-A-Amen" and says, "You won't crack up during this one, will you?" Shaking my head and smiling through my tears, I help them begin. And then we go on to:

"This train bound for freedom. . . .

"No more weeping and a-wailing. . . .

"Children git on a-board. . . ."

"A-A-Amen!"

Our "appropriate exercises" end.

The following Monday a note is discreetly dropped on my desk after school. It reads:

Dear Miss Gerber you

have been the nices

Teacher I ever had.

Just because your

skin is different
I still love you.
Will you for give
Me for all the wrong
things I done.
yes _____ or no _____
    from Jerome

. . . .

Do you forgive us, Jerome? yes _____ or no _____
—*Charlene Gerber Schildt, Atlanta, Georgia. Grade 3*

3. How Do We Help Children Choose to Live the Good News of Peace?

David Klahre

A FEW years ago I participated in the annual Moravian peace pilgrimage between Nazareth and Bethlehem, Pennsylvania. We gathered in the park at the beginning of the walk, sang Christmas carols, and heard the Christmas story. On that ten-mile pilgrimage, we thought about the birth and life of the Prince of Peace. Entering Bethlehem at dusk, we proceeded by candlelight procession to the historic town square. There we culminated our experience in worship and prayer as we renewed our commitment to allow Christ's peace to flow through us that we might live the good news of peace more perfectly.

Why did I choose to make this pilgrimage? I was nurtured in the way of peace as a child. Early guidance greatly affected my growth, development, and vocational choices. More recent service experiences as a first- and fourth-grade teacher, camp counselor, and college student personnel worker have shown me that the way of Christ is the only way to true peace. I wish to share this way in the following pages.

Living the good news of peace is positive social behavior

rooted in eternal dimensions. Following is an account of how a third-grade teacher helped children discover love, that eternal dimension, as the way to peace.

One of the most difficult, but most challenging and rewarding years of my public school teaching, began with a group of quite immature and low-achieving third graders. Because of building shortages and transportation problems, all of the children in my class were bused across town. They came charging into the room each morning, hurling accusations against the bus driver, each other, and anyone else who came to mind. I had to listen to all the grievances before I could even think of the business of academia.

Things came to a head one morning when the red-faced bus driver ambled into the room holding up a torn sleeve, which once belonged to a shirt, followed by an irate little fellow sputtering, "Just wait until my mom sees my torn shirt. You are in real trouble," punctuated by a few choice words. I suggested that the bus driver talk with the principal, and I would try to calm Mike. At this point I realized it was imperative that I work on some long-range behavior goals, rather than just trying to solve the immediate hassles of the day.

When the children arrived the next morning, I said, "Let's play a game first. *Then* I will listen to your stories." This appealed to them. "Follow instructions very carefully," I said. "Sit on the floor and form a circle." There were looks of scorn and disdain, until I said, "There's a secret about the circle, and when you discover this secret, there will be a reward." I sat in the circle with them and told each one of them something that I really liked about them. When I had finished, I asked if they would tell the people next to them something they really liked about them.

The climate in the room changed immediately. The tension was so thick it could have been cut with a knife. They bristled, and there would have been an explosion if it had not been for the prospect of losing the reward. One brave soul finally ventured to affirm the child next to him, and then there was complete silence. Somehow this had a calming effect. They were ready to retreat to the world of books, which was less threatening than sharing positive thoughts about each other.

We continued this circle every morning. Little by little more children were ready to affirm someone else. They came to look forward to the activity. After several weeks, the day finally came

when every child had spoken. I told them that they had discovered the secret of the circle and asked if anyone had guessed what it was. One boy finally spoke up and said, "I think sometimes we like each other!" Something really beautiful happened that day as they became aware of their feelings regarding one another.
—*Lois Schertz Schertz, Washburn, Illinois. Ages 8 and 9*

Emphasizing the primacy of love brought peace to the troubling situation in which these children found themselves.

Christians, particularly those in the believers church tradition, have seen living the good news of peace not only as a positive social behavior, but as a high calling of Christ. Peace living is not an optional commitment; it is a requirement of faith. Lois Schertz needed to maintain order in her classroom. And as a Christian, she did it by transmitting Christ's way of love to her students.

In this chapter, I will briefly outline the biblical background for peace and then discuss building blocks of peaceful living with the skills to aid in practicing it.

What Is the Biblical Basis for Living the Good News of Peace?

In setting the scene, an important idea to consider is the concept of *shalom/salaam*, Hebrew/Arabic for peace, perfect peace. *Shalom* has varied meanings, from a simple greeting to a meaning encompassing the will and vision of God. It is the latter that we will consider. *Shalom* embodies well-being, wholeness, harmony, joyful celebration, right relationships, peace, and fulfillment.[1] *Shalom/salaam* really says it all. Such a whole peace is the will of God for his people. One only needs to review the story of creation before the Fall of humanity to see that God had truly given his people shalom. In creation all was right and at peace. People were in right relationship with their Creator and in a right relationship with creation. They were happy, fulfilled, complete, and whole.

Some might consider the biblical view of creation idealistic from a human point of view. However, through the prophets we have God's promise of his continuing vision for his people:

In days to come the mountain where the Temple stands will be the highest one of all, towering above all the hills. Many nations will come streaming to it, and their people will say, "Let us go up to the hill of the Lord, to the Temple of Israel's God. For he will teach us what he wants us to do; we will walk in the paths he has chosen. For the Lord's teaching comes from Jerusalem; from Zion he speaks to his people."

He will settle disputes among the nations, among the great powers near and far. They will hammer their swords into plows and their spears into pruning knives. Nations will never again go to war, never prepare for battle again. Everyone will live in peace among his own vineyards and fig trees, and no one will make him afraid. The Lord Almighty has promised this.   —*Micah 4:1-4, TEV*

The royal line of David is like a tree that has been cut down; but just as new branches sprout from a stump, so a new king will arise from among David's descendants.

The spirit of the Lord will give him wisdom and the knowledge and skill to rule his people. He will know the Lord's will and will have reverence for him, and find pleasure in obeying him. He will not judge by appearance or hearsay; he will judge the poor fairly and defend the rights of the helpless. At his command the people will be punished, and evil persons will die. He will rule his people with justice and integrity.

Wolves and sheep will live together in peace, and leopards will lie down with young goats. Calves and lion cubs will feed together, and little children will take care of them. Cows and bears will eat together, and their calves and cubs will lie down in peace. Lions will eat straw as cattle do. Even a baby will not be harmed if it plays near a poisonous snake. On Zion, God's holy hill, there will be nothing harmful or evil. The land will be as full of knowledge of the Lord as the seas are full of water.   —*Isaiah 11:1-9, TEV*

Here we see that God's vision is a right relationship for his people in which all fighting, hatred, and selfishness are gone. God's vision for his people does continue. The cessation of fighting is not the end. Right relationships with God and with each other are the desired end. True peace or shalom is a spiritual peace, a peace that encompasses our relationship toward each other and our relationship with God through the good news of Jesus.

"The Peaceable Kingdom," animals appliqued on cloth.
Third and fourth graders under the direction of Joanne Holtzinger

Can experiencing personal peace prepare a child for accepting God's peace? A teacher who helped Rick stop fighting and begin to make positive responses toward others later learned of Rick's decision to make a positive response to Christ as Savior.

Rick, a rather large boy for his age, had a reputation as a bully with a quick temper. Observing his actions closely on the playground, I soon became aware that several smaller boys seemed to find delight in annoying Rick so that he would become angry and retaliate. Often the playground supervisor would only reprimand Rick, and he would find himself in trouble again.

Each time Rick would lose control of his feelings, he seemed to be remorseful and expressed dislike for himself. At such times, I would find a special place where I could chat with Rick without being obvious to the other children. We decided that perhaps it would be best if Rick simply walked away from those who irritated him. When I discovered Rick sitting all alone in the room while the others were outside playing during recess times, I knew this wasn't the solution. What Rick wanted was to be fully accepted by the other children.

Again, Rick and I had several talks. We agreed he would need to think before acting. He would need to *be* a friend before he would *have* friends. I was willing to help all I could, but only *he* could decide whether or not he really *wanted* to work for improvement.

Time passed, and Rick did seem to be improving. In every way I could, I publicly complimented Rick for his good behavior, and it seemed the class was quick to respond positively. Rick also improved in the neatness of his papers and in his handwriting. I often placed his papers on the bulletin board for all to see. When the class realized that I liked Rick and accepted him for what he was, they did likewise.

About the middle of the school year, we had a class discussion on mental and social health. At the end of that day, I found on my desk a carefully folded note in Rick's handwriting. "I have a problem with other kids. They always make fun of me. I tried everything, but it doesn't work. Sometimes I go somewhere to be alone. Once I thought of killing myself. Another time I was just plain sick about it."

I intensely wanted to help Rick. There was still time to do something for him. We had no school social worker or psychologist. Frequently Rick and I talked together. I affirmed him in every way I could. When he told me that things were better this year than last year, I immediately capitalized upon that positive note and assured him that things could continue to improve.

At the end of the year I received yet another note from Rick: "You are a good teacher, Mrs. King. I hope you keep teaching fourth grade. Good luck. With love, Rick."

As Rick progressed from grade to grade, I would talk with him as I had the opportunity. He always had a big smile and greeting for me. During a noon recess when Rick was in seventh grade, I noticed several eighth-grade boys attempting to get Rick involved in something which he obviously did not wish to do. I watched the proceedings as unobtrusively as possible. I feared that Rick's temper would flare out of control—precisely what the others wanted to happen. However, Rick kept his cool, the bell rang, and what could have been an unpleasant incident was avoided.

As Rick walked past me, I said, "I'm glad you controlled your temper. You really have improved!" Later his mother came to me and expressed her great appreciation for what I had told Rick.

Quite a few years have passed since I received Rick's note of despair, and I have had little contact with him. I do know, however, that he accepted Christ as his Savior and was baptized in the church where my husband had been pastor.

—*Lois Meyer King, East Peoria, Illinois. Age 10*

In the New Testament, we see God's vision of shalom in the ministry of Jesus, his apostles, and the early church. At Jesus' birth the angels proclaimed shalom to the shepherds: "Glory to God in the highest, and on earth peace" (Luke 2:14, KJV). In his first sermon, Jesus introduced his mission to bring good news to the poor, the broken-hearted, the prisoners, the blind, the wounded (Luke 4:18-19). In his Sermon on the Mount, Jesus identified peacemakers as children of God (Matthew 5:9, KJV), and cited love as the foundation for peace living (Matthew 5:38-48). At the Last Supper with his disciples, Jesus promised shalom: "Peace I leave with you; my peace I give you" (John 14:27, NIV).

Paul reminded the Christians in Galatia that they who had the spirit of Christ would live as Christ lived. "But the fruit of the Spirit is love, joy, peace. . ." (Galatians 5:22, KJV). Peter admonished members of the early church to search for shalom: "Turn from evil and do good; . . . seek peace and pursue it" (1 Peter 3:11, NIV).

God's will for his people will be accomplished! Christians experience the shalom relationship with God through Christ and continue Christ's mission of bringing shalom to others (2 Corinthians 5:18).

We need to realize that God's vision for the children who touch our lives is the same as his vision for all his people. Our goal as parents, grandparents, educators, and friends of children should be to help them be as whole as they can be, to have the needs of their bodies and spirits met. If our goal is to help children learn to live peacefully, we need to help them experience wholeness or shalom in the Lord. With careful and prayerful thought, this goal can become tangible and workable. Let us look at some ways the vision of wholeness and shalom can take on flesh. These are the building blocks of peaceful living.

What Is the Importance of Prayer?

One vital aspect in building wholeness is prayer. Children need to learn the value of prayer. The best way for them to learn is to see prayer in action. As adults working with children, we need to be active in prayer. Children need to know that true action for peace grows out of prayer.

Matt and Tim from my classroom participated with their parents in part of the Christmas peace pilgrimage I referred to at the outset of this chapter. They were present for the prayer service at the end of the walk. One beauty of the pilgrimage for me was the message it communicated to the children. Action for peace should always be accompanied by prayer for peace. We do not need great pilgrimages, however, to make this known.

The value of prayer can be shared with children any time we pray with them, whether it is for a sick friend, a problem at school, or a larger world problem. Sharing the Lord's wholeness, the Lord's peace, begins with prayer. Adults need to be in the spirit of prayer even when children are unaware.

As I tried to develop a feeling of acceptance and caring among my students on a daily basis, a current of strength through prayer was flowing unseen.

There was constant bickering and tension between the girls in my class. I used books such as *The Cay*[2] to develop understandings of self and those different from ourselves. We had group projects to help the children learn to work together. When the girls would come to a complete impasse, we had "jam sessions" to discuss problems and feelings involved.

Yet, with all my prayers and projects, it seemed as though we were spinning our wheels. The bickering and tension continued. Discouragement began to cloud my vision, and I was ready to completely give up.

One day the girls had a basketball game, and a player made a major error on the basketball floor. One of the girls sitting in front of me began yelling out to tell her how dumb her actions were. Another student sitting next to her said, "Don't yell at her! She's doing the best she can. That's what Mrs. Nice would say." I walked away, smiling and thinking, "Thank you, Lord, for letting me see that it's not all in vain." The bickering didn't completely stop, but I was able to see that progress was being made. My spirit was renewed.

—*Beverly Short Nice, Sterling, Illinois. Grade 5*

It was many years ago, but the picture is etched clearly in my mind. That September day Danny, with freckled face and tousled red hair, came into my third-grade classroom. He was larger than most of the children and not well coordinated. He was not a fighter, although first impressions could have put him into that category. But it was easy to see that he had inner conflicts.

I remember praying that I might find some way to become a real friend to him. God soon answered that prayer.

Early in September one of the science projects was to hunt for monarch worms on the milkweed plants and to bring them to the classroom. Danny was the first to find one of the treasures. I was delighted! He caught my genuine enthusiasm. For a number of days, he kept bringing in monarch worms! We got to watch the miracle from start to finish—from seeing the delicate and beautiful chrysalis being formed to watching the butterfly emerge and, minutes later, take off on gorgeous orange and black wings.

Danny didn't quickly become an *A* student. He never climbed to more than a *C* average that year. But he did make a swift ascent from near zero self-esteem to a feeling that he was a person of worth, admired by his teacher and his peers.

I am sure there were two special people who helped me to want to sense the needs, and especially the hurts, of young children—my mother with her sensitive, tender ways, and Mary Royer in her understanding way of helping teachers develop a caring attitude.

—*Elsie Burckhart Mast, Dalton, Ohio. Age 9*

How Do We Build Security?

One of the many blocks that builds wholeness is security; though taken for granted by many, it is important to wholeness. As with adults, if children do not have the basic necessities for daily living—a loving home, adequate food, and warm clothes—they are unlikely to feel peaceful. When children's needs for physical security are not met, they are likely to come into conflict with others who have what they need.

J. is an example of one who lacked a physical necessity. He

was intelligent for his age and functioned well in my first-grade class when he was not in conflict with another child. A common flare-up usually happened at lunch time. J. often came to school with an inadequate lunch. The other children always came with plenty. On more than one occasion, I listened to story upon story of how J. tried to take something from someone else's lunch. J. was obviously lacking what he needed to feel secure, satisfied, and at peace with the world he saw—his classroom. Without physical security, no one has a sure footing to begin making peace. Here is an example of how a good, nutritious breakfast to start a day made children more able to feel good about themselves and others.

> In a study of pioneer America, the culminating experience my student teacher and I planned with our fourth grade was a Thanksgiving breakfast prepared and served by the children.
>
> Interrelated learnings in music, art, math, science, nutrition, language, reading, and social studies were involved in preparing the simple, tasty food and attractive place settings. Since many of our children had to get their own breakfast at home or come to school with empty stomachs, we planned simple recipes which they could use at home for themselves and younger children. We had mush like the pioneers ate, and we taught the children how to cook similar hot breakfast food.
>
> We also wanted to help our pupils develop social graces through thoughtfulness to visitors and through their satisfaction in sharing pleasure with friends. They invited the college supervisor, the principal, and the superintendent.
>
> The children's joy in preparing the class breakfast led to new self-respect and self-confidence. They developed inner security that freed them to extend respect and friendliness to each other in the classroom. These traits are so basic in children's growth toward peace in school relationships and in all later social contacts. We teachers are sometimes unaware of the global and long-range significance of seemingly ordinary and taken-for-granted learning experiences.
>
> —*Mary Stutsman Lantz, Goshen, Indiana. Ages 9 and 10*

Security may also be related to social and emotional needs. When children do not feel accepted socially, they do not experience wholeness. A substitute teacher was able to turn children from ridicule toward respect:

> As a substitute teacher, I made it a point to get to the school as quickly as possible after I was called. But sometimes a teacher called in sick too late for me to get to school before it had begun.
>
> This happened one day when I was called to substitute in a third grade. When I arrived, the children were all in their desks, probably more out of fear of the strict first- and second-grade teachers on the same hall, than out of self-imposed discipline. The room was fairly quiet when I stepped inside except for one child sobbing noisily.
>
> D. O'Malley had her head in her arms on the desk, her red hair spread wildly around her. She came from a poor large Irish family—every child red-haired. I had met them in other rooms. The father was unemployed, the mother chronically ill. They lived on a little-traveled road. No doubt many mornings it was either get to the bus with uncombed hair or not get to school at all.
>
> I asked the class what was wrong. No answer. Clearly D. could not answer; she was too busy crying. I waited. Finally a girl said, "Some kids are saying she has cooties."
>
> I pulled my comb out of my purse and handed it to the girl who had spoken. I asked her to take D. to the restroom and help her wash her face and comb her hair.
>
> After they left, I was undecided about whether to scold the class for their injustice to D., mete out some general punishment, or try to find out who the name-callers were. I settled for saying, in a partially controlled voice, "D. does not have cooties, and you know it. You have hurt her feelings badly. Such a put-down is beneath this class."
>
> D. came back with her hair subdued. She gave my comb back and opened a book. Her eyes were red all day. I tried to unobtrusively encourage her in her work, and I saw little overtures of friendliness toward her during the day. The room had the possibility of being a good place for a poor child with uncombed hair.
> —*Helen Wade Alderfer, Scottdale, Pennsylvania. Age 8*

When children live with physical, social, and emotional security, they are more ready to live and work peacefully in the world.

How Does Learning to Communicate Relate to Peaceful Living?

Another building block of peaceful living is open communication. In a world of border clashes, cold wars, and terrorist threats, we can see the need to communicate in order to understand each other and settle disputes. Renita, one child I was privileged to have in my class, understood well that good communication is an important conflict-resolution skill.

Each day in my first-grade classroom, we had a time of sharing. The sharing usually included news from home, news about school, or any other news we might have. On this particular day, one of the children wondered why Great Britain and Argentina were fighting for possession of the Falkland Islands. I tried to give a simple explanation of the situation and then asked the children what they thought.

Renita usually had a solution or alternative for almost every predicament, and this time was no exception. She piped up and said, "Mr. Klahre, why don't they let someone watch [the Falkland Islands] for them while they sit down and talk it out?" I was impressed that Renita had begun to see the importance of communicating, in this case talking, as a way to solve conflict, restore relationships, and bring wholeness.

Another activity designed to help people express their thoughts and feelings is the Ungame. Doors of communication are opened by suggestions such as "Share something that you fear," "How do you feel when someone laughs at you?" and "Talk about a harmful moment." Through a forced silence due to nodules on her vocal chords, Rhea Zakich, originator of the Ungame, says she learned five secrets of communication. They are to listen well, don't criticize or judge what is said, talk from the heart, don't make a lot of assumptions, and show your love.[3]

If we give children opportunity to communicate, they will quickly learn by discovery the value it holds in the peacemaking process. Lois Schertz (reported at the beginning of the chapter) here describes further how her children's experiences in verbalizing freely led them to solve problems on their own and increased their sense of self-worth:

We continued with the class circle each day, sharing strengths, weaknesses, feelings of anger, loneliness, sadness. Toward the end of the year, the children proposed to me one day that when they were involved in fights on the playground, they might have their own small circle without the teacher, involving only the participants in the fight. It was used quite extensively. Although there were still days of frustration, fighting, and arguing, I was excited to see the children developing more self-confidence, improving their self-image, and accepting responsibility for their own actions in time of conflict. I feel this was a small but significant move in growing toward peace.

—*Lois Schertz Schertz, Washburn, Illinois. Ages 8 and 9*

Freely discussing problems with an adult friend and the Eternal Friend helps children to become more peaceful.

The first time seven-year-old Crystal came to visit at our home, she used words like "goo-goo" and "ma-ma" to get attention. During the two years of our friendship, she has learned that we will spend time with her. I have affirmed her verbally, listening when she has a story to tell, when she's been hurt by her older sister, when she's feeling lonely because her mother isn't home and she's locked out of her house. We talk to Jesus together. We bake cookies, crackers, pizza, and mix granola together. She goes shopping and visiting family with us. She is polite and respectful, blooming as she responds to the love of Jesus.

—*Glenda Detweiler Moyer, North Philadelphia, Pennsylvania*
Ages 7-9

We need to understand that before children can think of alternatives to a problem or solutions to conflict, they must be able to understand and use the language of living peacefully. This is particularly applicable to younger children. Do the children around us understand concepts such as happy-sad, if-then, and is-or? As the adults use these terms, they take on flesh for the children. For instance, we might say to a child, "*If* you share your blocks with Billy, *then* he will be happy." "It *is* time to eat now *or* the food will get cold."

Hearing, seeing, and doing are important in helping young

children develop the concepts and vocabulary of peace living. It is also important to remember that even older children who usually have better-developed verbal abilities still need to hear, see, and do. An old proverb might be an applicable model for our conversations with children. It goes something like this: "What I hear, I forget. What I see, I remember. What I do, I understand." The more children hear us use appropriate terms and participate with us in such language usage, the more they will remember and understand. Use language that makes for peace with children.

Karen Zaur in *A Manual on Nonviolence and Children* suggests that we teach children to choose a *useful* phrase in responding to people who are bothering them while they are playing or working. Examples are "Please stop it!" or "I don't like that!" [4] Sylvia took a similar approach when she communicated her feelings.

> We had always taught our children to ignore teasing and to control their feelings rather than to become physically defensive. As a kindergartner, Sylvia had long thick braids. In first grade she wanted them cut off, so I agreed and had them cut. Apparently the change was too great for her and her classmates, who teased throughout the day. When she came home that evening, one of the children said, "Good-bye, short haircut."
>
> Sylvia turned around and said, "Why don't you just say, Good-bye, Ugly Duckling?" That was the end of the teasing.
> —*Oleeda Sutter Albrecht, Morton, Illinois. Age 6*

Important to the development of linguistic concepts is children's awareness of how the voice affects meaning. Several questions are before us: Are we helping and encouraging children to say what they mean? Are children around us learning to be deceptive in their speech? Do their voices reflect appropriate feelings for the situation? Our children live in a society where they are bombarded by deception. Are our children learning the importance of Paul's exhortation in Ephesians 4:14-16 (NEB) to "speak the truth in love"? Speaking the truth in love is speech that communicates honestly, caringly, and factually. Read how the "truth" changed for fourth graders when they had actual contacts with black children.

> Many of the children in my fourth grade thought they definitely
> *hated* blacks. On Langston Hughes's birthday, I had a mother
> bring her two friendly little black boys along when she came to
> read his poetry. The boys freely circulated in the room. The chil-
> dren were so shocked. They had really never had close contact
> with friendly blacks before. Declarations of hatred changed to
> overtures of friendship.
> —*Elsie Eash Sutter, Goshen, Indiana. Grade 4*

Outlets for creative communication are necessary for wholeness. If children are to learn how to resolve conflict peacefully,
they need access to all types and modes of communication.
When children paint, draw, build, write, dramatize, or speak,
they are communicating. Access to many modes of communication promotes freedom to fully communicate.

PEACE

Peace is like a sunset
That shimmers on the lake.
Peace is like a smile
That no one can mistake.
Peace is like a bird
Singing sweetly to its young.
Peace is like a song
That not many of us have sung.

—*Andrea Milne, age 10*

Through the use of markers, fabric, varieties of paper, and
modeling materials, children of various ages interpreted their
understanding of peace.

Matt Grieser, age 9

"This is a duck swimming on the water quietly."
Kelly Short, age 5

"Peace is building."
Brent Falcón, age 5

Jeremy Garber, age 9

Rebecca Howland, age 10

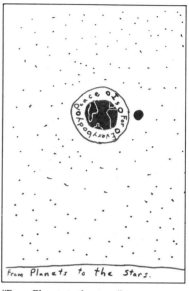

"From Planets to the stars."
Bryan Falcón, age 9

"The sun is peace and the heart is love.
Together it is beautiful like a flower."
Justin Kauffmann, age 9

Bobby McLaughlin, age 10

Colored tissue paper separated
by black construction paper
simulated stained-glass windows.
Matt Smucker, age 11

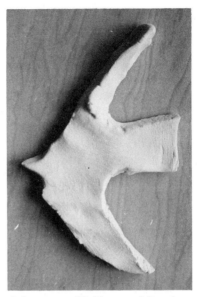

A dove was molded from modeling clay.
Artist unidentified

PEACE was etched in clay dough
on which a three-dimensional
dove was placed.
Artist unidentified

A dove was mounted on a background
of colored taffeta.
Joel Hartzler, age 9

The goal Norman and I shared was to create an environment in the home that modeled conflict-management and authentic caring relationships as the very fabric of our life together. Reconciliation was not to be seen as simply an abstract, unrelated idea.

We have tried to make our home a place where sharing feelings, information, and experiences can take place.

As a young child, Heidi learned to communicate her feelings through writing. The following is a poem she wrote to express her thoughts to her younger sister.

> You're nice sometimes,
> You're mean sometimes,
> but always you will Love,
> but always I will Love,
> ˙ and then we'll have fun,
> and then we'll run
> to a far-off lane
> where we'll start agane [again].
>
> Love,
> Sis

—Sharon Kennell Kauffmann,
Goshen, Indiana. Ages 8-9

Through out-of-class contacts, a Sunday school teacher won the confidence of a troubled girl who then communicated her feelings through writing.

Susie has been living with her grandmother for the past year. She is the oldest of six children. Her family situation has not been very stable for the past five or six years. Her father and mother are divorced, but neither one wanted the children. Both parents have served jail sentences in the past several years.

About the time Susie's father was released from prison and her mother entered, I began teaching the eighth-grade Sunday school class. On the first day Susie brought along her cousin Rhonda, whom she said was visiting church. The next Sunday she brought Rhonda again, saying Rhonda was in the eighth grade, too. I learned the cousin was really in the sixth grade. The following Sunday when I talked to Susie about it, she and her cousin started to cry. They said the girls in Rhonda's class were mean to her, and if she couldn't come to class with Susie, she wouldn't come at all.

They came regularly to my class for about six weeks. Then they began to go other places in the church instead of coming to class. They visited the mother's room or walked around in the halls. When I talked to Susie about it, she became quite disturbed and said, "No one is going to tell me what to do." We could have refused to bring her to Sunday school (she rode on a church bus), but I was just becoming aware of Susie's home situation at that time and felt that leaving her at home would not have been the right thing to do. As the oldest child, Susie had an almost unbearable weight on her shoulders.

I asked Susie how I could show her that I loved her. She shrugged her shoulders. I asked if she would go out with me some evening for supper; I'd take her shopping afterward and buy her something. Her face lit up, and she said she'd like that. We decided to go the following Tuesday. When I went to pick her up, she came running out to the car, saying she was sure I wouldn't come, but she was glad I did.

We had an enjoyable evening eating and shopping at Concord Mall. She said it was the first time she had ever been to a shopping mall. We went again about six weeks later. It cost some money on my part, but Susie became a changed person in church. She has been cooperative and has written me a number of notes which were more than enough reward for what it had cost in money.

These are excerpts from several of her notes:

> My Life Story
> My mom and dad got married when they both were 17. I was born when my mom was 18.
>
> My mom and Dad seperated when I was 9 I'm 13 now.

My dad is re-married and has 1 little girl by my step mom. her name is Kathy. The baby's name is Amberly. The baby is now 8 mos. old.

Guess who
Susie

Mary,

hello. I really enjoyed going shopping with you that really meant alot to me. I really do love my outfit. I never thought I'd ever get these pants that we been wanting for along time. You talking to me really made me feel like I was loved.

I was wondering if one of these days we could go again so I could talk to you about what is going to happen to us Kids.

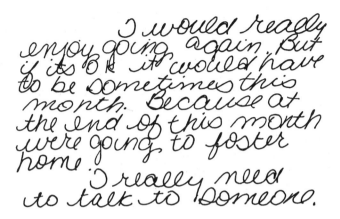

I would really enjoy going again. But if its ok it would have to be sometimes this month. Because at the end of this month were going to foster home. I really need to talk to someone.

—*Mary L. Yoder Bontrager, Topeka, Indiana. Age 13*

Another teacher became the person who understood the inner pain Daisy communicated through her actions. This teacher stood by her through a long grief process, much like Jamie's father in *A Certain Small Shepherd*.[5]

Daisy was a student in our small bilingual program with whom I worked individually on English and reading over a period of about four years. Although she had been in the program since kindergarten, by the sixth grade she was still barely reading on a first-grade level. Her intelligence was obviously more than adequate, but her moodiness seemed to indicate a deeper sense of confusion and self-doubt.

In her sixth-grade year, I met with Daisy individually every day and was determined to find some way to break the pattern of failure. Using the simplest and most interesting reading series I could find, we set up a system of charts. With these she could see daily progress and know the expectations for each week's work.

At first Daisy worked hard and seemed proud of her progress. Gradually the old moodiness set in with the onset of family turmoil in January. Her father had just left, her mother was laid off work, and her whole world was in chaos. Moodiness turned into complete withdrawal. Daisy would sit at her desk, head on workbook, and refuse to speak, even to answer simple questions.

I wanted to see Daisy through this hard time. So, since she

wouldn't speak, we sat. Every day for over three weeks we sat together at her study table for the thirty-minute class period. Sometimes I worked, sometimes I laid my head down (like she did) and rested. Usually I just sat, occasionally offering a willingness to talk, but never getting a response. As we sat in silence, I wondered how much longer we could take time for a student who had had so much attention through these six years, and who still showed no signs of progress in reading. But I couldn't desert her.

Daisy gradually decided to work again. I'm not sure which of us was more surprised (or more happy!) when at the end of the year her test results showed a complete year's progress in reading—the first measurable success in six years!

—*Brenda Hostetler Meyer, Goshen, Indiana. Grade 6*

How Can Children Be Taught to Do Problem Solving?

Children need to learn verbal skills to identify problems and decide what the best solution to the conflict is. Children should be able to ask questions: What do I need? What does the other person need? Can we solve this together? Do we need some help? Who can help us? For children to develop skills to resolve conflicts, we need to back off and assist the children in thinking through a problem, not do their thinking for them.

Becky, our adopted Korean daughter, came to join our family when she was nearly two. Our church family and neighborhood readily accepted her, and before long there were other biracial children in the area. We seldom thought about race. Becky's best friend was Laura, an adopted black girl her age across the street.

One evening when Becky and I were getting ready for bed, she was telling me more about her day in kindergarten. "You know," she said, "some kids call Laura 'chocolate bar!' " I could tell from the way she said it that it was upsetting. I asked why she thought they called Laura by that name. She said it was because Laura was black. After a while I said, "I wonder what kind of a bar they'd call me." Becky laughed and said, "You'd probably be a vanilla bar." Then I asked, "What would they call you?" She thought a while and finally decided she was a lemon bar. I said I was hungry enough to eat all three kinds, and we dropped the subject.

—*Marjorie Yoder Waybill, Scottdale, Pennsylvania. Age 6*

Last year one of my first graders came to school crying each day, clutching Father, and not wanting to stay. (The older sister was still doing this as a fifth grader.) I held the distraught child, and the class told him things they liked about him and ways they would help make his days more pleasant. Three months later he was walking to school alone with a smile; he even drew a school when he was asked to make a picture of his favorite thing.

—*Ardyth Hostetler Steckly, Hutchinson, Kansas. Age 6*

A class of sixth graders was guided to understand conflict management through playground research. Then applications were made to classroom situations.

Conflicts are common in all people's lives. Children should not feel that something is necessarily wrong with them if they are involved in a conflict. However, they should learn how to resolve conflicts. Several class periods were devoted to conflict resolution to help pupils learn something about this topic.

First, the pupils listed what they thought were some reasons conflicts between persons developed into quarrels. These were shared with the class, written on the chalkboard, and then classified and grouped under major headings: power hierarchy (explained to pupils), different interests, impatience, desire for same items. . . . The pupils worked on this activity and copied the groupings.

Later, the class was divided into groups of two or three and told to record observations of children at play several days during the noon recess. They were to look for (1) ways conflicts began, (2) words or gestures used, and (3) ways conflicts were resolved. The observing groups were at different places on the playground but remained unobtrusive and did not enter into others' activities.

Each small group recorded observations and reported their findings at a class meeting later that week. This time, observed behaviors were listed on the board and classified. We compared these observations with those of the original groups, and thus we confirmed or challenged earlier opinions. Conclusions were drawn from this process and recorded by the pupils. During this phase, disagreements arose, but the pupils tried to work toward agreement by asking questions and sharpening communication skills.

Here are some of their conclusions: (1) Some children had more conflicts than others. (2) Often younger children called for an adult or older children to intervene. Intervention was not asked for as often among older children. (3) Older children looked for alternative activities or avoided confrontations by walking away. (4) Few children apologized to others. (5) Some children compromised, took turns, or selected an activity everyone liked. (6) The few who had physical conflicts also had more conflicts with other children. (7) Children who were part of a group in which a conflict occurred, usually didn't try to help solve a problem but were saddened when it resulted in a physical or verbal exchange.

A class discussion was devoted to these conclusions. The pupils were asked to consider the reasons for the observed behaviors. They tried to put themselves in the observed child's place and imagine how the other person felt. Then they suggested alternative courses of action—both immediate and long-term.

The last class meeting was devoted to problem solving. The class was divided into groups of four. Each group was then given a sheet with several problematic situations for them to solve. Inevitably, differences of opinion surfaced, but the pupils saw that there had to be more than good communication skills. For the group problem to be solved, both would have to be willing to sacrifice. They realized that conflict resolution required give-and-take effort, but that more was accomplished in the long run, and participants felt better about the results.

Even though these pupils continued to have some interpersonal conflicts during the school year, there were fewer unkind remarks and quarrels. The pupils' level of conflict awareness was raised and so was their willingness to look for alternative ways of resolving differences of opinion.

—Hobert Yoder, Iowa City, Iowa. Grade 6

When children learn conflict-resolution skills by practicing them under the guidance of an adult, they become more able to use them without assistance.

I suggest that the two students in question find the quiet spot in the room and there talk over their differences. They are not to leave this spot until they have resolved the problem to the extent that they can live with it. This places the responsibility of their actions and the ensuing consequences directly on themselves without adult interference. The children then join the group with more understanding of another's feelings and with more tolerance of other viewpoints.

—*Verelda Zook Roth, Glen Ellyn, Illinois. Kindergarten*

We must be sure to involve children in peaceful conflict management at school and at home.

How Do We Help Children Make Choices Which Support Peaceful Living?

Children are exposed to society's values through television, videos, toys, and books. Often the values these resources emphasize do not encourage peaceful living. How do we guide children in handling these influences?

Last year my reading class evaluated current television programs. We took a poll of the most popular programs and then discussed why they were popular. The main reasons given were lots of action, humor, and identification with the characters.

We then discussed what a good television program should be and do. Good programs (1) are true to life and face current issues, (2) will not necessarily show all the problems being solved, (3) can be informative as well as entertaining, (4) will not feature violence or destruction of property, and (5) will show a family or a group of people caring for and about each other.

I was not surprised to hear that few (if any) parents discussed programs with their children. I was disappointed to hear that parents let their children watch programs with violence and emphasis on the supernatural without any supervision.

In my thirteen years of teaching, I have found that, with little exception, the best students watch the least television. They read more books, are involved in more physical activity (and are thus better athletes), and have more and varied interests than do children who watch television a lot. Children who watch more television seem to be hard-pressed to come up with creative ideas for writing stories or creating poems. A lot of television watching inhibits creativity.

—*John D. Christner, New Paris, Indiana. Grade 4*

Helping children evaluate toys sometimes has to be a "try it yourself" approach. After watching a TV commercial for a new toy car,
Jeff just had to have it. Excitedly he walked into the variety store
and bought the toy with his own money. As soon as he opened
the lid, he said, "It doesn't look as big or nice as on TV." After it
broke on the second day, he came to the conclusion, "You know,
you can't always believe what they tell you on TV."
                    —*Ruthann Brilhart Peachey, Goshen, Indiana. Age 4*

I have come to the realization (by reading about the subject and
through watching other children) that too much TV, and even
more specifically, violent TV programs (cartoons are especially
bad) can make children aggressive and violent in their play. So
our children are allowed to choose only one program each per
day from the offerings for children on the public TV network.
Many people are amazed that our two girls watch only an hour of
TV a day, but actually, it's often less. Although they are three-and-
a-half years apart in age, they play together well and creatively
without the interference of TV. In fact, they frequently become so
involved with their play that they even forget about "Mister Rogers' Neighborhood."
   We used to enjoy outings as a family at McDonalds. But then I
read that they are among the worst offenders in their sponsorship
of high-violence TV programs. Now we eat at a locally owned
deli—or make our own more healthy fries and shakes, for "Mc-
Donalds at Home" times. The girls love it, and we all feel better
after eating more wholesome food.
                    —*Sandra Gerig Glick, Freeport, Illinois. Ages 3 and 6*

I use open-ended stories to help children in decision making.
They enjoy telling what the wrong, thoughtless thing would be
and then the right, loving thing. The stories are about two children wanting the same toy, a mother who asks a child to pick up
toys, a sick child in the neighborhood, or. . . .
                    —*Marie Keeler Miller, Brevard, North Carolina. Prekindergarten*

The influence of a single book can have a lasting effect:

Our son delighted in the story of *The Little Engine That Could.*[6] The
little engine puffed along on the approach to the hill, saying, "I
think I can, I think I can, I think I can." The engine made it up the

hill and then said joyously, "I thought I could, I thought I could, I thought I could," as it chugged down the other side of the hill.

Our son adopted the engine's cry with many tasks he chose to do, such as stacking blocks, tossing a bean bag through a certain hole, and pitching a ball over the plate. I recall hearing him say once when in college that he conquered by the engine's cry.

—*Alta Eby Erb, Kansas, Pennsylvania, Indiana. Ages 2 to 22*

As I helped children grow in peaceful relationships, they were especially responsive to books, such as *The Happy Owls, Growing Pains, Stevie, Evan's Corner,* and *The Two Windmills.*[7]

—*Sara Alice Zimmerly, Homestead, Florida. Grade 3*

Discussing *The King at the Door*,[8] which contrasts humility and arrogance, can help support choices to promote peaceful living. Notice how a contact with an author left an impact on Bill's life.

Bill's father disliked him and constantly reminded him of this. I discovered that Bill could draw Lois Lenski figures better than anyone else in the room. On her birthday we wrote Lois Lenski a letter to send with a card Bill made especially for her. Before sealing the envelope, I inserted a brief note telling her a bit about Bill's tragic home life and poor evaluation of himself as well as his fondness for her books. When she answered our letter, she addressed the envelope to him and put a special note in for him. How proud he was! It was his first letter. I laminated it. He moved during the year, but took it along. When he returned eight years later, he told me he still had the letter.

—*Elsie Eash Sutter, Goshen, Indiana. Grade 4*

After I read aloud *Kelly's Creek*,[9] there was much less bickering and conflict on the playground.

—*Glenn Zoller, Goshen, Indiana. Grade 5*

Children need encouragement to identify and express their feelings to further peaceful living. Cooperative games and activities can offer such opportunities. Young children have an awareness of their feelings but often find it difficult to express them to others. During my three-year stint as a first-grade teacher, I often wondered how I could encourage my students to share informally with each other about their feelings without my assistance. Half-way through my third year of teaching, I discovered a feelings game.

The game was a suggestion from the kit *Discovery and Understanding of Self and Others.* The game is a simple board game that can be easily used by two or more children. The board contains four facial expressions—surprise, happiness, sadness, and anger, with a spinner (see illustration). All  the players are required to do is to twirl the spinner and tell one incident when they experienced the feeling indicated.

After a few class discussions about feelings and a brief introduction of the game, I placed the game with other free-time activities. The game became a popular item for free-time use. I found that the students enjoyed it not only because they enjoyed sharing with each other, but because there were always winners, no losers.

Why Not Fight Back?

How can we help children choose to live the good news of peace in the forgiving spirit of Jesus when we are faced with the question, But why can't I fight back? It is difficult to respond to that question. Adults too often find it easy to moralize with children rather than leading them to understand the situation from all perspectives. It is important in such situations to help children understand their own needs, the needs of others, and the perspective of the Prince of Peace.

On one occasion while discussing Jesus' teaching about turning the other cheek (Matthew 5:39), a boy responded that his father told him that if anyone hit him, he was to "hit him back." Not wanting to discredit the father, I asked the class what they thought Jesus would do. They, including this boy, thought Jesus would not hit back. I left it at that, hoping the boy would be able to make the appropriate response when the need arose. At any rate, it suggested to him an alternative to repaying violence with violence.

—*Lorraine Roth, Shakespeare, Ontario. Age 7*

To teach the wholeness of peaceful living, adults must lead children to understand the situation.

Because of inclement weather, my second-grade pupils were spending their regular recess period in the classroom rather than outdoors. During the hubbub, J., just a bit overage as a second grader, enthusiastically asked, "Miss Yoder, do you know what I'm going to be when I grow up? I'm going to be a bank robber."

Not knowing what to say, I said nothing. I felt that arguing with the boy was not the way to deal with the problem. That night I prayed, "Lord, what should I have said? How should I deal with this?" I received no apparent answer.

Many months later, J. again asked the question, "Do you know what I'm going to be when I grow up?" He gave the same answer, "A bank robber."

I knew it was time to do something. I feel the Lord put the words in my mouth. "Oh," I said plaintively, "if you'd be a bank robber, you'd take some of my money. I get paid for teaching school so I can buy the things I need. Someday I'll be old and won't be able to earn any money. I give the bank some of my money now to take care of for me. When I'm old and can't earn any money, I'll have the money the bank is taking care of for me.

"And here's your friend Dick. The bank takes care of some of his father's money. If you'd be a bank robber, you'd take some of his money, and—" I was rambling on when the boy abruptly broke in saying, "Oh, I'll be a fireman."

I informed the boy of the work of banks as it touched the lives of his friends instead of giving an impersonal challenge to an exciting adventure. This brought a most heartening response.

—*Rhea Yoder, Elkhart, Indiana. Grade 2*

I thought of asking my coteacher and our Sunday school class of fifth graders to help me write about nonresistance for *Junior Messenger*. On two different Sunday mornings, we allowed time for participation in a discussion of the meaning of nonresistance as fifth graders understood it. Samples of our conversations follow:

Ronnie: Last week at school we were playing baseball, and I hit a homer. Another guy was jealous and after the game he wanted to start a fight.

Teacher: What did you say?

Ronnie: I knew he was just jealous, and I said, "A Christian doesn't fight."

Teacher: What happened?

Ronnie: He just walked away.

Jim: Guys don't like to hear us say, "Love your enemies," and verses like that.

Craig: My teacher at school says if we do something kind to guys like that, it's like heaping coals of fire on their heads. He says we should not tattle about guys that want to fight. It is best to ignore them.

Jim: If you hit back, both are in trouble. If you don't hit back, then just one is in trouble.

Teacher: Do you think there might be certain times when it would be all right to fight back?

Beverly: Christians do not believe in fighting at all, because fighting can hurt someone.

Teacher: We remember that Jesus never fought. When people slapped him and hit him and spit at him, he didn't do anything or say anything. Fighting hurts, and Jesus did not want to hurt anyone.

Craig: It takes a bigger man to walk away from a fight.

Ronnie: If someone teases, just ignore him. He will soon stop. A fight is usually just over an ordinary matter. If you fight once, then you are labeled as someone who will fight. It's okay to wrestle for fun, though. But fights get into fists, and usually there's a black eye or something.

Teacher: Do girls ever fight?

Ronnie: Well, some of them bite and kick and trip you sometimes. And they fight other girls with words. They won't talk to each other for a while if they are mad or jealous or something.

Teacher: But all of us can ask God for help to be kind.

Jim: Some guys say you're chicken not to fight. I can say, I'm not a chicken. I am a Christian, and I don't like to fight. If I were a chicken, I would be clucking.

Craig: It is good not to take things so seriously. Humor helps.

Jim: Anyway, it's only because someone is jealous or something that he wants to fight. And besides, fights never settle anything.
Craig: A fight only makes another enemy.
Jim: If you do fight and lose, you're in a soup, and it's kind of hard to get out. But there will be no fight if *you* don't fight because the other guy always says, "You gotta throw the first punch." So if you don't throw it, everything's okay.[10]
                    —*Geraldine Gross Harder, Newton, Kansas. Grade 5*

Children, and even adults, need assistance to find alternative solutions to aggressive behavior.

As assistant principal and now building principal, I need to make frequent contacts with parents of children who have had a fight. I always stress with the children and with the parents that the children have options other than fighting. Fighting is not an acceptable means of settling disputes. We discuss the other options that the children could have chosen and will choose in the future.

I am always amazed at the number of parents who tell me that they told their children to hit back if someone hits them first. I have to do as much in educating parents as in educating children on how to handle disputes and problems in a nonviolent manner.

Our society teaches our children and adults to react violently. The people who believe in peaceful handling of disputes must join together in educating our society. We must speak against violence on TV. We must speak for nonviolent methods to handle problems.

                    —*Kay Freyenberger Frunzi, Denver, Colorado. Grades K-6*

Do We Pass Along the Story of Peace?

In the Christian way, we are fortunate to have a cloud of many witnesses who have gone before us and modeled the good news of peace. In our possession is a great oral and written record of peace. We should never fail to use these stories to give witness to the way of peace.

The 200 Sunday school children of the Universal Evangelical Association in Cotonou, Benin, had been singing for forty-five minutes while waiting for this unavoidably detained white person to show up. The African Independent Churches in Benin are fervent, fast-growing, and eager to learn more about the Bible. I was visiting them for the Mennonite Board of Missions and for the Interconfessional Protestant Council of Benin. In this church, while the children have Sunday school, the adults go throughout their neighborhoods, evangelizing. Then everyone meets together at 3:00 p.m. for Sunday worship.

I had learned to be prepared to speak on such occasions. This time I had four short stories of the way of love being lived, and a colored illustration to go with each. The first was the story of Jesus' crucifixion and his words of forgiveness to his captors. The second was of Stephen showing that the way of love was not just for Jesus to follow. The third was the story of Dirk Willems fleeing across the ice-covered canal, showing that the way of love was not just for Jesus and his followers in Bible times. The fourth was a recent story of a Christian, Adamu, from Nigeria, showing that the way of love was not just for Bible times, for long ago, or for other peoples, but also for Africans today. In all times and all places, this is the way Jesus wants us to live.

As these stories were translated from my French into the local Goun language, children and teachers listened attentively and seemed to agree. (Those who understood some of each language received a double dose!) Then we closed by singing a song I had learned in Benin, "Je suis chrétien jusqu'à la mort" (I'll Be a Christian Until I Die). They knew the song and sang enthusiastically, accompanied by the rhythmic shaking of calabash rattles and the striking of a brass gong.

The story of Adamu was one of twenty-seven African Christian peace stories that I collected and wrote as part of my Mennonite Board of Missions assignment. A book can do much more than one person can do. For example, this year one of these stories will appear in each of the four issues of a Christian children's magazine, *Tam-Tam*, published in French in Abidjan, Ivory Coast, at 20,000 copies per issue.

—*Marian Hostetler, Abidjan, Ivory Coast. Preschool-Grade 6*

Children learn that we value what we speak of and read about. We pass on what we find helpful. They can be so inspired by peace stories of their ancestors and other peacemakers that they will begin to live peacefully. *Coals of Fire, Peace Be with You,* and *A Friendly Story Caravan* are samples of quality works for children that pass on the good news story of peace.[11]

A teacher relates how he learned peaceful responses from his college professor which he applied in his classroom:

Raymond was *not* a good student. His span of concentration on subject matter was not long enough to make learning meaningful. When I started teaching, he had, from stories his peers told me, become a terrible discipline problem. Attempts at overt control and ridicule heaped on him by my predecessors exaggerated the problem and made him look for opportunities to rebel and throw the entire room of four upper-grammar grades into an uproar.

To my way of thinking, scolding and ridicule were inappropriate. This approach was not really *my* idea, but is attributable to the patience and devotion Mary Royer espoused and practiced.

On opening day the bell rang as a signal for all to enter and assume their assigned seats. All did, with one exception—Raymond. Immediately one student called his absence to my attention. Raymond was presumably trying me. I assured the entire contingent of students that when he was ready to enter the classroom, he would do so of his own volition.

Ten o'clock was recess time. Raymond had stayed in the lower-level playroom but then joined all of us in a game of softball. I saw some of the boys talking to him. Apparently he was determined to maintain his troublemaker status, because when the bell rang for assembly, he again elected to avoid the classroom.

At eleven the door opened and Raymond presented himself sheepishly and with embarrassment. I assured him that we were delighted to have him and requested all of the children to help him feel and become a part of our learning group.

I can't say that Raymond was a model thereafter. He tried my patience, but on return visits when I have met him, he delights in reviewing his initial encounter with me. He has fitted well into his Amish-parentage community, and I feel that the patient approach helped Raymond rid himself of a lot of animosity so he could live at peace in his community.

—*Gerald B. Miller, Charm, Ohio. Age 12*

How Long Does It Take to Teach Peace?

If we are to help children choose peaceful ways to resolve conflict, we must be friends with time. Peace often does not come quickly to children. If we truly value peace, we will live it and surround children with understanding and courage while they learn to accept and live peace. A country school teacher shares such an experience:

During my first year of teaching in 1931, I had twenty-eight fascinating children in all eight grades in a one-room rural school. Among them were three bright, flaxen-haired girls from Germany who were extremely defensive and ready for a fistfight or verbal abuse at the slightest provocation. Nobody knew why their father, Mr. S., reportedly one of Hitler's policemen, brought his family to our community. The preceding teacher resigned due to constant fighting among the children and because of Mr. S's death threats to teacher, children, and neighbors. Parents were afraid to let their children walk to school. While the German children were home for lunch, we discussed the need for peaceful solutions and going the second mile for the safety of everyone!

One day Ruthie, one of the German girls, was accidentally hurt at playtime. After school I went to Ruthie's home to express regret. Mr. S. warned that if anything happened to Ruthie, he would kill the child who hurt her. I reaffirmed my concern for Ruthie's recovery and our desire to be friends. Another time Gerlinde, Ruthie's sister, said, "I *hate* Wade! I will *never* forgive him!" When I asked how she could pray "forgive us our debts as we forgive our debtors" without forgiving Wade, she looked startled.

Because every child in our school had a lovely voice, we sang the cantata *The Children of Bethlehem* at our Christmas program. Differences were forgotten as all the children joined in sweet song to celebrate the birth of the Prince of Peace. Even Mr. and Mrs. S. came to our program and expressed thanks for it and for the girls' progress in school.

The rest of the year both children and teacher were alert and patient to avoid hostilities. After a year in a different school, the S. family made a surprise visit to my home. They described their new school as impossible and said our school was "like heaven." The next year they moved to a remote state where their disturbances and threats resulted in their deportation.

I shall always be grateful for the children who, in spite of aggravations and dangers, were willing to practice nonviolence toward a volatile, unhappy, transient family. We pray that the S. family's brief respite of peace in our little country school may have helped them to eventually find peace for their troubled lives.

—*Katherine Royer, Smithville, Ohio. Grades 1-8*

An additional account of Lois Schertz's class circle illustrates how Lois benefited from her own modeling.

We discussed loneliness, fear, and sadness. One morning I shared some things that had happened in my family and caused me to feel sad. The children listened quite intently.

The next week I sensed an air of excitement, giggling, and whispering. One morning a delegation of boys approached me and asked that I stay out of the classroom during a lunch hour. I protested that I needed to prepare lessons. They told me with an air of authority that they had talked to the principal, and he said it would be all right.

When the bell rang following the lunch hour, I opened my classroom door to the cheers of "surprise" and was bombarded with confetti made from the construction paper. The classroom was decorated with balloons and streamers. On my desk was a cake, candy, popcorn, cookies, and numerous other gifts.

I was overwhelmed. When I asked what the celebration was about, a child replied, "You told us last week that you were sad, so we wanted to make you glad." All this from children labeled by the system as troublemakers and potential juvenile delinquents! As the children became aware of their feelings and found that someone cared, they, in turn, were able to show love and comfort to someone else who was troubled.

—*Lois Schertz Schertz, Washburn, Illinois. Ages 8-9*

Modeling peace living is a lifelong task of growing toward peace. As we love and strive for Christlike living, we must constantly be in touch with the source of peace. A nursery school teacher keeps herself in tune this way:

In my four-year-old nursery class, I put either word reminders or Scripture verses on my bulletin board to remind me to be more loving or to smile. Just one glance at them helps me be a better example of Christ's love and forgiveness.

—*Marie Keeler Miller, Brevard, North Carolina. Age 4*

The teaching done through modeling often takes place without knowing how or when it happened. It is not always predictable. But it is always an active teaching element.

> Randy was from a poor home situation and was emotionally upset. He didn't trust anyone. What can a busy teacher with a room full of children do? I decided to show Randy I loved and accepted him just the way he was and that he was important. The change I could see in him was almost unbelievable.
>
> When I left that school, one of the teachers told a friend of mine that she always thought of me as a peacemaker. It was one of the neatest compliments I have ever received. But I can't tell you what I did to deserve it.
>
> —*Berniece Kropf Schmucker, Lebanon, Oregon. Grade 1*

Peace in our world begins with individuals who choose peace through experiencing wholeness and through seeing peace taught and lived in loving and caring relationships.

> College can be frightening, upsetting, boring, tiring. I had my share of doubts about my ability to be a teacher. Yet, whenever I walked into Dr. Royer's classroom, a sense of security and familiarity settled around me. The many books and displays, the pictures, the plants, her smile—it was like coming home, a little patch of peace in the midst of the complex college world. Her enthusiasm and faith in me—in all of us—renewed my excitement about teaching. She so openly believed in her students that we couldn't help but have confidence in ourselves.
>
> —*Sharon Schrock Beechy, Goshen, Indiana. College*

We need to teach children and adults to choose peace and share shalom! Let us prayerfully "go after the things which make for peace" and help one another (Romans 14:19, Basic). We look forward to the time when "nations shall not . . . learn war anymore," people shall live in peace, "and no one shall make them afraid; for the mouth of the Lord of hosts has spoken" (Micah 4:3-4, NRSV).

Interpersonal Relations

WHEN children experience inner peace, that peace is reflected in their relationships with others. A child who is loved can become a child who is loving. Children grow toward peace as we guide them to convey Christ's love in their relationships with others.

PEACE IS

Peace is caring for one another
Peace is having no war
Peace is being in quietness
Peace is having friends
Peace is having good ways to compromise
Peace is solving problems by talking
Peace is no put-downs to younger siblings
Peace is as warm as a sunset reflected on water

—Tonya Miller, age 11

4. How Will I Make a Place of Peace for Children?

Christina Neff Okamoto

IN mid-August a schoolroom is an empty place. The windows are clean. The desks are washed and polished. The empty bulletin boards reflect the afternoon sun. I study the quiet, waiting space. How will I make a home for children where they can become brothers and sisters? How will I make a place of peace? I think of the words I read and underlined:

> We were as gentle among you as a mother feeding and caring for her own children. We loved you dearly—so dearly that we gave you not only God's message, but our own lives too.
>
> —*1 Thessalonians 2:7-8, LB*

Ideas begin to flow. I'll put pictures of cats on this bulletin board especially for Ron. School and home seem impossible to him with his mother gone. Only his cat holds the world together just now. The reading tree with its bright book jackets would be nice in this area, with pillows and the rocking chair and beautiful books nearby. Charlotte's web spun from string would be perfect in the corner by the door. Soon we'll all be reading about Charlotte[1] with a brand new paperback in each child's hand while I read the story aloud. The Silverwind tape will be waiting in the tape recorder. Then there are the song-books and the guitar! The windows will be full of plants. There will be paintings on the wall. In those open shelves will be games, kaleidoscopes, art materials, centers for science and math, all saying, "Welcome, fourth grade! Come, explore new ways of learning and living together!"

What will these twenty-seven children bring? From school records and community contacts, I know they will bring many differences in nationality, race, religion, family patterns, health, economic background, academic ability, scholastic achievement, and feelings about school. Soon we will be together for the next nine or ten months. How can our classroom become a place of peace in which children may grow? I have many questions, and so will the children. Their questions will help us in our planning.

The headings of this chapter are six questions the children asked. In essence they are the questions of all children, everywhere, and in all times. They are basic for teachers and parents to think about in answering the question that is the title to this chapter.

What's Wrong with Anna?

The children came running to me. "What's wrong with Anna?" they asked. Anna's face was streaked with tears. First she had been angry, and now she was inconsolable. The group of serious little girls practically carried her to me. I took her in my arms and asked, "Anna, what's wrong?" She answered through her sobs, crying out the words:

> It's my little brother Georgie.
> He lives with my mom. I spent the weekend with them.
> He can't hear or talk right.
> I feel so bad because I used to fight with him.
> I walked him partway to school.
> It makes me sad when kids call him names.
> He comes to me. I tell him,
> "It ain't gonna do you any good to punch 'em out,
> Georgie. Just ignore 'em."

Georgie hugs me and says, "I love you, Anna,"
and runs off to play.
My mom helps him write little letters and sign his name.
It makes him feel special.
And he is special, special to me.
I miss him so much (more tears).

Together we planned a surprise package and letter to mail to
Georgie. A much-cheered Anna returned to her friends.

Children have so much on their minds. Robert was intently
reading his grade card when the question was asked, "What
does a report card not tell?" Quickly he replied, "What you
think about on the way home." Children are anxious about
themselves and about each other. They worry about their families and their pets and the world. They are troubled by the
things they hear and see. A teacher is challenged to see these
concerns from the child's point of view, to understand, to listen,
to interpret, to comfort.

Joe was having a miserable day. He was impossible. Tears
were running down his cheeks. In broken sentences he told me
that today his pig was being sold to Pantry Pride. It has been
said that a pet is a child's child. Children need loving ways to
say good-bye to their creatures, or they may continue to be
troubled and angry. Unshared grief can result in bizarre behavior, even after many years. Casey had a far-off look in her eyes.
Her hamster had died the night before. She said, "I feel like
writing *hamster* all over my paper."

Derek came with a tight little smile to tell me that his kitty
died the day before. I put my arm around him, and his eyes
filled with tears. I mounted a piece of lined paper on a fresh
white drawing sheet so he could write some special words
about his cat and draw her picture. He eagerly began the project.

Kirsten wrote about her feelings in this way:

As I dreamed, I saw pink blossoms waving in the breeze. In the
sunlight I could see my Grandpa. He was smiling with rosy
cheeks. Then I saw my hermit crabs; Gordon was smiling pleasantly with Herman the first and Herman the second. God was

taking care of them. They were happy with Him. Heaven was where they wanted to be. Everyone is safe and happy in heaven.

Often when children are quarrelsome or annoying, they are responding to stresses which they may or may not be able to identify. A teacher needs a creative imagination to see beyond the immediate situation, as when Joe came hurrying in from recess. "There's a tug-of-war going on in Scott's mind," he said, "and the wrong side is winning."

Scott was loud and impulsive. He had come storming into the classroom on the first day of school, a wild little motherless boy full of fight. If anything displeased him, he would crumple in a heap in the cloakroom. It seemed there was for him a continuous stream of crises. On the playground he could quickly explode into a mass of flying fists and angry words. His classmates worried about him and were valiant in their support.

After recess the children came urgently telling me that Scott had been in a fight with kids in another class. They said Matthew and Kristie from our room were in the hall talking to him.

Matthew then reported, "We told him that when he fights he only hurts himself. But he won't listen."

Barry and James asked if they could try to help him. Benjy and Brian wanted to go, too.

As Benjy left, someone whispered, "Fred went, too." Fred was a huge dirty, yellow stuffed dog that Benjy invested with wondrous personality! About a minute later a smiling parade entered the room with Benjy announcing joyfully, "Fred did it!" Scott brought up the back of the line, clinging to Fred, his face buried in the old dog's comfort. Everyone clapped!

One day Scott was furious with Susie for telling some people that his mother died in a car crash. He came to me and declared, "If they want to know what happened to my mother, they can come to me one at a time, and I will tell them."

Most of the afternoon, children unobtrusively made their way to Scott's desk to hear his story. He shared earnestly with each one. It was a hard story of leaving and being left.

As the children were preparing for dismissal, I said, "Make sure you take home everything that belongs to you." Scott took me by the arm. "Come on, Miss Neff, I'll take you," he said grinning.

In the weeks that followed, each child had the opportunity of being interviewed by the rest of the class. When it was Scott's turn, someone asked, "Who's your best friend?" Thoughtfully he replied, "Everyone in here!"

Small tokens of love may seem a poor remedy for the problems in a child's life. But such gifts can be blessed beyond what one dare even dream of.

> I am having a difficult year at school. These youngsters have so many problems—a product of incest, a boy picked up by juvenile officers, a girl with a slight mental handicap who wanted to kill herself yesterday by hitting her head with rocks. . . . In spite of all their problems, I have learned to love these motley twenty-seven. . . . Junior no longer yells at the top of his lungs that he hates us. . . . He put a note on my desk the other day with a little homemade gift saying he loves me.
>
> Oh, the time it takes to counsel, instill good attitudes, work through problems! Junior called me twice after school was out. . . . They were moving, and he kept the personal note I had written him. (I write a card to each at the end of the year.) He keeps it in an envelope by his bed, he said. Every night he reads it before he goes to sleep. He almost has it memorized.
>
> —*Roselyn Aschliman, Glendale, Arizona. Grade 2*

Each year brings class discussions relating to occult practices. Occult material in games, television programming, videos, and children's books is growing fearfully. Children encounter Ouija boards at parties. School libraries offer books devoted to the practice of witchcraft. Cable hookups bring the most gruesome experiences into living rooms and bedrooms.

Kathy told of how her mother, father, and brother were watching a horror movie. She was in the next room reading and couldn't concentrate because of the screams. She said that when she walked through the room, it looked sort of interesting, but she went upstairs and put "Honeytree" on the new little record player she'd purchased. I'd given her the record, and I was glad to think of her listening to these words:

> Day is done, Gone the sun,
> But we need not fear,
> Darkness comes that we may see the stars
> And know that God is near.[2]

One day the children had many worried questions about occult programs, bad dreams, and gruesome stories. After a long discussion of God's power and goodness and how it triumphs over darkness and fear, Brian said, "Thank you so much for telling us about these things."

Sometimes I feel like Gandalf, as he engaged in the conflict of a bitter hour when the place of peace was battered and worn:

> The rule of no realm is mine. . . . But all worthy things that are in peril as the world now stands, these are my care. And for my part, I shall not wholly fail of my task . . . if anything passes through this night that can still grow fair or bear fruit and flower again in days to come.[3]

Tony was glaring at me again. The heaviness of his expression weighed on me. I couldn't please him. He was "playing games" with the rules, pushing my tolerance in subtle ways. "Let's go!" I said. We headed for the time-out room down by the nurse's office. He was silent. Often he battled verbally. As he sat down on the chair in the quiet little room, I saw one crystal tear. I thought of the things that made the tear: the separation of his parents, the tragic death of someone he held dear, unanswered questions, loneliness. I asked him to write to me.

Several hours passed, and when I returned, this was Tony's message: "When I give you those faces, I don't do it on purpose. I do it because either I didn't understand, or I feel like crying and trying to hold it. It's just too hard."

Early the next morning we met to write his plan of action for return to the class. His ideas involved both of us. This is how it looked, signatures included:

> When I feel bad in the morning, I will come and tell you.
>
> Tony

When I see you feeling badly, I will come and talk with you.
When I feel badly, I will come and tell you so you can help me.

Christina Neff

On Tony's next spelling list, he signed, "Love, Tony."

How Come You Don't Yell?

This note appeared on the teacher's desk:

Your the nicest teacher I know.
Because your nice and do'nt yell
and you like the things I like, like cats.

Love,
Coni

Many children are accustomed to raucous television voices, loud music, and rough parental commands. Sometimes the classroom may become their only place of refuge. Marion Gerber comments from her experience as a kindergarten teacher in Orrville, Ohio: "One calms the waters by being gentle of voice." I am reminded of the words of Moses:

Let my teaching drop as the rain,
my speech distill as the dew.
—*Deuteronomy 32:2, NASB*

Eighteenth-century educator Christopher Dock wrote, "Often a child can be better trained and corrected and taught by kind words when harshness would be . . . in vain."[4]

Larry was very disruptive. . . . If it was time for music, he wanted reading or arithmetic, or vice versa. To show his displeasure, he turned his desk over, spilling the contents upon the floor. We went right ahead with what we planned to do, the other children coming to the circle of chairs. After working with the others for a while, I gently invited Larry to come sit by me. He came. I put my hand on his knee. I could feel the tenseness and anger leaving him. Before long his head was on my shoulder, and he said he was sorry. I gave him a hug and asked him what he would like to do now. He went back and picked up his things. This happened two or three times during the first eighteen weeks. He became adjusted and showed love to others.

Tommy was a little red-headed boy with a hot temper. His father and an older brother were in prison. Even though I stood between the girls' and boys' restrooms, watching and listening closely, a disturbance occurred. I went into the restroom and saw that Tommy had Bobby in a corner and was pounding his head on the hard tile. I took each boy's hand and kept them with me on the playground. After awhile, Tommy said, "I want to tell Bobby something." He told him that he was sorry, and he wanted to be friends. I smiled. They ran off to play, all forgiven.

—Minnie Sutter, South Bend, Indiana. Grade 1

If children know only unhealthy ways of handling frustration and anger, time out to think, talk, and plan may bring a sense of peace and purpose to replace yelling and strife.

David and Mike were constantly having differences regarding the rules and regulations during kickball and other games. Instead of trying to settle differences for them, we created a private place in the back of the room where they could go and share their feelings toward one another. Usually each came away from their meeting knowing how the other child felt. After sharing and informing one another, they had a feeling of relaxation and peace.

—Elizabeth Beyeler Jacobs, Goshen, Indiana. Grade 3

The first several weeks of one school year were exhausting. I wondered if I would survive. The level of activity was beyond anything I'd seen in the previous years. Could I be gentle as I longed to be? At the meeting of my Thursday evening fellowship group, I shared the frustration, the sense of helplessness I felt in meeting the needs of so many troubled children. Each member of the group volunteered to pray daily by name for the children in my class. The change was dramatic. Within the week, I felt the peace of Jesus growing among the children. In myself I sensed a strong, calm readiness. His peace was alive, aggressive, holding us together. I recalled a verse in Philippians:

Let your gentleness be evident to all.
The Lord is near.   —*Philippians 4:5, NIV*

I knew that we were daily being commended to the great Teacher, of whom it was said in Matthew 12:18-21 in the *Living Bible*:

Look at my Servant. See my Chosen One.
He is my Beloved, in whom my soul delights.
I will put my Spirit upon him. . . .
He does not fight nor shout;
He does not raise his voice!
He does not crush the weak,
Or quench the smallest hope;
He will end all conflict with his final victory,
And his name shall be the hope of all the world.

We experienced a year of special joy and peace. I didn't have to yell.

What Are We Doing Today?

Children come with the freshness of morning still on them. Sometimes it is covered with lettered T-shirts, breakfast crumbs, and cartoon voices. Other times it is dulled by growing layers of sophistication, fed by a culture that scorns innocence and mystery. But the freshness waits to be awakened.

I open Narnia[5] to them, and suddenly they are through the wardrobe and romping with Aslan. I ask them to write while the music plays softly, and new bright worlds grow on plain lined paper.

Sometimes we go out for a nature scavenger hunt and look for things that remind us of ourselves. Amy brought in a little milkweed puff. She said, "It reminds me of me because it's soft and nice, and I like to go out in the wind and blow around."

In a song of nature, Jenny wrote, "I can see love from the wind sometimes. I think God is blowing me kisses."

Kristie was studying the wooded hills from our windows. "The trees are together," she wrote, "the clouds are together;

it's togetherness that wants to mix."

Drew was celebrating spring. He had a faraway look in his eyes. He was slowly putting these words on paper:

> All life in which existence of love is present, thou shall ascend heavenward; as a flower or a tree comes up, not down. Though Spring comes with love but once a year, if you live with the Spring, it shall be year-round.

When interviewing prospective teachers, our curriculum director loved to ask, "Is education a preparation for real life?" He hoped they would say, "No, education is real life!"

Preparing for first grade is not sufficient reason for kindergarten. Being ready for second grade is poor motivation for first grade. Children might rightly ask, Do I ever get somewhere that is special all by itself? We need to celebrate the work, play, and wonder of *now!* It's delightful to become so wrapped up in the adventure of today that teacher and children even forget the difference of years. I remember the day when Benjy looked at me with twinkling eyes and remarked, "There have been fourth and fifth graders here all year, but *when does the teacher arrive?"* C. S. Lewis, in his autobiography, *Surprised by Joy*, recalls a favorite teacher:

> A boisterous, boyish, hearty man, well able to keep his authority while yet mixing with us almost as one of ourselves. . . . He communicated (what I very much needed) a sense of the gusto with which life ought, whenever possible, to be taken.[6]

Children love unexpected, unorthodox ways of learning.

> Variety can be introduced through many stories and songs throughout the day, not just at a storytime or a listening time. Stories and songs can spill like an artesian well in any setting and for every age whether in an Ohio eight-grade, one-room rural school, in daycare, in a Midwest urban American school, or a Ugandan international primary group.
> —*Lenora Dietzel Sempira, Charm, Ohio; Goshen, Indiana; Lombard, Illinois; Kampala, Uganda. Childhood*

To feel quiet and happy at the end of a day was more possible when the last activity on the schedule was what we called Uninterrupted Sustained Silent Reading. . . . Each person in the classroom, including the teacher, could . . . take a favorite book to any spot in the room and stay there as long as there was silence. That glorious aura of pleasant hush filled the room, and love of books grew as some crawled under the teacher's desk or on the windowsill or somewhere flat on their tummies on the carpet, and read for fun.

—*Thelma Miller Groff, Goshen, Indiana. Grade 4*

As a celebration of reading Marguerite de Angeli's medieval story *The Door in the Wall,*[7] the fifth graders created a castle room in an adjacent storage area. Tall Peter was up on a ladder painting turrets. He stretched to paint the edge of a stone and then leaned against the ladder to say, "This year is such a relief."

Korey and Julie told the student teacher, "In other classes you have to write misspelled words twenty-five times, and if you forget your name, it's two hundred times! This year, learning is what counts; the other stuff isn't so important."

Is a "creative project" something a child may do only when "work" is done? Or is creativity the way by which all the child's work comes to life? Children of the Creator need opportunities to be creative. A warm place of surprise, joy, and adventure is a lively, peaceful place.

Chatting about school, Sang commented, "There are lots of fun things to do in work. Every day is different, not like plain old routine. It's like coming into a circus."

Benjy declared, "This is the most wonderful school I have ever been to. It sure is hard to get bored here."

Brent saw on the chalkboard this list of work options:

> Complete math hunt.
> Do spelling cards.
> Work on magazine summaries.
> Continue bookmaking.

Pointing to each item he said, "I like this and this and this! I like everything."

An environment in which creativity is fostered is a place where children may express their thoughts more readily. The days become full of gifts given and received: "My poem, your picture, our idea. . . ."

Listening to *North to Freedom*,[8] we wait breathlessly while a guard releases twelve-year-old David from a concentration camp. We travel with him on his long, lone journey in search of his mother in Denmark. I ask, "How is your life different because you have heard this book?" The children write:

Gary: "You get loved just by listening to it."

Kay: "It sort of brought me closer to God."

Sue Ann: "Oh, I feel like crying for all that David has done to show me that we should be thankful for what we have! Our parents LOVE and CARE for us. . . . We are free . . . and everyone should be free."

Erma: "It made me want to not fight back. It made me love people more."

We ride the prairie with Laura,[9] swim the Chincoteague Channel with Misty,[10] bring the storks back to Shora,[11] zoom down the carpeted hall of the old inn with Ralph on his motorcycle.[12] Then we become illustrators and authors of our own books and write on themes dear to us: families, pets, hobbies, trips, treasures. We share our words aloud and experience joy and compassion for each other.

John Stevens, in his book *Awareness*, writes:

> Anything you can do to increase communication in your class will reduce your need to impose order by authority. The class will become more a place for listening and learning, and less a place for fighting and antagonism.[13]

One day I asked the children to comment on thoughts from George MacDonald:

> They need help from each other to get their thinking done, and their feelings hatched, so they talk and sing together; and then, they say, the big thought floats out of their hearts like a great ship out of the river at high water.[14]

Kirsten responded this way: "We can't learn alone. We have to learn together. And when we do learn together, we will always live together with the Lord." Children feel the acceptance of their gifts as they interact joyfully with materials and ideas and each other.

Can creative learnings continue in classrooms during national and international crises and conflicts? Yes, children need then, more than ever, the securities of fundamental freedom in questioning, reflection, acceptance of one another, and the release that comes through enjoying and creating beauty.

In 1941 my fourth graders were ready to sing a song from our Music Hour Series when Rodney warned, "We shouldn't sing that song by a German." We talked about the famous composer who lived long before World War II and knew nothing about the war. We talked about the many people in Germany who were just as sad about the war as we. Everyone relaxed and sang the lovely German song.

Pearl Harbor cast a special shadow over our fourth grade because Marilyn's big brother, Bob, was a naval officer there, and several days passed before we heard of his safety. Fire gongs called us to air-raid drills at school, and shrill sirens demanded blackouts at night. We discussed the fact that some of these sirens were probably manufactured in Japan. We decided it was important to obey them for our own safety even if they were made by an "enemy" country.

Our subsequent social studies unit on Japan brought protests. We agreed that our books and visual aids about Japan were prepared long before the war and had nothing to do with it. We talked about the many Japanese people who were worried about their brothers and fathers just as we were and who didn't want war either.

As the children studied about Japan, they were soon captivated by the artistry of the Japanese people. I was thrilled when Howard built a Japanese garden in his backyard.
—*Katherine Royer, Orrville, Ohio. Grade 4*

Hope must remain vibrant as children face their struggles daily. Darryl and I had shared fourth grade. He was now in eighth grade when he called and invited me for dinner at Burger King. I rejoiced to see him again. We talked for a long time over hamburgers and fries. He began to tell me the story of his uncle who had died. "My uncle was a strong man. He worked at Three Mile Island. But he got contaminated by radiation and lost a hundred pounds." Darryl's bright, sensitive eyes were full of tears. He continued, "When my uncle was dying, he asked me to come and sing for him. I took his hand and sang. I didn't like to see him that way."

Darryl went on to tell about his struggle with smoking and his efforts to get his friends off marijuana. As he got out of the car at his house, he sighed the words, "I wish everything would come to an end and the new world would begin. Then we could get rid of all the cruddy stuff."

On another occasion, Shelly and Francine were riding with me, discussing the things in the world that scared them and made them afraid. They were also reminding one another of the day when God would gather us and take us home. Shelly said thoughtfully, "It gives me expectation. I can just imagine a loving voice calling, and all the animals and the angels singing."

Sheri came visiting after school to tell me about a baby bunny she had helped. She hoped that if Whispurr (my cat) found it he'd be nice! "Not yum, yum," she said. As she lilted down the walk, she called back, "Peace on earth, you know!"

Suzy was writing about creation rejoicing. She concluded by saying that when the world ends, we'll be glad we were part of it all. I told her that I look toward a new world where there is no pain, no sorrow. All is beautiful, all free, all at peace. Her oft-troubled face came alive with joy. She hurried to her seat to tell her friend Tracy. Then she looked up, saying, "I want to be in your class forever!"

How Are We Doing?

Quoting from the book *Education for Peace: Focus on Mankind*:

> The teachers and schools are confused. . . . They assume that all students have or should have an intense desire to know things, a need for abstract thought and aesthetic experiences. Therefore,

they jam textbooks in students' faces and facts down students' throats. They disregard security, belonging, love, and self-esteem in their fanatic worship of knowledge, not realizing that the needs they are so casually tossing aside must be met first.[15]

Children need continuous validation as they work. I do not want students to equate a mistake in math or a poor spelling paper with personal failure. I want each child to feel the security of knowing that we begin where he or she is and we move on from there.

Kevin was not getting his work completed as usual because of personal concerns outside of school. His assignment was shortened, and he was promised a surprise if he could "pitch in." The next morning he came in glowing, "Not only did I finish course 1 in math, I started course 2."

> Nothing can be so disruptive of peace in a classroom as grades. When I assured my students that I checked mistakes so I would know what I still needed to teach them, the feeling of pressure to succeed and the incentive for cheating were reduced. My wise principal permitted us to use mostly *S* and *U* (satisfactory and unsatisfactory) grades.
>
> Less emphasis on grades made a comfortable climate for learning. Malcolm's comment, "I'm 'proving,'" well expressed the children's freedom and fun in progress. Gifted students enjoyed helping slower learners; and everyone rejoiced when Alvin, our special mainstreamed pupil, was successful. Because of prolonged illness and immaturity, two children were not able to keep pace with the others. But they did not feel like failures. They were grateful to repeat a year so they could learn with more ease and enjoyment. On the closing day of school, Harold, a superior student, didn't flaunt his superiority. He looked at his grade card, happily jumped up and down, and announced simply, "I passed!"
>
> Competence, not competition, had bound us together in a joyful help-one-another quest.
>
> —*Katherine Royer, Orrville, Ohio. Grade 4*

On the wall above the carrels in our classroom, this verse is written:

Each one of you has some kind of talent. Devote it to helping others. In this way God can use you to scatter all kinds of mercies. (1 Peter 4:10, *The Inspired Letters*, by Frank C. Laubach, Nelson)

Children need to be affirmed with notes and hugs and smiles. When a child shows special effort or accomplishment, I write a note for the child to take along home. As a class we make validation envelopes and fill them with notes for each other. The effects of such encouragement continues on and on. Jeff, now in middle school, called one evening. This was the conversation:

Jeff: "I'm doing okay in school. This is a smart kid!"

Teacher: "I know it. You always were smart."

Jeff: "Well, my sister doesn't think so, but as long as you and I know it, that's all that matters."

Praising children at parent conferences often brings about new understanding and teamwork between parents and children. After conferences one fall, a note from JoAnna appeared on the board:

I like my parent-teacher report. Thank you. Whenever my mom tells someone about what you said about me, I feel happy all day!

This winter we are having three-way conferences, including child, parent or parents, and teacher. We talk together around an attractive tea table with simple refreshments. Each child reads to the parent "My Life Story," shows samples of other work, and describes personal goals. The anticipation and courtesy with which the children welcome their parents, and the delight of the parents in the children's work—these have confirmed my feeling that at least one parent-teacher conference each year must include the child.

I had each child tape-record a message for their parent or parents entitled, "What I Like About My Parents." As I played the tape for the parents, many of them exclaimed with tears, "Did *my* child say that?"

—*Hazel Miller Kinzer, Goshen, Indiana. Grade 2*

Children and parents and teacher need such ties that bind their hearts in mutual love.

How Many Friends Do You Have?

Children gain many interpersonal skills by relating to a wide variety of people from beyond the classroom. They enjoy thinking of a growing world of friends as they meet each other's parents and grandparents. The other adults in the school become their helpers and friends. Our yearly plans are structured to include contact with younger children, elderly people, and handicapped people. I bring in personal friends and family to share talents and hobbies and good times from many backgrounds and interests—soccer players, artists, musicians, poets, historians. And so many others! Travelers are a special delight to the children. The stories of friends are many.

Each year we adopt grandparents at a retirement home within walking distance of our school. Beginning in March, we visit twice a month for a half hour, equipped with books, games, photos, hobbies, and presents.

One of the first years of the program, we matched little Lori with a lonely grandma. Lori herself was often troubled by family hurts and cried easily. I can see her standing by the wheelchair of her new grandmother, wiping the tears off the wrinkled old face. An attendant sharply reprimanded the elderly woman for crying in front of the child. Lori hastily said, "It's okay if she needs to cry. I don't mind."

Preparing one day for our visit to the grandparents, Peter volunteered to pray, "Our Savior, help us to see them for the special people they are inside."

Heather's face glowed with smiles after her first visit with her grandmother. These are excerpts from her written reflections:

> I read a book to her and every page she laughed. . . . I asked her what it was like when she was a little girl, and then we talked about our fathers, and I told her that my father was dead. She prayed for me and my mom and my brother and sister. . . . She prayed that I could be happy without my daddy.

One child wrote a year-end letter to his adopted grandmother:

> Dear Grandma,
>   Thank you for the tender loving care you gave me and all the other lovely things you gave me.
>
>   Your James

Here is the story of special friendships that grew out of a visit to a disabled friend of the teacher:

> The summer before school started, I brought all of my pupils in groups of four and five to my home. . . . We stopped to visit my friend Emma Hartzler, who is in a rocking bed during the day and an iron lung at night. She had them write their names in her guest book, and together we asked the pupils about their interests. Through the year we sent our newspaper to her so she was aware of what we were studying. . . . The children grew very fond of her. When we made jelly or bread or anything that was "sendable," they always wanted Emma to have some. In some cases, the children brought their parents to visit her.
>   —*Elsie Eash Sutter, Goshen, Indiana. Grade 4*

Children need to be prepared to act courteously. The kindness and understanding they receive and learn to give are fundamental to all relationships they will experience throughout their lives locally and globally. In planning for two days away from the classroom, I asked the children to write letters telling me how they would receive and encourage the substitute teacher. Following are excerpts from these letters:

> Dear Miss Neff:
>   When Mrs. S. comes, I will act like she is you and I will be very nice to her. . . . Any friend of yours is a friend of mine.
>
>   Your friend,
>   Sheri

Dear Miss Neff,
On Friday and Monday I will behave for Mrs. S. I will make her feel like she is our family.

Eternally yours,
Anna

Can I Come Along?

Peter was part of a sophisticated fifth-grade crew who campaigned for hard-rock records and grooved on being grown-up. Pete liked "freaking out" more than anything else. He was great fun, but I worried about him. One Saturday evening he and two of his classroom buddies came along to a contemporary Christian concert given by a group called Fireworks. The boys sat spellbound in the front seat of the auditorium. They were hearing the Jesus story in a way that surprised them. Afterward, I bought them the tapes they wanted, and the songs lived on. Steve would pop out from behind walls in the cafeteria or in the hallway, singing bits of phrases: "Out of the darkness and into the light!" Peter wrote his own Christian rock song:

HOPE

I was out of control a complete disaster
Until He came along with love.
He is the Lord with love I hoped for;
You're my only hope, my only hope.

So, Lord! please forgive all my sins,
Let me enter into your heart.
You are my hope, my sun and laughter,
You are the hope for me.

The atmosphere in the classroom grew more gentle, more caring.

One of the most significant ways to enrich the classroom environment is to have contact with a child outside the classroom. This greatly increases the warmth of rapport between teacher and child and in turn affects the atmosphere of the entire group.

I am delighted when my schoolchildren want to become my Sunday school and vacation Bible school children.

I continue to be inspired by Christopher Dock, eighteenth-century Pennsylvania educator and author of the first book on pedagogy in the colonies. He was known for his interest in every aspect of a child's life. Others praised him: "He shaped the mind, and more the soul . . . for he gave heed to heaven's guiding."[16] Daily he knelt at his desk with the open roll book before him, praying for his pupils by name. I have seen the gracious changes that happen *inside* a classroom, because of prayer, through which we can reach *outside* the classroom. Following are experiences of children who sensed God's presence and asked, "Can I come along?"

Lyn, eleven, was in my fifth-grade group. She wanted to come along to Sunday school. Her parents were divorced, and it made her sad. One Sunday I shared with my Sunday school class the way in which we can know Jesus. They all listened quietly. When the bell rang, Lyn and I went upstairs and slipped into one of the front benches. We sang. The preacher began his message. Suddenly Lyn was crying. I asked her what was wrong. She replied softly, "Found Jesus—now." After church, some of my friends gathered around to pray with her. She loved calling us family. I wrote a song for her:

> Little girl, golden hair,
> Sitting here beside me,
> You found Jesus,
> Angels singing,
> He is bringing
> New life to you.
>
> Tears begin in your eyes
> Waiting here before Him—
> Jesus loves you,
> He's been calling,
> Now you're falling
> In love with Him.

She asked me to share the song with our fourth- and fifth-grade class at school. Before I sang and played it on my guitar, she came to the front of the group and explained:

> I believed in God but I didn't talk about it or tell people. The Bible was in the back of my drawer. Then several Sundays ago, Miss Neff started taking me along to church. The preacher said something, and it made me think of myself. I started to cry. I began to believe more than ever.

Everyone clapped. Casey said, "That was a nice song."

I gave Lyn a *Living New Testament.* We used colored pencils to mark verses for each other to read. Once she called by phone to say that she'd hunted for an hour to find a verse for me. This was the note that came marking the Bible page:

> I hope you don't look
> upon this as being small,
> for when I looked at the words,
> they looked ever so large to me.
>
> With love,
> Lyn

The verse was this:

> May God our Father and the Lord Jesus Christ
> give you his blessings and his peace.
> I always thank God when I am praying for you.
> —*Philemon 1:3-4a, LB*

Another day Lyn called. "I was thinking about how I was before I got into your classroom. I used to think that it was my ideas and my religion that changed, and that I was still the same me. But I realized that I am not the same me. When someone bumped me, instead of saying, 'KNOCK IT OFF!' I just told him to please watch."

A song that touched me deeply was written by a troubled little girl. She asked one day in a frenzy of tears, "If my mom says I'll go to the devil, will I?" I told her about Jesus. She listened intently. She wanted to receive his love. She wanted to open her heart to him. I saw the healing begin. This is the song she wrote and sang to me:

> You took me from the meanest one
> And gave me to the greatest One,
> You took me from the devil
> And you gave me to God.

I see her now during vacation Bible school. As a high school student, she has asked to become a teacher's helper.

As I teach, I pray. I watch the peace that grows in a class when children sense the enfolding presence of the Lord Jesus. They are his children; to him they belong. I was commending the class one day for their remarkable writing, their brilliant ideas. Jennifer said delightedly, "God helps us to express our feelings." Jake looked over his shoulder and responded, "God helped Jennifer express *that!*"

We share a public school classroom. I speak only those things of God that arise naturally as we talk and work together. The call of Jesus and the longing for his shining peace are strong within us, and so it comes forth everywhere. With each year Jesus brings a growing sense of unity and peace into our midst—a sense of home, and Home.

● ● ●

P.S.: After thirteen years as a public school teacher, I am a homemaker and mother, and a resource person in various church, school, and community programs. I continue to enjoy contacts with my now-grown fourth- and fifth-grade students who come to share their life journeys with me, my psychiatrist husband, Jeff, and our son, Stephen.

5. How Can We Encourage Empathy and Guide Peaceful Interaction?

Carolyn Smith Diener

MAHATMA Gandhi wrote, "If we are to reach real peace in this world, and if we are to carry on a real war against war, we shall have to begin with children." [1] Guiding children to show love and concern for others may be one of the most important contributions adults can make in working toward peace and justice in the world. Children do not automatically come into the world as caring, sharing, helpful, peaceful individuals. We must nurture them to establish positive relationships with others. Parents, teachers, Christian educators, and all adults who have a direct influence on children must encourage them to develop caring behavior.

During my years as a mother of three daughters, a teacher of public school kindergarten and church school, an instructor in the department of human development at the University of Alabama, and a lecturer in the division of education at Indiana University Southeast, I have begun to understand the process by which children develop altruistic or caring behavior—and its importance! Peacemaking and conflict management require empathy for others rooted in understanding and respect.

Once I asked a group of college students in a preschool development class to play hypothetical parent. They were to name qualities which they as parents would like to see their children acquire. The students listed personal traits such as happy, outgoing, honest, smart, and healthy.

I was disappointed that none of the students mentioned any of the caring qualities which children (and adults) need to develop in order to interact peacefully with others. Such qualities include self-respect, trustfulness, honesty, sense of fairness and justice, appreciation for others, empathy, sympathy, desire and ability to share, kindness, desire and ability to settle disputes without force or violence, generosity, cooperative spirit, helpfulness, and assertiveness with kindness.

These qualities come under the umbrella term of altruistic or prosocial behavior. *Altruism* can be further defined as helping others without expecting tangible rewards, self-sacrifice for the good of the group, and selfless concern for the welfare of others.

In our highly competitive world, many parents may not really want their children to be altruistic. We give lip service to the importance of caring qualities. Yet our society seems to put high value on getting ahead at all costs and being happy. It takes courage to be a person who genuinely cares for the feelings of others. We must show children how to have that courage.

> I'll never forget Richie; a fun-loving, curly haired, handsome nine-year-old, always vying for attention, whether for a compliment or for chastisement.
>
> He had been taught from early on to stand up for his rights. A fist was a handy tool to attain his goals. What he believed or chose to believe for his own benefit was the course to follow, and this he defended to the end.
>
> Richie refused ever to admit that he was wrong. A ringleader and class idol with determination, he became a bully, mistrusting me (his teacher) and most adults. His parents' broken marriage had upset his world of trust and love.
>
> One day I wrongfully accused Richie of a misdemeanor. Since he was constantly in trouble, it was an easy error. When I later

discovered my mistake, I openly apologized and asked for his forgiveness. This act was almost incomprehensible to him since Richie never admitted a wrongdoing himself. For an adult to make such an admission was unheard-of in his experience.

Slowly thereafter, Richie learned the secret of peace, the chief components being love, forgiveness, and trust. It was the turning point in classroom control; the eye contact between teacher and ringleader became warm and trusting. Richie finally learned a new road to peace.

—*Irma Ebersole Bowman, Akron, Pennsylvania. Age 9*

How Do Children Learn to Care?

Dorothy Kobak is a psychiatric social worker with the New York public schools and an authority on the topic of "Teaching Children to Care." She maintains that too little attention has been paid to our responsibility for developing caring individuals. We are all interested in children's IQs (intelligence quotients). We should also be concerned about their CQs (caring quotients). Dr. Kobak feels that a higher CQ leads to emotional health and personality growth, as well as mental health, elevated academic achievements, improved school management, and input for a responsible commitment to society.[2]

As my Sunday school class of four- and five-year-olds assembled about our round table, I observed one girl whose eyes were filled with tears. When all were seated, she burst out crying "Before we came to church this morning my father, and mother said ugly words to each other."

The teacher and other children cried with her. When she saw all the tears of sympathy, she wiped her eyes, and so did the rest of us. She spoke no more of the conflict she had heard. She was comforted in her distress. We prayed and had a happy time together.

—*Alta Eby Erb, Hesston, Kansas. Ages 4-5*

Charles Smith discusses the significance of emotions in developing caring attitudes.[3] Emotions allow us to be affected by events, to experience feelings. If we had no emotions, we would not react because we would not care. Emotions enable us to communicate with others and understand one another better.

> Mrs. Kamps, our school social worker, suggested that I identify with the particular emotion John was experiencing at a specific moment in order to be of the most help to him. For example, when John was so angry with Jim for knocking over his block tower that he hit Jim, I might respond something like this: "John, I see that you are very angry with Jim. I am tempted to get angry at people sometimes, too, so I know how you feel. But I cannot let you hurt Jim. Let's talk about what happened and try to find a better way to solve the problem." Thus, I was telling John that his actions were unacceptable, not John himself. John learned that it was not unusual to feel angry, but that he must learn acceptable ways to handle his anger.
> —*Verelda Zook Roth, Glen Ellyn, Illinois. Kindergarten*

As adults, we want children to express their feelings in positive and appropriate ways. We want them to know that men and women, young people and old, all feel sad, afraid, happy, disappointed, and frustrated. But, as with *The Little Brute Family*, we want them to find the "little wandering lost good feelings."[4]

> I have used fingerplays and poems to help children identify feelings.

> FEELINGS

> Sometimes on my face you'll see,
> How I feel inside of me.
> When I'm proud I beam and glow,
> But when I'm shy my head hangs low.
> —*Author unknown*

A familiar traditional song suggests responses to certain feelings.

> If you're happy and you know it, clap your hands;
> If you're happy and you know it, clap your hands;
> If you're happy and you know it, your face will surely show it;
> If you're happy and you know it, clap your hands.

If you're angry and you know it, tell a friend. . . .
If you're sleepy and you know it, close your eyes. . . .[5]
—*Susan Hess Hurst, New Holland, Pennsylvania. Ages 3-5*

How Do Children Develop Empathy?

When children recognize their own emotions, they can begin to understand emotions in others and begin to empathize with them. Empathy includes being able to put oneself in another person's place, to walk in their shoes, to view a situation the way another person is viewing it. As children grasp how others are feeling in a particular situation, adults can guide children to understand the most helpful ways to react.

We had a unit in my fourth-grade class on people with mental and physical handicaps. The students shared what they read in a variety of books on the subject. We took "An Unfair Hearing Test" which showed us, via tape recorder, what persons with a hearing loss hear.

We viewed the filmstrip *Walk in Another Person's Shoes*, about a boy with a learning disability. The filmstrip showed how he saw two balls instead of one coming toward him in a ball game, and he wasn't able to block out background noises when the teacher gave directions. We talked about how we could befriend these children and help them to compensate for their disabilities.

Dot Hansen from the Association for the Disabled of Elkhart County (ADEC) talked to us and did some activities with us. We learned to be thankful for our minds, to understand those with disabilities, and to search for ways to help them.

—*Marty Suter, Elkhart, Indiana. Grade 4*

After reading an article on handicaps which emphasized that we all have limitations, we discussed disabilities. The children became more accepting of each other and of others' handicaps as we blindfolded ourselves to feel braille pages, and used earplugs and crutches. We also learned that we all have limitations. One book that the children loved was *Howie Helps Himself.*[6]

—*Ann Klink Herendeen, Goshen, Indiana. Kindergarten*

While working for a private school for handicapped children being housed in a public school, I found myself next door to a regular classroom.

None of the children coming into my classroom each day would ever be mainstreamed into other classrooms. So we tried mainstreaming in reverse. The third- and fourth-grade youngsters next door responded wholeheartedly. First, we had an open house for any parents of third and fourth graders who expressed a desire to work in our classroom during a recess or noon period. Following this introductory visit, the parents could give permission for their children to work in our classroom at scheduled times.

The third and fourth graders were open and avid learners. With new understandings, they returned each day showing enormous love and caring. They approached each child with some awe and fear and numerous questions. They knelt beside little Chris who would never see, talk, or walk but was very sensitive to sound, touch, and vibrations. As they learned that the beautiful blue eyes of Chris could not see, they would choose an auditory toy carefully and approach little Chris, calling his name, gently manipulating a toy with him, and telling him stories.

More children volunteered than could be scheduled. By the end of the year, a number of children expressed their hope that sometime they might become teachers of special children.

—*Arlie Hershberger Weaver, Phoenix, Arizona. Grades 3-4*

At Broader Horizons Institute, a program for individuals with mental handicaps, I observed students helping their friends. Each time the bell rang, mobile mentally handicapped students would surround the mentally and physically handicapped to push their wheelchairs. It was necessary for them to take turns since only two students were permitted to assist each physically handicapped friend.

—*Karen Diener Thompson, Atbara, Sudan. Ages 8-12*

Adults can help children identify with the loneliness of the rejected through the use of carefully selected literature for children. *Crow Boy* and *The Hundred Dresses* are among the powerful loner stories.[7]

Adult empathy is important to a child. "Empathy says, 'How you see things is important to me. It is worth my time and effort to be with you in your feelings. I really want to understand how it feels to be you because I care.' " [8] Empathetic understanding by adults brings warm feelings of comfort and safety to a child.

What Is the Importance of Parents and Other Significant Adults to the Growth of Caring Behaviors of Children?

As infants have their needs met, are fed, kept warm and dry, and are cuddled, they learn that their caregivers are loving and dependable. Researchers have found that strong attachment of the infant to the mother seems to spark an early interest in others and may be a necessary component of empathy as each infant feels, *I am a person of worth*. Without a sense of self-esteem, it is difficult for a child to be able to empathize with others.

A noted observer of child development states that "there is abundant evidence that the basis for confident, responsible, cooperative adult personality lies in interpersonal relationships within the family characterized by consistent and genuine concern for the well-being of others, sensitivity to their needs, and generosity in fulfilling those needs." [9]

Children who do not experience loving concern in infancy may feel that they have no reason to trust others, and therefore no sense of responsibility or empathy toward others. How does an adult help build trust with a child who does not feel that others can be trusted?

Twelve-year-old George came to Yoder School having known much rejection. The first three months were difficult ones for all of us. George found it almost impossible to trust others. Efforts on the part of teachers and students seemed ineffective and resulted in disruptive behavior.

In a conversation with our daughter Rachel, I received an insight into George. Rachel and her husband, Duane, had adopted a child, three years of age, who had known nothing but rejection and hurt. She said that when Timothy finds it difficult to receive kindness, she holds him close and lets him cry until the ugly feelings are gone. Ah, I thought, I wonder if George has had similar experiences.

Shortly after Christmas, George was rude to a child who had done something kind to him. I asked him to join me in the office. His face was tense, and he seemed to brace himself for punishment. I turned to him and said, "George, I know nothing about your experiences before you came here, but you know how frustrated both of us have been this year. George, my daughter told me how her adopted child responds because he has known much rejection. When he has ugly feelings, she holds him close until he knows that she really cares. I understand your feelings. Have you been rejected when you did kind things to others so that you want to reject them even when they want to be kind?"

George looked at me with beautiful brown eyes filled with tears. He unashamedly put his head on my shoulder and cried. So did I! It was not the end of the problems, but it was the beginning of a new relationship with teachers and students.

—*Esther Eash Yoder, Grantsville, Maryland. Age 12*

One of the best gifts parents can give children is the knowledge that they are loved and respected. In this way a child feels secure enough to be able to reach out and show kindness and care for others. Parental nurturance contributes to the development of consideration, kindness, and sympathy.

Parents are the most significant socializers of children. Parenting techniques have a pronounced effect on children's behavior. A parent who uses threats or physical force serves as a model for aggressive behavior on the part of the child. When parents reason with children, they demonstrate their respect for them and also indicate the standards they hold. A parent who points out the rights and wrongs of the child's action models concern for others and the effect of one's behavior on others. In this way, empathy is developed. How parents work out conflicts will in a large measure determine how children learn to work out conflicts with others.

When our son was fifteen, he experienced a disciplinary action at school that made him feel isolated from his family. He violated a school code, and consequently, the school policy of suspension was implemented. One aspect of the policy included making a phone call to the parents' home explaining the reason for the suspension.

When we arrived home from work that day, there was a note from our son on the kitchen table simply explaining that he would be going away to camp nearby and that there would be a phone call from school. He requested that we do not look for him or his camping spot.

After we received the phone call from school, we understood more clearly why our son wanted to be alone for a time, but we were sad that he felt unable to share the problem with his parents. When his sister who was a junior in high school came home, she said she thought she knew where her brother likely went at the camp and volunteered to go looking for him. Because of her capacity to empathize and to reach out to others, we believed her suggestion to find her brother was a good one.

Several hours later our daughter returned and reported that her search was successful. She had had a satisfactory visit with her brother and had a message for the family from our son. The message was carved on a twig: "God Loves Me." (The twig is still kept in a special place reserved for family mementos.)

Our son did not return to the house until the following morning after his parents left for work. That evening he and his family were able to share the problem and work at restoring relationships within the family. The love and concern of the family, and especially that of a caring sister, facilitated a healing of interpersonal relationships.

—*Frederick E. Meyer, Rittman, Ohio. Age 15*

Parents are not the only socializers of children. Other significant adults also serve as role models for children. Family members, teachers, ministers, and neighbors are among those who help mold the child's behavior and attitudes. Parents should provide contacts with the types of adults who model the qualities they wish their children to develop.

Before persons can teach peace to others, they must experience this peace within. Then they can provide a peaceful environment in which the child can develop. Children sense the extra dimension.

One day Duane, one of my fourth graders, said, "The nicest lady waited on me at the store. She must be one of Jesus' helpers."

—*Miriam Stalter Charles, Elida, Ohio. Grade 4*

I don't recall ever planning, "I am going to teach peace today." Hopefully, it was an interweaving of my thoughts, actions, and words prompted by the love of Christ.

Several years ago I met a woman I had taught at least twenty years earlier. She introduced herself and said, "I'll never forget you and the time when my friend and I had a disagreement and were angry. You had us talk it over and shake hands."
— *Carrie Yoder Diener, Topeka, Indiana. Age 11*

In my four-year-old nursery class, there was some moving around and kicking and bumping each other during story time. I put small pieces of masking tape on the carpet and put each child's name on the tape. I explained that they were growing up and could find their special places on the floor. They were all anxious to find their seats, and I did not have problems with them rolling into each other.

I found that emphasizing the positive and ignoring the negative also helped this problem. We're so apt to condemn the rowdy, but noting the good behavior makes others want to be recognized too: "How nice and quiet Jimmy is sitting."
— *Marie Keeler Miller, Brevard, North Carolina. Prekindergarten*

Teachers may find that bringing in resource people whose work involves them in helping people is an excellent way to inspire children to want to help others. The school principal is an important but often overlooked resource. If the principal is aware of teachers' efforts to help children acquire peacemaking skills, she or he may become more conscious of ways to reinforce such efforts.

Several resource people were helpful as they shared some of their life experiences during opening sessions in our Sunday school junior department. Lela Sutter, school nurse, told of her nurse's training, experiences as a voluntary service worker in Texas, and some of her experiences as a school nurse in a suburban high school. In another session, George Gerber, an older member of the congregation, told the group about a diary he has kept for many years. He encouraged them to write something every day relating the good times and the hard times. He shared parts of his own diary written when he was about their age.

At the end of each session, we gave each student a few minutes to write or sketch something they remembered about the person they'd heard and/or something that person had said. These items were incorporated into a bulletin board display called Someone You Should Know. I was impressed with the way the children listened and empathized with the experiences of these individuals. The questions they asked of these two resource people indicated they had listened with understanding, thoughtfulness, and appreciation.

—Margaret Kauffman Sutter, Lombard, Illinois. Grades 4-8

A beautiful opportunity came to my class one year to learn firsthand the culture and needs of people beyond our community. Homer's Aunt Valerie was home on short furlough from years of serving as a nurse on the hospital ship *Hope*. Aunt Valerie accepted our invitation to visit our classroom. We sat spellbound as she told how the doctors and nurses loved and helped children in suffering countries. That afternoon a third of my class walked home taller and prouder than they had ever felt before, because Aunt Valerie, like them, was black.

—Leona Yoder Hostetler, Urbana, Ohio. Grades 3-4

How Do We Help Children Learn the Difference Between Negative Aggression and Assertiveness?

Children are socially dependent on the family; they move out into the church, the neighborhood, and often into a nursery school or daycare center. Failure to develop positive relationships with peers during childhood has been found to be related to later maladjustment. Since being exposed to kind and generous peers seems to reinforce prosocial behavior in children, it would be wonderful to expose children to only positive influences. However, sooner or later, likely sooner, children will be exposed to children and adults who have not developed the interpersonal skills which we value.

Seven-year-old Darren had emotional and behavioral problems as a result of a difficult home situation during his preschool years. Darren and his parents had been attending our church for the past two years, and his behavior was improving. When Darren's mother called and asked if my son Josh could stay overnight with

Darren, I wasn't comfortable with the idea and thought Josh might refuse. Instead he said, "Sure! He must have thought I was the best kid at his birthday party."

Josh went willingly. I worried that the two boys might get tired of each other and that Darren might return to old behavior patterns. The next morning when Josh came home, I asked if he had a good time.

"Yes," he replied, "and Darren's dad made us eggs for breakfast!"

I shouldn't have worried that night—children are often better peacemakers than adults.

—*via Marie Moyer, Hatfield, Pennsylvania. Age 7*

Adults do not want children to feel that they must always give up what someone bigger, stronger, or more aggressive wants. Parents must help children know how to be assertive enough to maintain their rights, while at the same time trying to understand the other child's behavior and how to help that child. How can adults help children develop skills in being assertive, and yet kind?

With four children in our family, invariably someone takes something that belongs to a brother or sister. This often starts a fight. I have been talking to my children about asking courteously for their toy rather than demanding it.

We recently moved from a private home in a small town to an apartment complex in a medium-sized city. Conflicts often arise on the apartment playground because of the great many unsupervised children and because we are people from many different backgrounds with differing expectations for our children's behavior.

My son Nathan learned the wisdom of courtesy while playing outside here. He frequently takes a ball out with him. One day he forgot to bring the ball back inside. The next day he saw a boy with his ball. He went over and asked if he could have his ball back. The boy returned it with no problem. When Nathan lost another toy, remembering the ball incident, he said, "Maybe if I see someone with it and ask nicely, they might give it back."

—*Elizabeth Miller Broaddus, Terre Haute, Indiana. Age 6*

We also need to help children understand that they can cause aggression in others by their actions, such as teasing, provoking, and name-calling.

> During the study of the emotions in a health unit, I asked the students to write about how they would respond if someone called them names such as Freckle Face, Pop Eyes, or Fatty because they thought that they were different. Together we discussed the papers without revealing names of students.
> —*M. Irene Slaubaugh, Montgomery, Indiana. Grade 5*

Children who are intimidated by an aggressive child need help in learning to tell the other child in words that they don't like what is happening. I saw five-year-old Freddie chasing Kevin on the playground and constantly pulling on Kevin's coat and hood. Kevin yelled, "Stop that!" Freddie continued. Kevin was getting so frustrated that he was nearly ready to cry or hit. Kevin stopped suddenly and said, "Freddie, it makes me so angry when you pull on my clothes. Just tag me on the back, and then I will run and chase you." Kevin is learning to put into words exactly what he is feeling.

Since television has been found to affect the level of aggression of children, parents need to monitor the types of programs watched by their children. Teachers are aware of the effects of television program selection on children's behavior.

> The children of our school were for the most part from non-Christian homes. Their games at school took on the forms of the then-famous television and radio heroes. Cops and robbers seemed to be the only interesting and exciting game they wanted to play—hiding behind trees, bushes, or buildings, shooting at each other, and then playing falling dead.
>
> A Bible lesson on the commandment that says, "Thou shalt not kill," led to a discussion of what this really means in life. We decided that it wasn't right to play what God says we should not do. We worked on other games such as darebase or kick-the-can, until these games were just as exciting as cops and robbers.
> —*Margaret Ulrich Strubhar, Culp, Arkansas. Grades 1-3*

Programs such as *Mister Rogers' Neighborhood*, which encourage cooperation, empathy, sharing, and sympathy, can have positive effects on the development of prosocial behavior.

How Can Parents and Teachers Encourage Cooperation and Help Children Learn to Solve Conflicts Creatively?

Since young children enjoy using grown-up words, parents and teachers can discuss with children the meaning of the word *cooperation.* When children are solving conflicts peacefully or working together successfully, adults can give positive feedback such as, "I like the way you are cooperating to build that tower of blocks." Children may begin to imitate the adults' positive comments and tell each other, "I like the picture you painted."

A five-year-old with a history of hostile and unfriendly behavior toward other children was beginning to respond to the positive comments he had heard. While working cooperatively on a special project with another child, he commented, "Hey, we're really cooperating, aren't we, teacher?"

> In my classroom we hold weekly class meetings on Friday afternoons. During these meetings, the children discuss problems they have with their peers; solutions are given by the students. My role is to serve as moderator. At these meetings we also present good things that happened. We close by having a child sit in the center of the circle while the class, one by one, says, "I like you because. . . ." Class meetings are held sometimes when a problem arises, and the child with the problem can't wait until our regular class meeting time.
> —*Ethel Henry Rush, Doylestown, Pennsylvania. Grade 2*

> I am amazed with the ability of children to find excellent solutions to their interpersonal conflicts. I try to help the students clarify what the issue is and then solve the problem with a minimum of help from me. Last week Calvin took Jeff's eraser and broke it into little pieces. I had Calvin and Jeff each tell me what had happened from their own point of view. The issue was clear.

Jeff felt he should be paid for the eraser.

I asked the two boys to go to the back of the room and decide how to solve this problem. In a few minutes Calvin came up and said, "I am going to give Jeff my milk the next time I buy a hot lunch. Jeff always brings a sack lunch and twenty cents to buy milk. He will have twenty cents to buy another eraser on the day that I give Jeff the milk." I felt the boys had solved their conflict in a creative way.

—*Jane Zehr Birky, Wheatridge, Colorado. Grade 3*

Children can discuss ways of avoiding conflict. In the author's kindergarten classroom, an aggressive and egocentric child had a history of hitting, biting, pushing, kicking, and spitting at the other children. He was absent for several days. Although the child had shown marked improvement in his ability to control his emotions, he still needed considerable help. The other children needed help in knowing how to respond when he was aggressive. On one of his days of absence, the book *Let's Be Enemies*[10] was read.

The following discussion ensued:

Teacher: "What is an enemy?"

Child: "Someone who does mean things to you."

Teacher: "Have you ever had an enemy?"

Child: "Well, Freddie used to do a lot of mean things, but he is getting better. He still hits sometimes."

Teacher: "What do you do when Freddie hits you?"

Child: "I tell him to quit it; that I don't like it."

Another child: "I just walk away and play somewhere else."

Teacher: "What does the teacher do when Freddie hits someone?" (This question was asked to reinforce the idea that although she can't always prevent the action, the teacher will not ignore it.)

Child: "She brings Freddie in and has him hit the punching bag instead. She tells him it doesn't hurt the bag when you hit it, but it hurts children when they are hit."

Teacher: "Yes, we are all trying to help Freddie be more friendly and more gentle. I won't let him hurt you if I can prevent it."

At What Age Can We Expect Children to Be Able to Understand the Qualities of Kindness, Empathy, and Sharing?

As hard as we might try, none of us reaches the perfection of being kind, loving, and generous *all* of the time. We know that children will not *always* be kind and loving. If adults try too hard to encourage caring behavior, children may become over-anxious, or may feel guilty over situations for which they had no responsibility. We do not want to have unrealistic expectations for children's behavior; neither do we want to expect too little of them. As adults interested in children's development, we would do well to familiarize ourselves with resources on behavioral norms such as *Infant and Child in the Culture of Today.*[11] Knowing what to expect of children at different developmental stages can keep us from developing such an extreme social conscience in children that they feel they have the whole world on their shoulders.

Each year in science and health class, we study the effects of cigarette smoking on human beings. There are always several students who become concerned about their parents' smoking. In discussions with them, they express the fear that the parent will develop lung cancer. Some children tell me that they destroy or hide the cigarettes at their houses, thinking that this will help the parent break the smoking habit. Of course, instead of the hoped-for result, the child often receives verbal abuse and sometimes even great anger from the parent. A confused child then wonders how to help, yet not be the cause of such emotional outbursts.

Over the years I've come to the conclusion that one good way to help my students is to make sure that they understand that they themselves are in no way responsible for their parents' habits. We are each responsible for our own actions and cannot force change upon others. Then I suggest that they go to the parent and say something like the following: "Dad, I love you very much and I want you to live a long healthy life. I worry about you when you smoke. Will you please quit smoking for my sake? Is there anything I can do to help you quit?"

—*Maxine Schrock Miller, Wakarusa, Indiana. Grade 6*

For many years the theories of Jean Piaget, noted Swiss psychologist, have held that young children are too egocentric to empathize or to understand another's point of view and thus to act altruistically. Recent research as well as our own experience and examples cited by parents indicate that young children are not always egocentric and are indeed capable of empathizing. Children may sense sadness by the expression on the face of someone they love, and then they respond in ways appropriate for their age level to comfort the saddened person.

> When Rachel was three years old, her grandpa died unexpectedly. We suddenly found ourselves dealing with some very perceptive questions about death and grief. We found Rachel to be sympathetic with her dad and grandmother. She went out of her way to help them. She hugged them often and patted their hands. She constantly assured them that she loved them. She asked questions about how Grandma was feeling and why. Then she would try her best to comfort her and assure her that we loved her.
>
> After we returned home from the funeral, she "wrote" Grandma several letters telling her she loved her and missed Grandpa, too. She said she was writing to Grandma because Grandma was so sad.
>
> —*Marilee Roggie Schoolcraft, Goshen, Indiana. Age 3*

Marian Yarrow, chief of the laboratory of developmental psychology at the National Institute of Mental Health, has studied children between the ages of ten months and two-and-one-half years. She has found babies to show generosity and young children to have the capacity to show kindness and compassion.[12] Concern may be shown in concrete ways, such as offering a child who has fallen off a climber a bite of cookie.

> Our youngest daughter, Starla, just two, had received a Fisher-Price music box for Christmas. It was her favorite toy, and she played with it every day and carried it around much of the time.
>
> When we received word that the adoption agency had a boy ready for us to adopt, we began planning a trip to Calgary to get him. The children were going with us and were not only excited about the trip but very excited about the prospects of a new baby

brother. (Even though he was seventeen months old, they called him a baby.)

Each one of the girls was planning what she would do to welcome her new brother. Starla said right away she would give him her music box. It became her responsibility to take the music box along and be sure he got it. At the appropriate time, Starla gave him the music box. Three years later it is still a highly treasured and shared toy of both.

—*Verla Fae Kauffman Haas, Bluesky, Alberta. Age 2*

Yarrow concludes that caring behaviors are promoted when parents give children a strong message that they must not hurt others, and when they show altruism toward their own children. The age of eighteen months seems to be a critical time for children to be led in the direction of either altruism or selfishness.

It is encouraging to note that in a follow-up study done of the infants when they were five, most were still empathetic. It appears that kindness can be taught, both by training and by interaction with kind adults.

Our family had been in a small prayer group with five other families for five years. When one member became ill with cancer, we made visits to see him at his home. Our preschool Kelly befriended some of his out-of-town grandchildren. They came to play at our house several times. As our friend became more and more ill, we often discussed his condition with the children.

The day he died we picked up our new little friends, and we talked of their grandfather being in heaven with Jesus. That evening Kelly sat down and wrote a letter to her friends: "Dear Laura and Katie, I am sorry about your grandpa. I am sad, too. Love, Kelly."

—*Mary Jo Hartzler Short, Goshen, Indiana. Age 5*

Between ages six and nine, children respond mainly to an immediate and specific distress felt by another. As they mature, they can begin to understand more general distress such as poverty, illness, and oppression. They can begin to understand the problems of a whole group or class of people, as well as the distress of just one individual.

Our fifth-grade class showed unusual concern when a school in Oklahoma was shattered by an explosion which killed several people. They empathized so deeply that I was caught by surprise when they wanted to know what *they* could *do* for that school.

One child proposed that we give that school our money from fines. In trying to learn neatness, they had assessed a five-cent fine for lockers left open and for leaving books or pencils on desks after dismissal—to aid custodians. We had only $3.45, money that was to go for pizza for them on the last day of school. I accepted their idea for the time being; they felt so good just to make that sacrifice.

Before the day ended, we had $9.65. Children who went home for lunch told their parents who sent back dollar bills; others gave the change from their cafeteria money. One child wasn't going to eat lunch so she could give her lunch money. (I wanted to cry!)

In further discussion, we decided to send children's books to put into the Oklahoma library in memory of those who lost their lives. What love and empathy and generosity were displayed!
        —*Idella Zuercher Nussbaum, Orrville, Ohio. Grade 5*

What Are Some Strategies Parents and Teachers Have Used to Teach Children to Interact Peacefully?

"Every day at 1:45 I am going to sit down with my children or my class and spend fifteen minutes teaching them to be kind." We all know that this is a foolish statement. Positive feelings toward others are not usually taught on a schedule, but as situations arise. Someone has said that values are caught, not taught. However, adults must be sure that they use the opportunities that arise to help children learn altruistic behavior.

Parents and educators must first be aware of the many opportunities to help children learn to care and share.

It was always my concern as a Sunday school teacher or superintendent to be informed about illness or tragedy in the homes of the children. All of these experiences were shared, and we prayed for each child during the Sunday school hour. I recall when one of our families lost its home in the 1965 tornado, Donnie lost all his toys. The children brought money, and we bought a beautiful semitrailer truck for him.
        —*C. Kathryn Yoder Shantz, Goshen, Indiana. Grades 1-2*

As a relatively new parent, I was surprised, but pleased, to observe my daughter learn to take turns with her cousin while they played together. It's a familiar scene: two children want the same toy and are clinging to it for dear life, yelling, "Mine," at the top of their lungs. In this case, Heather (four years old) shouted to Lyris (two years old), "You have to take turns!"

I thought, "There's a good solution," but said to Heather, "Lyris is two years old and doesn't know *how* to take turns; you are four years old. Can you show her?"

I helped by setting a timer for thirty seconds (to begin with). Heather agreed that Lyris could play with the popcorn popper first. After that my only involvement was to reset the timer (for longer intervals as the sharing game progressed). The play continued peacefully, and Lyris wanted to take turns long after Heather had decided to play with other toys.

I acted as facilitator, not dictator, in the situation. Since then I've learned that it's not so unusual for young children to play peacefully, if adults give quiet guidance instead of imitating the grabbing, screaming children. For example, "I'm taking this toy away until you learn to play without fighting!" After this experience, Lyris knew what taking turns meant, and she was ready to do it with other playmates. She has been a good "teacher" too!

—*Beverly J. Short, Denver, Colorado. Ages 2-4*

Kindness must be voluntary and come from the heart. Forcing children to share or to apologize when angry does not show kindness on their part but is simply forcing the child to accept the power an adult wields.

When children feel competent, have self-worth, and are respected by others, they are then able to reach out to others with loving acts. Children sometimes amaze us with their ability to respond with kindness and gentleness.

Excell had almost been declared an outlaw. He was at odds with other children on the school bus. Several deviant antics and antisocial behaviors had sent him to the office. The principal was perplexed over his conduct.

On this occasion, Excell dropped a book from his desk. Debbie, his neighbor across the aisle, reached down in an unassuming manner and proceeded to pick up his book for him. While she was raising her head, Excell hit her on the head with his knuckle.

This incident called for a class discussion. "Why did you hurt someone who was trying to help you?" "Why did Debbie wish to pick up Excell's book for him?"

Debbie replied, "Even though Excell is naughty, I still wish to be nice to him."

Ah—how's that for responding with kindness?

—*Dorwin Carrol Myers, Kokomo, Indiana. Grade 5*

Learning to express appreciation for the efforts of others and to affirm others just for being themselves—these are wonderful traits to have. All of us know how we feel when some unexpected praise or support comes our way. Children need this reinforcement from adults in their lives as well as from their peers. Being able to *give and receive* love are both important qualities to develop and especially significant on an intergenerational level.

Children and older people—what a neat combination! Each year I plan a unit on grandparents and older friends. This always opens the opportunity for the children's own grandparents to come in and share a hobby, or to simply share a snack time or mealtime with us. I also try to involve older people from the community who have a special interest in young children and have some extra time which they would be glad to spend with us.

Throughout the year we have a continued relationship with older friends at Fountainview Nursing Home. We visit them several times a month, either in small groups or the whole group. We sometimes plan special stories and games around holidays, or we just go and spend time visiting.

One day last spring was designated as Children's Day at Fountainview. We went and sang with the people, ate refreshments with them, and sent helium balloons up into the sky with the residents' names and addresses.

It is so special to see a wrinkled hand holding a small child's hand, or to watch a resident giving one of our children a ride in a wheelchair! The smiles from the children and the older people alike are a rewarding and peaceful sight!

—*Linda Harshbarger Heiser, Goshen, Indiana. Ages 3-4*

For two years on Valentine's Day, we in kindergarten have made it a combination Valentine's Day/Grandparent's Day. We prepared by emphasizing how special older friends were. We made

Rice Krispie treats, decorated the room appropriately, and invited grandparents and older friends in for a short program of singing and fingerplays. The older friends shared their favorite memories of school. They appreciated being remembered and felt loved by the children who are so uninhibited.

—*Ann Klink Herendeen, Goshen, Indiana. Kindergarten*

Last year our first-grade class exchanged visits with persons residing in a local nursing home. Our entire class went to the home once a month and the elders, as we came to call them, visited our classroom every month as the weather permitted. Six to ten of them came, mostly in wheelchairs, carried by a van especially equipped for them.

On our trips to the home, the children read to the elders, played games and did art work with them. When they came to our classroom, we planned a variety of activities: We talked with them about life and school when they were young, we sang for them, we all churned butter, and we ate school lunches together.

The children quickly learned to push wheelchairs carefully down the halls. They learned to share the opportunities for helping because there were fewer elders than children. We dealt with understanding elders who cried and those who wanted to hug us all.

While at the home, the children observed that one elderly lady's bed was covered with crocheted items and stuffed toys, gifts from friends. The children had learned to love Maggie, who also visited us. Eventually one child asked, "Why does Maggie get so many presents?" The children answered it easily—not that people love Maggie, but "because *Maggie* loves *people*." Incidentally, plans have already been made for my next year's first graders to continue this project.

—*Mary Maple Berkshire, Elkhart, Indiana. Grade 1*

Children sometimes spontaneously offer nurture and kindness to a classmate who is hurt or sad. Five-year-old Olympia in the author's classroom was the only black child in a group of eighteen children. She lived with her mother and disabled grandmother in a house which would be considered poor by most standards. Her grandmother had been disabled when shot in a robbery while doing her laundry at a community laundromat.

Olympia was gentle and genuinely concerned for every child. If a classmate fell on the playground, Olympia helped her up, led her over to steps to sit down, and got a wet paper towel to hold on her scrape or bump, while patting her and talking to her soothingly. Olympia performed kind acts daily. Her mother and grandmother had shown her much love which she was passing on to others.

> My husband was seriously injured in a logging accident. My nephew in second grade was deeply concerned. His classroom teacher had the class write cards to my husband, allowing classmates to empathize with my nephew while cheering up my husband.
> To acknowledge the class gesture, my husband and I visited the classroom and read one of our favorite books.
> —*Catherine Lehl Rheinheimer, Topeka, Indiana. Grade 2*

Just before Christmas, five-year-old Sally in the author's kindergarten classroom was discovered to be a diabetic. She would need to have a special snack of diet soda and graham crackers each day. Would her classmates accept the fact that she had soda pop, and they were to drink milk? Most fives value conformity and do not want someone else to have something they do not have.

To help the class understand the need for Sally to have a different snack, she brought a toy bear, a needle, and a vial of insulin. At group time she demonstrated for the children how to fill the syringe and give a shot to the bear. We made a simple statement that Sally had a special need for a shot each day, which her mother gave her at home, and that she needed a special diet. The children have never commented on the fact that her snack is different and perhaps sometimes preferable to their own.

On Valentine's Day a mother who sent a valentine cake for the children showed she cared for the child who couldn't have cake by bringing a heart box filled with nuts, sesame seeds, and sugarless gum.

Resourceful parents and teachers will always be on the alert for ways to encourage taking responsibility for helping others.

At the small elementary school where I taught, there was one severely physically handicapped girl. She wore braces on her legs
and had no feeling from the waist down. The students throughout the school felt serious responsibility for Laura and would
help her in any way possible. She probably had more friends than
any other child in school. The staff made a conscious effort to encourage students to help Laura in a way which would make her
feel a part of the regular school activities. Children took great
pride in her accomplishments. I remember a girl telling me, "This
year Laura can get upstairs by herself." The students and staff
gave Laura a standing ovation when she completed the require-
ments for the President's Physical Fitness Award.

—*Jennifer Sprunger Spykman, South Bend, Indiana. Grades K-6*

Children may find it comparatively easy to show kindness
and help persons obviously in need, such as those disabled, ill,
or in nursing homes. It may be more difficult for them to support the efforts of peers in their classes or siblings in their
homes.

A week spent as "secret spies" helped my class of third graders to
express appreciation for the kind acts they observed among their
peers and to receive praise and affirmation from their peers. To
begin the week, the secret spies drew names of the persons
whom they would observe for any positive, helpful, or thoughtful
actions or words.

At week's end, identities of the secret spies were revealed in a
circle meeting. The children expressed appreciation to their
"spyee" for at least one thoughtful act observed during the week.

—*Carla Griebel Mishler, Nappanee, Indiana. Grade 3*

Since giving children responsibility for helping others at an
early age is positively correlated with empathetic behavior, parents and teachers should look for opportunities which encourage children to help one another. When there is a new baby in
the home, young children can assist the parents by bringing a
diaper to them, bringing a rattle to the baby, and in a myriad of
other ways. In the classroom, children can help by tying shoes
for those who cannot, zipping the jackets of others, feeding
pets, washing tables, and watering plants.

Many times in my kindergarten group we would sing, "What can I do, what can I say, to make Mother happy today?" Then some youngster would pantomime things like picking up toys or drying dishes, and the group would guess what the children were doing.

One day at home, little LeRoy did something for his mother, and she spoke her appreciation. LeRoy answered, "That's the way I make my mother happy."
—*Rhea Yoder, Portland, Oregon. Kindergarten*

In our neighborhood, several concerned Christians sponsored and taught summer Bible school for two weeks, every evening, Monday through Friday. With my seven-month-old baby and gardening, my housekeeping was postponed. The last Friday evening, all teachers met at my house to evaluate the two weeks. One of the seven-year-old students riding home with one of the teachers saw my dirty kitchen floor and voluntarily washed it! His thoughtfulness blessed me so much!
—*Glenda Detweiler Moyer, Philadelphia, Pennsylvania. Age 7*

I have a strong feeling that children should learn to appreciate others and be responsible for themselves and others. So each year, for over ten years now, after observing my new third graders begin school, I group them in four work-study groups. These are not instructional-performance level groupings. I aim to include a variety of abilities and personalities in each group. These groups work at study stations individually, in pairs, or as a group, depending on the assignment or activity.

Throughout the year we have other groupings on a short-term basis for science and health. These four groups, however, remain the same, with *each* student having a six-week period in which they are group leader. Obviously, I choose the first leaders carefully, but not necessarily the best students academically. Then they take turns. "Smart kids" are often most surprised at what they learn from others.

One of our goals through the year is to each try to be a group member who not only develops skills but who gains an awareness of the needs of others and a better understanding of how to help them. We are not without conflict; yet I feel that working out our problems with my guidance plus much input from the larger group really helps my third graders develop responsibility for their own learning and the learning of others.

I have found it valuable in child-parent relationships to involve our third graders in our first parent-teacher conference, so it is a three-way or four-way conference, depending on whether both parents are able to come. With each report card I also send a personal letter discussing positive growth in the ability to work out solutions in cooperation with others. My feedback from parents, and later older students, has convinced me we do make third grade a growing year.

—*Nancy Virgil Groff, Goshen, Indiana. Grade 3*

How have children been encouraged to support efforts of their peers? Anne Gunden's class discussed the fact that all persons have areas in which they can use help. There are those who can give help.

Our group was composed of children with a wide range of abilities. Fifth-grade social studies focused on the United States. The health series studied "Me": What makes me feel as I do? We are all different, and yet each one has worth and can help others in some way.

To correlate health, social studies, and spelling, we used a big map of the United States and had children design planes to fly to different places on the map as they progressed in spelling. After discussing how we all have areas in which we could use help, the children agreed to help each other with their spelling in this study unit. Friday afternoons became an exciting time for all. Some pupils were supposed to have at least three or four words correct. They were glowing as they flew their planes to different states, and those who had helped them were just as elated. Spelling became an exciting part of our week. Instead of competition, a lot of concern and love was evident.

The enthusiasm generated by the cooperative project reached parents, too. When they came for a conference, the first thing they wanted to see was the map.

—*Anne Wenger Gunden, Goshen, Indiana. Grade 5*

Another way in which children may learn to respond with kindness is through contact with animals. By caring for an animal, children learn the importance of taking responsibility for a being which is dependent on them. Pets respond to a child's gentleness and kindness.

How cute is a baby opossum? Certainly not as lovable as a fluffy baby kitten or a lively little puppy, you might answer.

Yet, through the eyes of several fourth-grade girls in our Honduran school, two orphaned baby opossums became the center of their motherly attentions for several weeks as they nurtured them with loving care. A nest of leaves, grass, and rags was made in an old tub. Water, milk, and fruits were provided daily. The baby opossums were cuddled, petted, and talked to sweetly during many spare moments of the day.

Caring for these homeless little creatures whose mother had been killed by a dog may lead these children, as they grow up, to treat kindly also the many thousands of refugees and homeless youngsters around the world.

—*Robert Duane Lehman, La Ceila, Honduras. Grade 4*

Here are examples of generosity shown by children when they shared or gave a possession to another person who needed or wanted the item:

My first-grade son came home with the news that his teacher at his parochial school had a sister dying of cancer. His teacher was sad. He wanted to show his care. That night he chose his favorite stuffed animal—a special one a Sunday school teacher had given him—to give to his teacher the next day. He said, "I'm sorry about your sister." Later I told his teacher how special the stuffed cat had been to my son. She kept the cat a year, then returned it and told him how much it helped.

—*Ardyth Hostetler Steckly, Houston, Texas. Grade 1*

Packing Christmas boxes is a yearly tradition for the children at Mazapan School. They bring in food, clothing, and toys to share with those who are less fortunate in material possessions. The boxes are colorfully decorated by the students and personally delivered to the families a few days before Christmas.

Stories are read during the year describing people who have spent their lives helping those in need. In response, the children often mention how they shared some of their things through the Christmas boxes.

—*Robert Duane Lehman, La Ceila, Honduras. Grade 4*

Remembering how one felt in a new and strange setting can help a child be empathetic with others facing a similar situation.

I breathed a prayer as each of the children left for school that morning. We had just arrived at our assignment in India. Since the school year was well under way there, these three new students had a special challenge as they tried to find their places in this unfamiliar school setting.

As a family, we had talked about their fears and their hopes for the year, and we had tried to prepare them for what we hoped would be a rich school experience.

Later that afternoon, our usually reserved seventh grader came bounding in the door. Excitedly she told us of her day and how warmly she had been received. And then she said, "I'll never act the same toward a new person in my class again. I never knew how lonely one could feel and how good it felt to be accepted."

—*Marjorie Schertz Liechty, Mussoori, India. Grade 7*

Before a new classmate arrives, children can begin to empathize with how the child might feel on the first day of school in a strange place. They can describe how they think they would feel in this situation. We can outline positive ways in which they can assist the new child in getting acquainted and feeling more secure.

The children could role-play the situation, with one posing as the new child, one taking the part of a member of the class, and one assuming the teacher's role. This would have a positive effect on how the children react as the "stranger" arrives.

As a substitute teacher in a fourth grade, I noticed one girl having problems being accepted by her peers. At recess we discussed the morning, and I found she had entered that school about two days earlier. That afternoon in the science room, she suddenly asked to go see the principal. When he came back with her, we found the problem of name-calling had been continuing across her table in science while I was busy with other students. The principal ex-

plained to the class the girl's problem of being new. He also impressed upon them the importance of accepting all persons in the school and allowing them freedom to be themselves.
—*Ellen Penner Ebersole, Wichita, Kansas. Grade 4*

Kindergarten children experience apprehension similar to new students when they enter school in the fall. I try to plan a busy, joyous first day in the new kindergarten setting.
—*Maxine Mumaw Yoder, Jimtown, Indiana. Kindergarten*

When a child was faced with leaving the familiar classroom setting to move to a new school, a teacher skillfully turned sadness into joyful anticipation.

Usually first graders are sad and reluctant to leave when a family moves during the school year. Instead of giving a farewell party, which usually made them more unwilling to leave, I began using our last minutes together in a sharing time. The classmates took turns recalling experiences they had shared and giving the departing child special wishes for continuing good experiences in the new school setting. The students who had hesitated to leave began leaving with a smile and eagerness for the future.
—*Ardyth Hostetler Steckly, Houston, Texas. Grade 1*

The empathy of parents aids children in gaining strength in new experiences.

As we prepared to move, we took pictures of our friends and mounted them in a photo album for each child. Since we moved, we made scrapbooks about our friends in Washington, D.C., whom we left behind. On days that have been particularly difficult, we sit down with the photo album, put some good music on the stereo, and talk about our friends.

Making new friends has been particularly difficult for our children. Finding friends is scary but important. We have used *The Trip* and *We Are Best Friends.*[13]

Justin was concerned that he wouldn't know anyone in his new school. We had read *Will I Have a Friend?*[14] So we got it out to reread. He requested that book to take to preschool the first day and the second day. The third day Justin proudly introduced me

to his new friend, Eric, "Just like the story, Mama."
—*Maribeth C. Shank Shank, Goshen, Indiana. Age 4*

In review, children who are generous and helpful are likely to be empathetic, self-confident, understanding, respectful, and advanced in moral reasoning. They are likely to be children of nurturant parents who model caring behavior, use reasoning in discipline, maintain high standards, and give their children responsibility at an early age. Children are more likely to be kind and helpful when they feel happy and successful, when they are rewarded for helping, and if they are given responsibilities in helping others.[15] The warmth of their models also appears to have a positive effect on children's helping behavior.

Therefore, knowing these facts about children should prompt parents, educators, and all those who are in positions to influence children to do the following:

1. Discuss with children their own feelings and how others feel.
2. Model behavior which is generous, kind, empathetic, considerate, and compassionate (in other words, to show that they care deeply for others).
3. Have realistic expectations of the capabilities of children of various ages.
4. Give opportunities for sharing with and helping others at an early age.
5. Respond positively when the child exhibits helping behavior.
6. Encourage interactions with kind adults.
7. Help children solve conflicts creatively.

These seven principles can be found in the following account.

It was a rainy morning when the children in Newton, Kansas, went to Bible school. It had rained hard during the night. Telephone calls came to the church office that Sand Creek was overflowing its banks, and not all of the parents could get their children at noon.

Some of the children were afraid. "Don't worry," the teacher said. "Your parents are safe, and we will take care of you until they can come for you."

It was the worst flood that anyone could remember in Newton. Many houses were flooded, and some people had to be taken out of their homes by boat.

When Bob got home from Bible school, he and his friend David discovered that the telephones were out of order. Bob was a ham radio operator, so he and David offered their services to Mennonite Disaster Service. The boys got on their trusty bikes and delivered messages all over town.

Red Cross workers and Mennonite Disaster Service gave clothing and food. Many people could not go home for the night, so they had to sleep in temporary shelters or were invited to homes that were not flooded.

For several days volunteers hosed out basements, and women helped to clean household items that were full of sticky, slimy mud. The Bible lesson for one of these days was on sharing. But rather than using the lesson book, the teacher asked the children how they had shared during the flood.

Bob and David told about delivering messages. Neil said they shared their hose.

"We found some extra clothes in our closets," Sara said.

"Mom and I made sandwiches and vegetable soup," Karen told her class.

"Jimmy and I shared stamps and toys because Mike and Nellie's floated away," said Carl.

"We shared our boat," added Nathan.

Years later Bob and David, these same boys, answered a call to go to Denver to aid in an emergency one weekend while in college. One summer they offered their services to help a desperate need on an island in the Caribbean. They joyfully shared their time, energy, and expertise through active peacemaking. This is empathy rooted in action.

—*Geraldine Gross Harder, Newton, Kansas. Grade 5*

6. What Has Celebration
to Do with Peace?

Beth Hostetler Berry

I BELIEVE that there is no more important task today than educating children toward peace. Since our oldest child began picking up violent play from his young neighborhood friends, I have had a more personal concern for helping children grow toward peace. Sunday school and nursery school teaching assignments on the Indiana University campus called for creative ways of celebrating to promote peace.

This chapter reflects the many experiences I had with children and adults over the years as I taught in public school, camp and church school settings, teacher education at Goshen College, workshop settings with other adults, and primary curriculum writing for Herald Press. It also reflects the home and church in which I grew up near Orrville, Ohio.

Being a parent in Goshen and Bloomington, Indiana, and for a year in Costa Rica, I have a personal interest in designing family celebrations for my own family which includes my husband, Lee Roy, and our three children, Joe, Malinda, and Anne. I hope you, too, are challenged to fashion your own celebrations of peace in ways that make people happy, while not hurting another person or group of people or the earth.

Why Do We Celebrate?

Why is celebration part of living? How can we use events celebrating life passage and traditional holidays to promote peace? What new holidays might we celebrate to promote peace development? I explore these questions in this chapter.

One of the qualities of our humanness is the ability to celebrate. All peoples of the past and present in any location on the face of the earth seem instinctively to observe events of their lives. This celebration includes elements of the past. As the writer of Ecclesiastes suggests, "For everything there is a season, and a time for every matter under heaven: . . . a time to keep, and a time to throw away" (Eccles. 3:1, 6b, NRSV).

Along with those things we want to keep from the past, we celebrate with those around us the present moments of our lives. But celebration then reaches into the future as it becomes the beginning of the rest of our lives as well as the lives of generations which follow us.[1]

Increasingly I realize the value of celebrations as faith-sharing events. Children grow in their faith as they hear us share our faith. When our children were young adults, I read about the Family Cup of Blessing as a symbol for family celebration.[2] Ours is a special one-of-a-kind crystal goblet which we got from registering at a jewelry store when Len and I were engaged to be married. We've used it to celebrate joy as well as sorrow.

At Thanksgiving time family members list reasons for which they give thanks. Following a concluding prayer, we pass around the Cup of Blessing, filled with a beverage chosen specifically for the occasion. Likewise, at Christmastime persons share ways in which Christ became real that year, followed with the passing of the Cup. At birthday celebrations we affirm the person of honor before passing the Cup as we did when a son-in-law joined the family, or at the birth of a new baby, and at the time of my mother's death. The Cup of Blessing was included in the dedication of our home following a move to a new location.

This common but special drinking utensil became a bond to help us maintain a sense of common destiny and a fresh hope for the future. It is a tangible symbol filled with the juices reflective of and made a part of our family tradition.

The tradition is carried on by our son, who along with his fiance, has selected a Cup of Blessing for their family.
—*Linea Reimer Geiser, Goshen, Indiana. Intergenerational*

While celebration is part of our humanity, it is grounded in the spiritual aspect of that humanity. The deepest roots of celebrative joy are expressed thus by the psalmist:

O come, let us sing to the Lord;
   let us make a joyful noise to the rock of our salvation!
Let us come into his presence with thanksgiving;
   let us make a joyful noise to him with songs of praise!
For the Lord is a great God, and a great King above all gods. . . .
O come, let us worship and bow down,
   let us kneel before the Lord, our Maker!
—*Psalm 95:1-3, 6, NRSV*

An understanding of the meaning of the great Creator God's relationship to us his children brings celebrative joy to lives even in the midst of the negative aspects of our humanness—disease, hunger, poverty, war, brokenness, malice, and greed that are everywhere present. We celebrate to restate our hope in life and in the future. Our celebration communicates tangibly to us and to our children that we believe life is God-given and thus good, there will be a future, peace is a possibility, and hope is one reality that must never die.

How Can Our Celebrating of Life-Passage Events Educate Children Toward Peace?

Peacemaking involves building up innerpersonal well-being along with interpersonal and intergroup cooperation, mutuality, and community. Or, conversely, peacemaking works toward restoration of relationship with God, between human beings, and within human beings. How are these goals enhanced by the celebrative activities in which we engage?

Families celebrate at the beginning of each child's life. Parents might send a gift in the child's name to an organization supporting less fortunate children, to Save the Children,

UNICEF, or a local nonprofit daycare center. Later, the children may see records of such gifts while they peruse their baby books. Then they know that already at birth they were sharing with others or were recipients of loving gifts other than material possessions.

Sharing with other families in celebrating a new birth might include giving childcare time or a meal to the family.

> When a pupil was to have a baby in the family, I contacted the mother to ask if I could bring supper to the family. She had her choice of having the meal brought while she was still at the hospital or after she came home. In *every* instance, the mother wanted it brought when she was home. I also brought a small gift and talked about how much I enjoyed my own children and the big responsibility each one brought. In many cases, the mother brought the child to school several times so we could measure the growth and rejoice in the development of the child.
> —*Elsie Eash Sutter, Goshen, Indiana. Grade 4*

After birth, the yearly celebrations of that event are rich opportunities for peace building. While in Costa Rica, I attended the birthday party of two-year-old Andrea. First thoughts were that this overwhelmed little child did not understand all the action and hullabaloo. Yet my lasting impression was that it was not an age-group party. Present were grandparents, great-aunts and -uncles, cousins of all ages (babies through young adults), as well as aunts and uncles. This was one setting which cultivated the strong sense of family present in that society. While some activities were especially for children, all ages enjoyed the breaking of the piñata. They were bonding intergenerational relationships.

How do we move beyond cake, ice cream, expensive gifts, and competitive games to birthday celebrations that also include healthy foods, gifts of personal love, and cooperative games which will foster the building of relationships?

> Birthdays were special in our home. There was always a cake or pie or watermelon, or anything the birthday person chose to hold the candles. And, of course, there was a prayer for the birthday

person and a token gift. But what the children and we parents enjoyed most, was the special birthday "time." At bedtime, the others went to their rooms, but the birthday child got to stay up with Nelson and me. We three sat in the living room and read through the child's baby book together.

Each child had (and still has) a baby book which was really a large scrapbook of their first two years, described with photos and story. From age two on the book simply had photos. Hearing the stories and seeing the photos always brought laughter, questions, and exclamations! One of the children at the age of sixteen requested that we go through the book on his birthday because he had always enjoyed that special time together. The books will be a gift to the children when they leave home.
—*Marjorie Yoder Waybill, Scottdale, Pennsylvania. Childhood*

One of the traditional elements of a birthday celebration is cake and ice cream. In our family we include this birthday dessert but also encourage enjoyment of other foods by letting the birthday person choose the day's menu. We state that the food must be cooked at home and provide a reasonably balanced diet for the day. Our five-year-old chose the following menu for her birthday:

Breakfast	*Lunch*	*Dinner*
Rice Krispies	Bologna sandwich	Fried chicken
Milk	Fresh pear slices	Creamed potatoes
	Milk	Carrot sticks and
		cucumbers
		Orange juice
		Birthday cake
		Ice cream

—*Elizabeth Miller Broaddus, Terre Haute, Indiana. Age 5*

In our family, birthdays are very special. The birthday person helps choose a special meal including the type of cake. Sometimes we eat out, and the birthday person chooses the place. Our evening is family-oriented with family activities or games. One year our church youth group sponsored a roller-skating party on the night of one child's birthday. She chose that as our evening's activity. One year we visited the Pittsburgh Zoo.
—*Suzanne Beechy Kauffman, Scottdale, Pennsylvania. Childhood*

Carl's second birthday fell on a school holiday, so we were able to celebrate the whole day as a family. When Carl got up, he found a row of snapshots of baby Carl to the present Carl on the wall above the couch. On the couch were several birthday packages from the United States—all books—so he and Mom looked at the books while Dad made breakfast. After breakfast we mixed up some gingerbread cookies, and Carl helped put on eyes and buttons before the cookies went into the oven.

Since we'd given Carl a gift when baby brother was born two weeks earlier, we hadn't bought a birthday present. But after breakfast, Dad got an idea and started drawing simple pictures on a piece of cardboard for a puzzle. Carl helped with suggestions—he wanted a bunny and a cookie man. Mom cut out and colored the pictures while Dad pasted the first cardboard onto a stronger back and made holes for punching out the puzzle pieces. Carl wanted it put together for him at first, but with some help, encouragement, and practice, he was soon proud to do it all by himself. He's still using the puzzle two months later, minus one piece. When I found the piece lying on the floor, chewed to a pulp, I asked Carl about it. "Carl ate the cookie," he said.

In the late afternoon we invited the neighbor family up to help us enjoy the gingerbread men with some ice cream. Dad saddled the horse and gave rides. Then the adults sat and compared birthday customs and the traditions in America and Lesotho while the children played. Company gone, at the end of a fun and memorable day, we were all tired. As we read one of the new books at bedtime, we realized that we had forgotten to take any pictures. We snapped a few quick ones in pj's.
        —*Brenda Hostetler Meyer, Quithing, Lesotho. Age 2*

We told our daughters their adoption stories when they were small. From the time they were old enough to understand, we celebrated two special days each year for each girl. One was her birthday, and the other special day was the day she joined the family. The latter day we called her Family Day. It was celebrated by doing something together as a family. The activity was one chosen by the person whose Family Day it was. So instead of feeling that being adopted was a handicap, our daughters felt that in celebrating Family Day they had something some other children didn't have.
        —*Mary Shank Lehman, Goshen, Indiana. Childhood*

Some years the birthday treats at school were the gifts Indians showed the white man—such as popcorn, turkey, potatoes, or sweet potatoes. This went along with Indiana history.
—*Elsie Eash Sutter, Goshen, Indiana. Grade 4*

Once a month a party was given for all those in our class having a birthday that month. The parents were invited to attend the celebration. The teacher planned the party and selected foods that correlated with the month's activities. The selection included fruits, vegetables (carrots and celery sticks were favorites), tiny peanut butter sandwiches, Jell-O, cheese, crackers, various shaped cookies, popcorn, ice cream, milk, and fruit juice.

Sometimes the teacher and children worked together to prepare pudding, applesauce, or vegetable soup. Other times parents helped them make ice cream in a big freezer. For the birthday children, it was a day of happiness, of feeling important. For parents it was an occasion for rejoicing.
—*Pauline Yoder, Elkhart, Indiana. Kindergarten*

Birthday celebrations can affirm the one having a birthday. I found it helpful to have a birthday affirmation bag for the birthday child. The day before the birthday, I decorated a big bag with a picture and the child's name. On the day of celebration, I taped the bag to the child's chair back or desk. Then I encouraged children to write or draw birthday messages to put in the bag. These affirmations could be signed or unsigned. At the end of the day, the birthday child took the bag home. My students enjoyed this, and I found it boosted self-esteem and provided purposeful free-time activity in the classroom as well.
—*David Klahre, Souderton, Pennsylvania. Grade 1*

At the beginning of the year, I cut out and hem a dirndl skirt. On it I draw rectangles for each of the children in the class. Children draw whatever they want in their spaces—some even sign their names. After all the drawings are finished, I complete the skirt and wear it whenever there is a birthday party.

On the day of the celebration, each classmate draws a picture of the birthday child and copies the child's name beside the picture. The entire group writes a chart story about the birthday child. Some years I send these charts and pictures home with the birthday child on the day of the party. Other years I run off a copy of the story for each child in the class. At the end of the year, I assemble the stories and pictures of the birthday child into a book. Each child then has the picture he drew of the birthday child along with a copy of the class story about that child.

At the party, parents are *strongly* urged to attend along with younger siblings. Parents share a hobby, talent, or interest with the class. These have ranged from learning a few phrases in a foreign language to seeing a cast put on the arm of a child.

The one with the birthday is given a construction-paper crown with that child's name written in glitter and an application for a library card (if it is the sixth birthday). Some years the birthday child is allowed to choose a start from one of the classroom plants, which is potted in a cottage-cheese container.

Unfortunately, many of the children I deal with have always been on the receiving (rather than the giving) end of good things. They have had little opportunity to do things for others or to give of themselves. It is a real joy to see them learn how much fun it is to create a special day for someone else. In the long run, this valuable lesson for the entire class is probably the best reason of all for our birthday celebration.

—*Marilyn Miller Morris, Goshen, Indiana. Kindergarten*

Finding creative ways to celebrate birthdays at home often eliminates the need for buying and awarding prizes—which can cause much grief! If you enjoy traditional parties, rather than purchasing lots of expensive party goods, help the birthday child use markers to decorate inexpensive white cups and napkins. Provide materials for the children to construct hats as one of the party activities. Let the birthday child help make a small gift or favor for each of the invited friends. Hunt for some "new" games in which everyone is a winner. For example, hide puzzle pieces (suiting the puzzle to the children's ages) and have all the children hunt for the pieces and cooperatively assemble the puzzle as pieces are found.

Graduations, weddings, and anniversaries are other events to celebrate. Are there ways to be sure relationships, commitment, and caring are seen as the primary ingredients of those events? I remember how I used young nephews to carry the gifts into the reception room at my wedding. Now I wonder what kind of impression of weddings this job gives to children!

A family tradition for college graduations of nieces and weddings of nephews has developed in our family. I organize the making of a friendship quilt, sending out a letter of explanation and direction along with a quilt square to relatives and friends of the person or couple. Grandma does the piecing and oversees the quilting. Our children plan and draw their squares. The finished product is a one-of-a-kind quilt which holds in it memories of times, places, and relationships.

In July my husband, son Nate, and I went to Minneapolis, Minnesota, to meet our daughter coming from Korea. Kayann was eight years old and could speak no English except for a few words. In August, two weeks after Kayann came into our home, Dennis and I were to celebrate our tenth wedding anniversary. My idea of a great celebration is first of all intimacy, being alone with Dennis, just the two of us doing something special together.

But this year I was presented with a problem. Seven-year-old Nate was having a difficult time adjusting to Kayann's presence in our home, and Kayann could speak little English. Could we justify engaging a babysitter at this time? But it was our tenth anniversary. Could I give up my intimate celebration in the interest of our family? I finally decided, yes, we were needed at home. However, my need to celebrate was still present, and I began to think of my options. We would celebrate at home.

I took the children shopping with me, and we purchased wedding bells to hang from the ceiling, streamers to loop from corner to corner, nut cups for mints and nuts, and candles.

Our dining room had a large picture window opening up to the flat Iowa terrain. But the trees in our front yard gave a graceful touch to the landscape, and with the August crops in the fields, it was a most peaceful setting.

Nate, Kayann, and I began decorating. The language of celebration is universal, and Kayann, with her limited English, joined in the spirit, grabbing Nate and dancing about the room.

After the dinner was prepared, I slipped upstairs and dressed in my wedding gown, veil, heels and all. The candles were lit, the room was decorated, our wedding album was laid out on a nearby table, and I was escorted into the room by Nate and Kayann as a surprise to Dennis. It was a gorgeous August evening; the company was delightful, the food delicious, the setting magnificent. I don't believe that I shall ever have an

anniversary that I will enjoy or treasure more than the one
celebrated with Nate and Kayann.

—*Marian Kauffman Miller, Manson, Iowa. Ages 7-8*

On the various occasions when "gifting" is usually involved,
helping children find ways to give of themselves to others is a
positive way to develop caring rather than selfish attitudes.
Most children do not have adequate sources of money to buy
the material gifts they might wish to purchase for others. They
can give of their time and energies, two items which children
usually possess in abundance.

M. Melanie Svoboda compiled a unique list of ten "Best Gifts
Anyone Can Afford." Although they do not cost a dime, they
are priceless because they are gifts of self.

1. The Gift of Listening
2. The Gift of Affection
3. The Gift of a Note
4. The Gift of Laughter
5. The Gift of Playing a Favorite Game
6. The Gift of Doing a Favor
7. The Gift of a Cheerful Disposition
8. The Gift of Being Left Alone
9. The Gift of a Compliment
10. The Gift of Prayer [3]

The following idea would be a gift that children of all ages
could give, and it would also be appropriate for graduations,
weddings, anniversaries, and other occasions.

For our daughter's sixth birthday, we made and gave a coupon
book that she prized above all other gifts, carrying it around with
her for several weeks. The book[4] consisted of about a dozen
coupons she could redeem anytime during her sixth year. They
ranged from inviting a friend to spend the night to choosing the
menu for dinner one evening. Other favorites were a lunch out
with Daddy, three dollars to spend on anything, and taking the
family out for ice cream. Our daughter's enthusiasm for this
family-style birthday gift has reached a few of her friends who

have since received similar coupon books for their birthdays.
—*Sandra Gerig Glick, Freeport, Illinois. Age 6*

With a special type of fabric crayon available at sewing and craft shops, children's paper and crayon drawings can be permanently ironed onto cloth. Hot pads, pillows, aprons, or wall hangings would be some possibilities for items that could be made featuring the children's art, enabling them to give a part of themselves in a unique gift for a variety of occasions. The age range for which this is appropriate runs from the time a child can hold a crayon through teenage years.

The way in which other life-passage events are planned can contribute to promoting peace. Special celebrations will result if we think sensitively about individual family members and their particular experiences. As my sister approached her fiftieth birthday, our family discussed the many contributions she had made. Being single, she had never been feted at the special anniversary celebrations many people have. My husband suggested we surprise her with a special party.

We invited relatives and friends, asking them to bring, as gifts, remembered anecdotes or words of affirmation. The evening of the party we arranged a display of some of her tangible contributions—books she had written, pictures she had painted, and artifacts from her Algerian sojourn. As the group assembled, the surprised honored guest was treated to an evening of affirmation and appreciation which concluded with a litany written for the occasion. Our three children were involved in planning the event and helping with the refreshments. We hope they caught the idea that we enjoy celebrating the variety of gifts those among us possess.

Occasions such as child dedications, death of a pet, first day of school (nursery school through college), baptism, voluntary service, mission appointments, new job, dedication of a new home—these can become special times of celebration. A collection of songs, Scripture passages, or compilation of prayers written by family members on these occasions become treasures of a family heritage. Family reunions can be a celebration of the spiritual legacy passed on by a common ancestor as memories of faith-building traditions are shared.

The final celebrative event of each of our earthly lives is our physical death. Do our celebrative events at death communicate to our children the agony and ecstasy of human sorrow and joys, of loss yet with hope? Or do they convey only fear, anger, and bewilderment? Do we teach by example that nothing in this world is worse than death, or that values, commitment, and oneness with God are what we live and die for? One of the favorite hymns of martyred Martin Luther King, Jr., includes this thought: "If I can help somebody as I go life's way . . . then my living will not be in vain." The song illustrates his life and death. When we celebrate the quality of life lived on earth and the entrance of the soul into God's presence, this will speak to children of the importance of relationships and self-giving.

> Our children's experience of their grandpa's death was not one of sudden separation or jarring tragedy. They were aware of his illness for more than a year, and it was part of our daily concern and sadness. Yet they could sense Grandpa's joy as he set goals and met them: trips to his Michigan cottage, visits from his children and grandchildren, meals together on winter evenings, a table he built for the family to gather around. When he was too ill to leave his bed, the grandchildren played nearby in the kitchen, often talking with him about birds and squirrels eating outside the window or helping him drink with his special "bent" straws.
>
> Grandpa stayed at home until he died. The boys knew how serious his illness was since my husband Jon stopped his hospital work to help care for Dad as he grew weaker. When he died, Jon called us over to join Grandma, Aunt Julia, Aunt Mary, and their children before Grandpa's body was taken to the funeral home. The boys saw Grandpa lying in his bed in his final sleep. They sat on our laps and cried and prayed with us as we asked for strength to face life without him. They were part of our grieving.
>
> Before Grandpa was buried, the children joined us at the funeral home for a prayer-and-song service. They saw the pine coffin that some of Grandpa's sons made, and when it was time to close it, the children helped. It was a sad good-bye. We miss Grandpa very much. The boys still have questions. But they sensed with us the relief from suffering brought by death, and the lack of fear Grandpa had as he placed himself in God's loving

care. They anticipate seeing him in heaven.
—*Janet Nase Smucker, Goshen, Indiana. Ages 4-8*

Children do learn what they live. As we give attention to relationships above things, we plant the seeds of self-giving rather than greed, mutuality rather than self-aggrandizement, hope rather than despair.

> One thing our family has found meaningful is a family hug. It helps celebrate the closeness, caring, and support of one another on happy occasions, during traumatic times, or upon resolving interpersonal tension. All members of the family gather together into one tight hug, perhaps with a short prayer.
> —*Cara Frey Ulrich, Archbold, Ohio. Intergenerational*

Are There New Ways to Celebrate Old Holidays?

"Families need rituals, traditions, moments to be treasured in later years. We all hang the facts we learn onto our feelings. If we remember a warm, nurturing, celebrating family, we can better understand and participate in the family of God."[5]

As with life-passage events, many of our traditional holidays have roots reaching back for many centuries. Their origins and meanings have changed as the cultural context has changed. To maintain celebrative richness, we need to cast away aspects no longer meaningful and keep those that still have meaning, even as we add new meanings from current experiences.

In the multinational nursery school where I taught, we celebrated Valentine's Day as "I Love You Day." During rug time, I told the children individually that I loved them (most in their particular first language) and mentioned one thing I especially appreciated about each. For snack we had friendship fruit salad made from fruit they had brought in to share with their friends. We had baked banana honey bread and spread it with cream cheese. This was a good accompaniment to the heart-shaped cookies Eric had made at home as his valentine for each of his friends. We really didn't miss the sugar and chocolate valentines. Teachers could ask older children to research the probable origins of this particular saint's day and encourage them to make cards for their friends rather than simply purchasing them. All ages of children could use Valentine's Day as a day to celebrate friendship and to affirm friends and family.

> It was Valentine's Day. The first grade of Bushnell School was invited to visit the Knights of Pythias Home to give a musical program and share with the residents there. How busy we were, making valentines, learning to write "I Love You," and practicing our songs and stories!
>
> When we arrived at the home in the afternoon, we were directed to a special place from which we watched the residents come into the assembly room—some in wheelchairs, others walking slowly with canes, and some being led by nurses. But what attracted the most attention was a blind man led by two kind nurses. He trembled and walked slowly. The children were so impressed, for just a few days before I had read the story of Jesus healing a blind man in our morning Bible story time. A little boy came to me and said, "If Jesus were here, he would help that man!" How beautiful is the faith of a child!
>
> After our program, each child gave his or her valentine to an elderly total stranger, and said, "I love you!" It was a bright spot in the day and a lesson of love the children never forgot.
>
> —*Bertha Yoder, Springfield, Ohio. Grade 1*

St. Patrick's Day also affords a time to introduce children to the life of a Christian missionary. The significance of remembering Patrick is more interesting than just wearing green and talking about leprechauns. Plant some belles of Ireland, prepare potatoes after finding out their significance to Irish and American history. With older children, explore the roots of the modern Northern Ireland tragedy of bloodshed and the misery of war. What solutions to the discord can the children project? How can such conflicts be avoided in the first place?

We hope every Sunday is a celebration of God's people giving thanks for the resurrection. The Christian church's position has been that Easter Sunday is the focal point of the church year. However, in children's eyes Christmas may overshadow Easter. Christ's death and resurrection are seemingly more difficult to share with children than his birth as a baby. Perhaps the primary goal in sharing Easter with children is to communicate our joy that Jesus is alive, as in Katherine Royer's lyrics:

> I am so happy on Easter Day;
> I am so happy, I sing and say,
> "Jesus is risen! Glad Easter Day!" [6]

Toward that end, one year the nurture committee at Berkey Avenue Fellowship in Goshen, Indiana, planned an Easter event for the fellowship's children, ages four through twelve, the Saturday before Palm Sunday. The children enjoyed coloring eggs. They constructed and filled baskets to be given as tray favors at a nearby nursing home. They used posterboard, markers, and stickers to create "Jesus is alive!" bookmarks for themselves. As they gathered in the sanctuary for a time of singing and worship, eggs were hidden in the fellowship rooms for an egg hunt. The hunt and refreshments were followed by a trip to the nursing home to deliver the favors. We walked through the halls and lobby singing Easter songs.

This joyful celebration provided an alternative to the community egg hunt where hundreds of children scramble and shove to find numbered eggs that are turned in for prizes. Winners as well as disappointed ones who found only plain eggs—they all probably leave confused about the meaning of Easter.

Berkey Avenue Fellowship also had a large tree branch set up in the foyer, sporting a banner carrying the words Jesus Is Alive. All persons in the fellowship were invited to hang blown-out, decorated eggs on the tree. The egg, as a symbol of life and as descriptive of the Trinity, was introduced during children's time in the worship service: An egg has a shell, a yolk, and a white. You need all three parts to know all about an egg. Likewise, the Trinity has three parts—God, the Father; Jesus, the Son; and the Holy Spirit.

Easter might be followed with a celebration of Pentecost. One year we had a birthday cake in Sunday school to celebrate Pentecost as the church's birthday. Discussion can move from the birth of the Christian church to that of one's denomination and particular congregation, according to what would be most meaningful to children at different ages. While a relatively small group of early believers spoke in many languages on that special Pentecost many years ago, today the church embodies in its membership the many languages of its varied peoples and cultures—a cause for celebration, acceptance, and unity rather than rejection and fragmentation.

Unfortunately, some of the bitterest wars in history have been so-called religious wars; some of the worst cruelties and injustices ever perpetrated have been done in the name of faith. Older children read of these events in their study of history. If we recall in celebration our oneness in Jesus, we can help them better understand faith and build commitment to peace, especially within the faithful. We would take a big step toward peace in the world if all Christians agreed not to kill each other.

Arbor Day is another traditional although not widely celebrated holiday that has much potential for peace building. As James, age seven, said, "Peace is trees, not stumps." [7] Living at peace with the physical environment in which God has placed us is intimately connected to our living at peace with other humans. We might celebrate Arbor Day with that focus.

Beside the usual planting of trees and reading of *A Tree is Nice*,[8] there are other ways to help children celebrate our commonality with our earth. We can take a cue from Michelle's comment, "Peace is planting flowers on a clear day."[9] Help children beautify their surroundings by planting flowers or by picking up trash. Other possibilities are cooperative leaf-identification games, taking bark rubbings, or thoughtfully planned nature scavenger hunts.

I watched five-year-old Daisuke as he gazed in wonder and respect at the tiny ladybug who could walk upside down on the underside of a leaf. He cautioned others to be quiet as they watched. In contrast, Johnny came along and grabbed the ladybug, imprisoned it in his fist, denied he had it, and finally was coaxed into letting it go free. Our responses to our environment have too often been like Johnny's.

We can promote the importance of peace and celebrate the joy of peace with our earth. This happens as we plan study units on insects and birds and trees as well as those on space travel or transportation. It also happens as we include hikes and gardening in our family activities as well as attending ball games.

Some adults exemplify their concern for the earth by active support and/or involvement in groups dedicated to abolishing nuclear weapons from our planet. Such persons can also speak loudly by example to children, be a reassurance to them, and provide avenues for their own involvement as they mature.

The Las Animas Nuclear Freeze Group participated in Ground Zero Pairing Project with cities in Russia. I was a part of the group and involved my third-grade class. We used Ground Zero Education materials to study Russia. We got Seeds of Hope packets from Fellowship of Reconciliation and sent marigold seeds as a symbol of peace to Russia and to our congressman. On one side of the packet in Russian and in English was printed:[10]

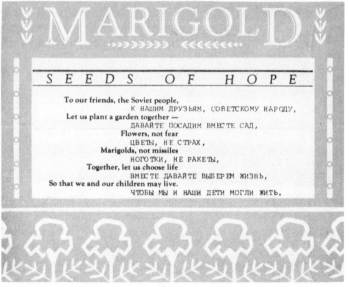

We had a speaker who visited Russia and a school there. We wrote letters and sent art work and pictures of ourselves to the Russian children. My third graders got bookmarks and other materials available from Fellowship of Reconciliation.

It was rewarding to see the attitudes of the children change as the year progressed. It was encouraging to have other teachers ask to see and use some of the materials.

—*Irene Rhodes, Las Animas, Colorado. Grade 3*

We might revitalize May Day as a time to pleasantly surprise neighbors and friends with a gift of field or homegrown flowers in homemade baskets hung on their doorknobs anonymously. Decoration/Memorial Day is another May holiday which involves the use of flowers to express love. Around May 30, friends and relatives beautifully decorate with plants and flowers the sites where their loved ones have been interred.

To educate children toward peace, we can expand the traditional meaning of Decoration/Memorial Day. We can make it into a time to remember, not just the military personnel who died in battle, but also the innocent civilian victims of war who outnumber the combatants. Use this occasion to affirm life and weep for the terrors of war.

The Fourth of July and Canadian Dominion Day provide appropriate times for examining your family's roots. Why did your ancestors come to the United States or Canada? Share family faith stories in this context. Help your children look at their country evaluatively. As we celebrate our country's espoused ideals of "liberty and justice for all," we need to celebrate those times and occasions when this principle has been a flourishing reality.

We also need to help our children understand historical and current situations in which this principle has *not* been a reality for many people. What do we appreciate and find celebrative about our country? What are our concerns for our country? Maybe this is the time to write a letter and share gratitude and concerns with state or provincial representatives, the president, or the prime minister. A special prayer breakfast, praying for national leaders, may be a good way to celebrate.

In October our nursery-school theme for Halloween week was "Autumn." We focused on orange and black colors and foods, baked pumpkin pie, made paper-bag costumes, and in general tried to concentrate on pumpkin fun rather than on ghosts and ghouls and scary things. A "Festival of Leaves" might be another theme for this fall celebration. It is the custom of the Goshen College Laboratory Kindergarten to collect money for school supplies where they are needed overseas, and to accompany the collection with a study of that country.

Other groups make treats/favors to take to shut-ins or hospitals.

"Halloween is a night of spirits, and has a history rich in religious traditions. It is historically All Hallow's Eve, the night before All Soul's Day, decreed by Pope Gregory to honor all the dead saints. Halloween costumes started in medieval times when churches displayed relics of saints. Those parishes too poor to have relics let parishioners dress up to imitate the saints." [11] Older children might be introduced to these origins. Can they suggest ways of returning their activities to the focus of celebrating the lives of those no longer on this earth?

> We at Trinity Mennonite Church believe our celebration at Halloween time to be consistent with Christian commitment and a lot of fun for children and adults alike. We have an All-Saints Party at the meetinghouse on October 31. Everyone is encouraged to come dressed as a saint. We have three categories: Old Testament, New Testament, contemporary. We ask that each "saint" give one additional clue beyond the above category.
>
> Following the guessing of saints, we meet in the fellowship hall for games such as bobbing for apples and smashing each other's balloon. Then we have refreshments. Every child is given a bag full of goodies to take home. Other concerned Christians from our community are now joining us for this Halloween alternative.
> —*Mahlon D. Miller, Morton, Illinois. Intergenerational*

The Fellowship of Hope in Elkhart, Indiana, has also developed an alternative Halloween celebration. Barbara Rody Cataldo reports:

> The most meaningful act of our celebration is the way we begin the evening—the lantern walk. This custom is borrowed from the Society of Brothers. Each person who wants to take part finds or improvises a lantern. The walk begins after dark at a home about a half mile from the meetinghouse. Along the way, individuals and families join in with lanterns. We sing as we walk—songs about light overcoming darkness and about Jesus, our light.
>
> When we reach the meetinghouse, we gather in the parking lot, forming a large circle, singing more songs, enjoying each other's lanterns and the joy on the children's faces. This is a moving tradition with strong symbolism.

I'm grateful to be part of a church that is both serious enough and playful enough to have taken the time to develop such a redemptive alternative to an uncomfortable holiday.[12]

Janet Martin shares her Halloween experiences:

On Halloween evening the children of the church, accompanied by their parents, are invited to dress up as a Bible character and meet at the church or at the house of one of the members. They are encouraged to study up on their Bible character and to be ready to answer questions. There are games and quizzes, fruit and cookies, and fun for all. This does not answer the question of what to do for those children who come to our door, but it does help when our own children ask, "Mommy, what can I be at Halloween this year?"[13]

If you still prefer the traditional trick or treating, consider the following adaptation as noted by Leona Weaver Schmucker:

I'm grateful that my parents shared their concern about the meaning of Halloween and the rituals that have become a part of that holiday. My mother had a most Christian response to trick-or-treating. We dressed up, like others, and went door-to-door. Instead of asking and threatening, we carried a bag of goodies which we helped prepare, with a sign which read:
If you guess who we are,
we'll give you a treat.
That's the most creative compromise I've heard of during the past thirty years. My mother's positive response made an indelible imprint on my eight-year-old mind.[14]

We usually eat more than we need in a world where many people are starving. This obviously is not an appropriate way to give thanks in November. At nursery school, we shared the old folk tale *Stone Soup*[15] with the children. It tells how greedy people were tricked into sharing their food with hungry people. Our classes made no-stone soup for our thankfulness meal. Each child was invited to bring a vegetable which was chopped and added to the soup pot. We were glad to share with each other and did not have to be tricked to do it! Indian corn pone complemented the soup.

Sharing an international meal with friends during Thanksgiving season can initiate awareness of persons in other parts of our world. We can give thanks for others as we experience their unique foods, language, and dress. Also, we can give money to our mission boards to support sharing Christ's gospel of peace in that country. The Family Mission Thanks-Giving materials[16] are one example of resources toward these goals of understanding and sharing with thankfulness.

> I remember with pleasure one Thanksgiving season when our family was living in a new community. We were too far away to visit family, so we went to a local nursing home and asked for a "grandma" to share Thanksgiving with us. Our eight- and nine-year-old daughters were a bit shy at first since our guest was not very outgoing. They soon began showing her some of the things we had brought back from Africa, moving her around in her wheelchair, and generally trying to help her to have a happy time.
> —*Marian Brendle Hostetler, Belle Plains, Iowa. Ages 8-9*

Here is a musical prayer for a meal shared with lonely, elderly, new-found or long-time friends. Use the tune of "Edelweiss."

BLESS OUR FOOD

Bless our friends, bless our food;
Come, O Lord, and sit with us.
May our talk glow with peace;
Bring your love to surround us.
Friendship and peace, may they bloom and grow,
Bloom and grow forever.
Bless our friends, bless our food,
Bless our sharing together.[17]

—*Author unknown*

A teacher practiced Thanksgiving in this significant way:

> At Thanksgiving time I wrote a personal, different note to each child in my class, telling them why I was thankful for them.
> —*Elsie Eash Sutter, Goshen, Indiana. Grade 4*

Another teacher adapted her Thanksgiving study to the needs of her Appalachian classroom.

In November, I usually combined a study of Indians as a bridging activity between a seeds-and-plants unit and a food unit. I could usually count on one or two children to have an Indian grandmother to spark interest. At this level we concentrated on Indian life, how they helped the Pilgrims, the first Thanksgiving feast, foods Indians have contributed to our diets, the traditional Thanksgiving dinner, and their *own* dinner. From there we went into their first "academic" food unit.
—*Joyce Gingerich Zuercher, Harlan, Kentucky. Grades K-1*

Christmas is a golden opportunity to stress love and peace.

Little Baby Jesus came on Christmas Day;
Little Baby Jesus slept upon the hay;
Little Baby Jesus was God's only Son;
Jesus came because He loves us ev'ry one.[18]

I was in a setting where various religious groups were represented among the constituent families one year at Christmas. Hence, I struggled with how to share the meaning of the Advent without offending the Muslim, Unitarian, and possibly Buddhist and atheist families represented. In order not to compromise my faith, I focused on Jesus' message of peace, a concept that all would support. We made a banner with the word *peace* written in all our languages, and the children used markers to add decorations. Daisuke's contribution to the banner was a broken arrow, a Native American symbol for peace which we had learned prior to Thanksgiving.

guideline: insert broken-arrow illustration here

As we developed a Christmas alphabet, *A* stood for the angel and its message of peace on earth, and *D* for the dove, the peace bird. We learned American, English, Spanish, African-American, and German Christmas songs. We celebrated Sweden's St. Lucia Day and the Jewish Hanukkah. We heard the biblical Christmas story as well as the Russian story of Babushka and the traditional "Visit from St. Nicholas." I believe we felt that we can all be friends and live peacefully together.

Sensitivity to holidays of other cultures and religions throughout the year is appropriate. Particularly in December, we can make children familiar with the eight-day Hanukkah celebration of their Jewish friends. They can enjoy making and eating special foods of the holiday such as potato latkes and playing games with the dreidel, a four-sided top.

David was a Jewish boy whose father was a rabbi. He shared the meaning of various Jewish holidays with us. He also participated in our Christmas programs and parties.

—*Minnie Sutter, South Bend, Indiana. Age 6*

Christmastime is a special time with family and friends. My fourth-grade class shared with members of their family and friends by performing a Christmas play and serving simple refreshments to their guests after the play. All the children had a small part in the play about a family who chopped down a forest tree for Christmas. The forest animals wanted to surprise the family while they slept one night and decorated the tree with nature objects from the forest.

We all cooperated to make simple costumes, invitations, and programs for the play. The day before the performance the children worked together making two kinds of no-bake candy to be served as refreshments for the family members and friends who came to the play. Not only were the guests pleased to share in this Christmas celebration. The children were also truly delighted that they had been able to work together to give to their family and friends in this way.

—*Geneva Hershberger, Hazard, Kentucky. Grade 4*

For quite a number of years at the annual Christmas PTA programs, my pupils (fourth, fifth, or sixth graders) would present a choral reading and my latest Christmas song. The choral readings always were from the musically cadenced King James translation of the Christmas story. This way, children in the public school memorized Bible verses.

—*Paul S. Liechty, Decatur, Indiana. Grades 4-6*

While serving as principal at Harrison and Union Township schools, the question of Christmas trees and gifts was raised. Children were encouraged to bring clothing, toys, and canned food as gifts for needy people. These were distributed by the Goshen Salvation Army and Nappanee Open Door. The warm smiles were evidence of the joy the students felt as they helped others during the holiday season.

—*Samuel W. Martin, Nappanee, Indiana. Grades K-6*

While earning money to finish college, I worked for a family whose mother was seriously ill in the hospital. At Christmas, Eddie, the sensitive son, was hurting and lonely. In a gift box for him I put only the instruction, "Look for a package in the hall closet." In that was another direction. By the time he had searched for five such packages, he found his gift in a most unlikely place. This helped him over a difficult day. His eyes sparkled.

—*Elsie C. Bechtel, Bowmansdale, Pennsylvania. Age 9*

Instead of a classroom Christmas party and traditional gift exchange at our primary school, we made a trip to a nearby nursing home. We sang familiar Christmas songs and distributed boxes of Kleenex covered with brightly decorated handmade wrapping paper to residents of the home.

—*Eleanor Davidhizar Shoup, Mishawaka, Indiana. Grades 1-3*

During the Advent season each year, we celebrated by having Advent suppers with special guests. Each of our four children invited a favorite teacher and family for one of the four nights. They helped plan the menu, decorate the table, and plan the special after-supper activity. It was something they talked about as soon as the new school year began in September—deciding which of their teachers would be invited.

—*Elsie Eash Sutter, Goshen, Indiana. Ages 5-22*

I vividly grasped the need for making Christmas a time of sharing, affirmation, and *hope* for children when I heard several fifth graders singing this version of "Joy to the World":

Joy to the world, the bomb has come.
Let earth receive its doom.
Let everyone evaporate,
Let everything disintegrate,
Let buildings crumble, too,
All over me and you,
All over our parents, too.

What a sad sign of the times when children originate and sing such a song. Surely we need to find ways of celebrating the coming to earth of the Prince of Peace—which will revive hope.

Last Christmas, since our family was planning a trip to Florida during the last half of the Christmas break, we dispensed with "boxed" gift giving. Yet as Christmas Eve arrived, we did gather to give gifts of a different sort. Each family member was to write on cards something they liked about each of the others. The six of us gathered in the living room to pass out our "gifts." One or two who had not written something gave their "likes" verbally. It was an experience of positive affirmation and sharing for our family. One of our younger boys said that this Christmas was as good as any, even with the "boxed" gifts.
—*Elaine Yoder Unzicker, Goshen, Indiana. Ages 7-15*

Our family went caroling each year, taking along homemade gifts such as elderberry jelly or candles. We visited the children's school principal, and school and Sunday school teachers (present and past!). There were as many as 20 people on our annual list. This was our favorite Christmas celebration. One year our married son and wife came home from graduate school for twenty-four hours so they could take part in this favorite activity.
—*Elsie Eash Sutter, Goshen, Indiana. Intergenerational*

We had a dying birch tree in our front yard that needed to be cut down. To make the job easier and more fun, my husband Owen, our nine-year-old son, Steven, and I cut the tree into Yule logs. We tied the logs together with red ribbon and delivered them to all our friends with fireplaces and wood-burning stoves.
—*Eleanor Davidhizar Shoup, South Bend, Indiana. Age 9*

Sharing of ourselves with family and friends certainly is one of the joys of the Christmas season. Once when we attempted to communicate the *meaning* of Christmas to preschool and elementary aged neighborhood children, we planned a Christmas sharing party for them. As one of the activities, I read *The Christmas Pageant*,[19] and then we had simple props available for the children to put on their own pageant. Refreshments included goodies from the piñata we had made.

Are There New Holidays That Could Well Be Celebrated?

We need not be rigid about the nature and form of our celebrations. Memorializing a past event even has educational significance. In Joshua 4 we are told of twelve stones being set up near the place where Israel crossed the Jordan so that "when your children ask their parents in time to come, 'What do these stones mean?' then you shall let your children know, 'Israel passed over the Jordan here on dry ground' " (Josh. 4:21-22, NRSV).

Most of those who set up memorial celebrations hope that they will have this kind of ultimate significance.[20]

As we celebrate the memory of people and events, we provide a reason for children to ask why. We might add a few more birthdays of heroes or heroines to our calendar of holidays, as well as days that focus beyond our own nationalistic events. This year at school and at home we had a birthday party around January 15 to commemorate the birthday of Martin Luther King, Jr. We read a children's biography and listened to the "I Have a Dream" speech on a record available from our local library. This special day can be followed by observing Black History Month in February. Appreciation of African culture as well as African-American gifts can be celebrated.

To celebrate Black History Week, the following poem appeared in a *News Pilot* magazine for first grade with a full-page picture of a dejected black child.

Sometimes when I'm lonely,
Don't know why
Keep thinkin' I won't be lonely
By and by.
—*Langston Hughes*

After studying the picture, my first graders added hungry, tired, hated, and crying to describe the child. I set the words to music. The children loved to clap the syncopated rhythm.

Hope

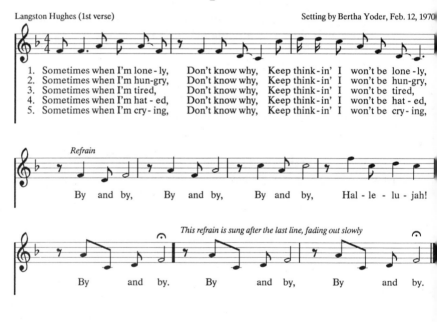

Langston Hughes (1st verse)   Setting by Bertha Yoder, Feb. 12, 1970

1. Sometimes when I'm lone-ly,   Don't know why,   Keep think-in' I   won't be lone-ly,
2. Sometimes when I'm hun-gry,   Don't know why,   Keep think-in' I   won't be hun-gry,
3. Sometimes when I'm tired,   Don't know why,   Keep think-in' I   won't be tired,
4. Sometimes when I'm hat-ed,   Don't know why,   Keep think-in' I   won't be hat-ed,
5. Sometimes when I'm cry-ing,   Don't know why,   Keep think-in' I   won't be cry-ing,

Refrain

By   and   by,   By   and   by,   By   and   by,   Hal-le-lu-jah!

This refrain is sung after the last line, fading out slowly

By   and   by.   By   and   by,   By   and   by.

—*Bertha Yoder, Springfield, Ohio. Grade 1*

Our son once had a good friendship with a Chinese child. We saw an article in the children's *World* magazine containing descriptions and recipes for celebrating Chinese New Year. This began our tradition of having a special meal to celebrate that event, from wonton soup to fortune cookies and even chopsticks. We hope our children's experiences will preclude their ever viewing oriental people as a "yellow tide" or in other less-than-human terms.

In Costa Rica, the first Sunday of September was widely celebrated as Children's Day. Special parties and parades feted the children and made them feel special. The second Sunday in June is Children's Day in the United States, but it is certainly not an event of widespread significance as it should be. Universal Children's Day falls on October 2 while International Children's Book Day is April 2.

Grandparents' Day in September seems to be largely an idea of Hallmark Cards, but it is a special day with potential for highlighting loving intergenerational relationships. As eight-and-a-half-year-old Clifford says, "Peace is love that is passed on from generation to generation."[21]

> Family Peace Day, an intergenerational event, allowed families to explore a variety of facets of peacemaking. The Peace and Social Concerns Committee of the Franconia Mennonite Conference and the Women's Missionary and Service Commission sponsored a Family Peace Day for families of elementary school-age children. Families rotated around interest centers to learn various aspects of peacemaking: Ancestor Peacemaking featuring storytelling, Peer Peacemaking with open-ended stories, noncompetitive games, Family Peacemaking illustrated with puppetry, and Worldwide Peacemaking taught by an oversized puzzle. The day ended with John Lapp talking about biblical peacemaking.
> —*Beverly Myers Ehst, Perkasie, Pennsylvania. Intergenerational (via Marie Moyer)*

How might we celebrate the birthdays of Nobel Peace Prize winners Mother Teresa (August 27) and Jane Addams (September 6)? September 27 is Native American Indian Day. Might the gifts of the Indians be highlighted on that day as well as at the time of the American Thanksgiving Day? Also, consider special days of global significance: World Literacy Day (January

8), World Day of Prayer (March 6), World Health Day (April 7), World Environment Day (June 5), Hiroshima Day (August 6), International Day of Peace (second Tuesday in September), United Nations Day (October 24), World Community Day (November 7), Universal Bible Sunday (the Sunday before Thanksgiving), and Human Rights Day (December 10).

How Does Celebration Enable Us to Experience Joy in Daily Living?

Authentic celebration flows from a basic joy and affirmation of life. We all live through times when it seems impossible to celebrate. The grief, terror, or despair of the moment may seem too much to bear: celebration seems not to be possibile. If we have cultivated mutuality, caring, and our relationship with God, we will have the resources to return to joy.

Unfortunately for many people, celebration does not flow from joy; it is but a momentary escape from a reality too hard to bear. To celebrate, one must use enough alcohol or other chemical substances to get "happy." The fun really starts when everyone is a little "tipsy" or "spaced out." In today's society, "party" has become a verb meaning to drink.

We want children to find God-given joy in experiencing their past, present, and future in the company of relatives and friends. We want children to realize that celebration cannot be created or enhanced by chemical substances.

Perhaps thoughtfully planned special times of celebration will help us move toward approaching our everyday living in a more positive way. Can we begin looking for something redeemable or celebrative in each ordinary day? If we cannot find anything, maybe we can begin creatively planning to do one thing each day that is a step toward celebrating life and building peace. It might be as simple as a warm, sincere smile or a listening ear, a love note in a lunch box, or a special hug.

A wise grandmother said, "Children can't 'don't'; they have to 'do.' " We hope that our sharing with children the "do's" of celebration will contribute to their "doing" peace.

Global Relations

OUR PERSPECTIVE of the world family grows out of our own family experiences. With a view of God's world family, children grow to understand injustices which arouse anger and conflict and precipitate wars. Children are the world's future. We build toward peace when we prepare children to find ways to bring love and joy to others.

I WALK

I walk
  on dangerous paths
  where I may fall into evil hands
  at any moment.
I walk
  where many were killed
  where hatred and revenge lurk
  around dark corners
  and Satan himself
  may come from his burning castle.
I walk
  through a land dark red with blood
  and black without the light of Christ.
But the Lord walks with me
  and I am not afraid
  for in Him I find peace.

—Alison Dick, age 10

7. How Can Children Develop Awareness of Their Global Family?

Lois Meyer King

MANY persons agree that peace is more than the absence of conflict. Rather, it denotes action and involvement. One educator has said, "Peace involves the appreciation of other people, regardless of differences in sex, race, ethnic origin, language, culture, or mores."[1] Teaching children appreciation of others is imperative if there is to be peace in the world.

Some of my fondest childhood memories are of large family gatherings during which much animated conversation occurred. Such discussions almost always included global issues, and I sensed the loving concern for the welfare of others regardless of race, creed, or nationality.

My parents and other members of my extended family were my earliest teachers, with the church, school, and community exerting much influence later. Wherever people gather to talk, listen, share, and work, teaching is in process. As people enjoy potluck dinners together; share tree trimmers, tents, and trailers; make quilts and assemble health kits, attitudes and values are passed on and skills for peace building are developing.

Children imitate and absorb what they hear and observe, whether positive or negative.

I cannot recall anytime in my life when I have not been surrounded by literature of various types. My parents, although busy providing for the physical needs of their six children, nevertheless did not neglect providing for the spiritual, intellectual, emotional, and social needs as well. Since they were devout Christians, the Bible was given priority, but we also read other books, magazines, and newspapers. Only illness or other emergencies kept us from attending school or church. Even though my parents had limited financial resources, they encouraged us to prepare for college.

The congregation in which I was nurtured was unusual because of a comparatively high level of education. Several missionaries had been sent abroad and were held in high esteem. Relief workers also helped bring the needs and the understanding of other people in our world to our attention. When I, as a young adult, returned home after spending summers doing social and religious work with migrants and with persons of another race in the inner city, I was warmly welcomed and affirmed by the congregation. Now, for over thirty-seven years, I have been a pastor's wife in six different locations. Ten of those years were spent in the inner city with another race and culture.

I am sure it was an answer to prayer when one of my uncles offered to lend money for my oldest sister to attend college. That began the chain reaction in which we siblings helped each other through college, and five of us became public school teachers. Others in my extended family also emphasized the value of education. For five years before marriage and for a total of twenty-four years, I was a public school teacher of intermediate grades and emphasized the importance of global awareness.

In this chapter I give some methods and suggestions as to how the home, the church, and the school can cooperate in developing within children a positive awareness of a world family.

How Does the Home Help Children Begin to Develop Appreciation of Others Worldwide?

We want children to be able to appreciate people who are different and far away. Children are an integral part of immediate and extended families, and their experiences in those families play a strategic role in developing such appreciation. Children must have a healthy attitude toward themselves and their own families before they can have similar attitudes toward the world family. As parents and teachers show love, respect, and trust for each other and for each individual member of the family, positive self-images will develop within those members. Children nurtured in this type of environment will more easily transfer similar attitudes to their world family.

> When two-year-old Kelly welcomed her baby brother into our family, we tried hard to remind her of all the things two-year-olds could do that babies couldn't. So later on at age three, as I put Kelly to bed, I prayed aloud, "Thank you for our good daughter, Kelly. Amen." She said, "But, Mommy, you forgot Brian! And dear God, thank you for our *dear* baby Brian. Help him to be good, and not hit me, you know, God. Amen."
> —*Mary Jo Hartzler Short, Goshen, Indiana. Age 3*

"The way to peace develops best in the kind of home environment where conflicts are handled creatively. This occurs more readily where there are extended relationships, where more adults are connected with children, where more support is possible."[2]

Helping children realize that their families' backgrounds are special can build appreciation for the larger world family. A way of strengthening family bonds used by one creative teacher involves the families in birthday celebrations at school. The birthday child introduces parents, grandparents, and younger siblings to the class. One by one classmates introduce themselves to the families. Often the parents then share a hobby, talent, or interest with the class, thus helping children appreciate the abilities of their own family. Often, for the first time, children are aware that their families are special people who possess valuable talents and abilities.

Close family relationships have suffered where the extended family is scattered. This increases feelings of isolation, loneliness, and of being disenfranchised. Personal and social alienation often develop. Age groups have become more and more separated as the number of people over sixty rapidly increases and they live out their retirement years in special buildings or communities built exclusively for the elderly.

Children develop respect and appreciation for the older generation when their elders are given a place of importance. When we tap the vast reservoir of love and wisdom found in older people, we provide children with a dimension of continuity and a new sense of hope. We want the young to receive special attention from loving adults who have the time and patience to listen to and communicate with them. Then they gain a vital sense of relation to the past, along with guideposts for the future. Schools can capitalize on these personal contacts with the past and students' place of origin.

> One year we had an unusual opportunity to help kindergartners visualize an extended family spanning four generations. During Family Week, our kindergartner Jonathan, his mother and father, his four grandparents, and three great-grandmothers came to school. They sat in family tree formation one generation behind the other beginning with Jonathan. His parents talked about their children, Jonathan and his sister. His grandparents talked about their children, Jonathan's parents. His great-grandmothers talked about their children, Jonathan's grandparents. After that formal presentation, the grandparents read to the children, books such as *Is Anyone Home? Grandpa's Garden Lunch, What Time Is Grandma Coming?* and others.[3]
> —Kathryn Aschliman, Goshen, Indiana. Kindergarten

> If you want to foster feelings of belonging, help children create their own family trees and relate ancestral stories. It is also important to help children enjoy and learn the language of parents and grandparents whose first language is not English.
> —Vernon and Bonnie Sommers Ratzlaff, Tuba City, Arizona. Grades 1-8

Children who live miles away from their relatives will catch the joy and excitement of parents who involve them in planning and sending gifts for special occasions. Preparing for a long trip to visit grandparents can be a time of eager anticipation. We can encourage them to correspond with their distant relatives, exchange audio and video tapes, and write their own original books of family stories past and present. As children grow in their ability to read and write, they can enjoy books on family histories.

When children live far from close relatives, an extended family might be "created." This could include persons living nearby, such as an "adopted" grandparent or persons living within the household.

We've found that living with other adults has been a good experience for our young son Carl. In Goshen we lived in a household, and here in Quithing, Lesotho, we opened one room in our house to a single woman who works at school. Having those adults as friends means that other adults can be natural friends, too.

We always try to introduce adults as well as children to Carl, because names are important to him, even though he doesn't always remember. We had a supper guest last week, a stranger to Carl. Carl asked his name over and over. After supper, he asked one more time, "Who's that?"

We said, "Stan."

Then, grinning, Carl announced, "I want to play with Stan!" A new friend!

—*Brenda Hostetler Meyer, Quithing, Lesotho. Age 2*

For eleven years we were part of an extended family which included (at various times) other families with and without children, and single adults of different ages and ethnic backgrounds. We interacted with "brothers and sisters" in the household while engaging in weekly household discussions, participating in events important in the life and culture of other members, and sharing tasks based on interest and need rather than traditional roles. We had access to skills not present in our nuclear family. We learned through observation how others relate inside and outside of family settings.

—*Ellen Penner Ebersole. Wichita, Kansas. Intergenerational*

Rural families hosting children from urban areas and vice versa provide many opportunities to teach appreciation for other cultures and ways of living. At times there can be conflicts because of cultural differences and suddenly being in close living quarters with "strangers." There are especially beneficial results when homes host the same children several years, thus building lasting relationships.

> The first time I remember a black person in our home, our two small daughters were hosting Vicky and Jeanette, two little black girls from Chicago. As they were getting ready for bed, I heard Jeanette comment, "Boy, Vicky, you're really black!"
>
> With a sigh of relief, I thought, "Jeanette, I'm sure glad it was you who said that."
>
> This year one of our daughters has a black roommate at college.
> —*Neva Miller Beck, Archbold, Ohio. Ages 6 and 9*

Not only are children's perspectives enriched by relating closely to others of various cultures, but discerning adults are also beneficiaries. When our family moved to East Peoria, Illinois, from Chicago, our next-door neighbors became our good friends. The first summer, we hosted children from Chicago and did so several subsequent summers. Our children, the neighbor's children, and the black and Hispanic city children presented a lovely picture as they played games, rode bicycles, and operated the motor cart in our yard.

Later, my neighbor lady told me, "My daddy taught me to hate blacks and Catholics, but I never did really think he was right. Now I know for sure that he was wrong!"

Families may make it a practice frequently to host children or adults of other cultures and races. Such hosting will provide a setting where children may develop flexible expectations of human behavior. This in turn will enable them to approach contacts of less-familiar people with a more respectful and open-minded attitude. The ability to ask and appreciate others' perspective is an important skill for understanding and relating to different cultural groups. This skill can become highly developed over a period of time.

Our daughter and a black girl were the only girls in a Sunday school class of boys. The girls became good friends, and Joyce spent every Sunday at our home. They worked at Spruce Lake Camp together. Joyce went on to work in the Mennonite Hour Office and to attend Eastern Mennonite College. Now she is married and has a daughter, is active in a Mennonite Church, and teaches at the local high school.

Our family has belonged to the Pittsburgh Council for International Visitors. Having people in our home from all over the world is a common experience for our children. I'm sure it helped our daughter who lived in Morocco for six years. They now have many visitors from overseas in their home.

—*Winifred Erb Paul, Scottdale, Pennsylvania. Lifetime*

Our youngest child is adopted and is a Meti (part Native American) by birth. Our girls are fiercely proud of him, and we have often talked about the Indians' contributions and how they have been treated, including how they are portrayed in TV programs. A year ago some neighbors were keeping Indian children as foster children. Lillian, our oldest daughter, became good friends with the foster girl in her class at school. Many times Lillian expressed herself strongly: "I just can't see why they treat Indians *that* way! They're people just like us!"

—*Verla Fae Kauffman Haas, Bluesky, Alberta. Age 12*

Hosting international students is an excellent way to help children develop an awareness of a global family.

We invited international students from nearby colleges during holidays and weekends. We hosted a foreign-exchange student from Chile for a year. She became like another family member during that time.

—*Oleeda Sutter Albrecht, Morton and Tiskilwa, Illinois. Childhood*

Often these students keep in contact with their host families for years. Occasionally a host family finds it possible to visit the student's native country, which enriches the experience further.

The importance of meaningful contacts with international students cannot be overestimated since most students become leaders in their own countries. As both the host families and the students learn to appreciate the variety and customs of other cultures, there will be less likelihood of using violence in resolving conflicts with people who are different.

University settings, with their many students from other countries, are excellent places for children to develop a global awareness as they interact with playmates from many lands. They learn to appreciate and accept each other without regard to color, race, or creed. Their accepting attitude is directly related to that of the adults around them.

> While my husband was doing his graduate studies at the University of Iowa, student housing became our home. Our three-year-old son enjoyed an international playground with his three best friends coming from Costa Rica, Egypt, and Iran. Not one incident but rather a sum total of daily feud and fun with his friends served as the background to build a "world image," preschool style. I needed only a small globe to show where José, Ahmad, and Mehrdad came from, and where they would someday return to live.
>
> That world image took a new turn as one afternoon our son, in a moment of serendipity, discovered that his friend Ahmad from Egypt lived in the same country as one of his favorite Bible characters, Joseph. Historical time held no meaning in his preschool development—that happy discovery was sufficient.
>
> Five years later, with our son tuned to world events, those global relationships are a nugget of gold building peace and good will toward all people. Iran means Mehrdad and his family to us, Egypt is Ahmad, and José is Costa Rica. Somewhere in this adult world of power struggles, there are little boys loved by their families. That realization forms a significant slant toward peace.
> —*Christine Yoder Falcón, Iowa City, Iowa. Ages 3-8*

Organizations such as the American Field Service and the Mennonite Central Committee (an inter-Mennonite relief and service organization) provide opportunities for longer-term hosting.

> My husband and I are long-time members of the Mennonite Church. We wondered whether our sons would learn the way of peace since they did not live in a traditional Mennonite community. Eight Mennonite Central Committee Exchange Visitors

lived in our home each for a period of six months and taught us to be sensitive to the worldwide search for peace. They were people from Switzerland whose father and brothers were in the Swiss Army; people from Colombia whose families were frightened by riots of the working class; people from Indonesia who were troubled by Islam-Christian conflicts in their land. Each person shared with us of family and national cultures. Gradually, our sons began to note the limitations of common stereotypes. Yes, they were learning the way of peace.
—*Marie Kanagy Stevanus, Amarillo, Texas. Childhood*

Opportunities to teach the ways of peace while living in another culture have been used successfully in some families. Our family lived in Chicago for the first ten years of our lives together. The majority of our neighbors and of our church were black, but that fact became quite insignificant as we learned to know one another as people with names and personalities.

Especially meaningful was our relationship to "Granny," a frail-looking elderly lady who became like a mother to me and a grandmother to our children. She fulfilled a real need in our lives since our own relatives lived many miles away. As a family, we have often discussed how relating to Granny has greatly enriched our lives. This richness also benefited the family of God as Granny daily promoted peace by her forgiving spirit and loving ways.

Through the years that have followed, our children, now adults, still keep in contact with Granny. When Granny celebrated her ninetieth birthday, she was thrilled with our return to her beloved church to help her commemorate the event. Our children—to whom she refers as "my children"—had remembered to send her birthday cards, which greatly added to her enjoyment.

When our children were growing up in Mathis, Texas (a Spanish-American community), there were many neighbor children who often came to play. Eventually I found them playing cowboys and Indians. I approached the whole group and asked them if they knew how Indians really lived. We discussed how Native Americans make pottery and weave cloth, and how some groups of them move from place to place or build hogans. I suggested that if they wanted to imitate Indians, it would be better to build tepees or hogans and to make pots. They were soon playing something else.

I regret that we did not have a good public library and I could not follow up with reading material and authentic activity suggestions. We did not have TV at that time. When we got one, we did not allow the children to watch westerns. Sometime later when a minority person asked twelve-year-old Tim, "Who always gets killed in cowboys and Indians?" he honestly did not know. Innocence freed him to appreciate the Indians' contributions.
—*Ann Burkholder Conrad, Mathis, Texas. Age 12*

Fortunate are the children who are able to spend some time living or traveling with their families in another country. Observing and participating in the culture around them, they can more readily identify with other children.

My husband, Rick, and I took advantage of an opportunity to take our daughter with us to Japan and Korea. Our family developed an awareness of a world family by staying with a Mennonite missionary family in Japan and with Korean friends.

Language was the biggest problem. As we watched our daughter interacting and communicating on the train, at the park, and in the pool with Oriental children of all ages, we realized there are many ways to communicate effectively without knowing the correct words.

It was well worth the expense to take her along on the trip. We feel she will never forget the kindnesses shown and the many friendships we all made while visiting the Orient.
—*Sarah Roth Smucker, Lusby, Maryland. Age 5*

Other families have lived for longer periods of time in other lands while in mission, service, or other work assignments.

Rick joined our family by adoption when he was five years old. Half a year later, a black Nigerian student came to live with us while attending college. During the year that he lived with us, Rick often showed signs of resentment toward the student, like refusing to sit by him at the table. The initial jealousy probably had nothing to do with skin color—just a threat to his new status in our home. Yet, subsequent experiences seemed to show a color prejudice emerging.

When Rick was thirteen years old, our family accepted an African assignment. During that time, Rick worked for three months on a water project in a rural area and developed a good relationship with one of the workmen—a community leader. Before our departure for Swaziland, we visited Bhembe at his village—and Rick gave him his prized slingshot as a farewell gift (because Bhembe had admired it earlier).

Now, back in Goshen, Indiana, Rick speaks positively of a Kenyan student who has a locker next to him. He also told what fun they had together at a recent party. The key? A positive attitude toward and complete acceptance of blacks by our family coupled with an opportunity for him to develop personal relationships with those of another culture.

—*Marian Brendle Hostetler, Goshen, Indiana; Mbabane, Swaziland*
Ages 5-15

Our sons, Robert and Thomas, both have a keen interest in world affairs. Robert served in Brussels, Belgium, under the Mennonite Board of Missions. Thomas spent several weeks one summer in a work camp in East Germany.

In our family we promoted global awareness and understanding in various ways:

1. Reading—books, news magazines, newspapers, periodicals
2. Watching TV news
3. Hosting visitors from other cultures in our home
4. Living in other countries—Japan, England, Ghana
—*Miriam Stalter Charles, Goshen, Indiana. Childhood*

How Can the Church Help Children Develop Appreciation of Others Worldwide?

The church can work closely with the home in fostering appreciation for those of other countries. We realize that the home and extended family are primary in aiding young children to gain an awareness and appreciation of a world family. Yet the church family is larger in size; thus the children's world is expanded. In this setting, basic teachings of Jesus Christ, the Prince of Peace, are taught and lived by adults who provide positive role models for the children in their midst. As children observe adults creatively resolving conflicts and expressing concern and love for each other, they learn values that remain with them for life.

> The Bible story one Sunday was about Joseph; the Bible verse was "be ye kind." As introductory background for the lesson, the children made a chart, listing their names and the number of brothers and sisters in their own families.

"Be ye kind."

	Brothers	Sisters
Nancy	2	0
Roger	2	1
Jean	1	1
Neil	1	2
Judy	1	2
Jeff	2	0
Carlyle	2	0
Becky	1	1

> The children talked about playing and working together and drew illustrations of ways they had shown kindness or had kindness shown to them at home. For example, Jean drew a picture of herself helping her younger sister ride a tricycle.
> As a summary, we reviewed a story from the children's nursery Sunday school days, which included the lines:
> "You can be kind and friendly in play, and make children happy the very same way Jesus did when he was a boy."[4]
> The children responded with thoughtful smiles of assent.
> —*Mary K. Nafziger, Goshen, Indiana. Grade 1*

One writer states: "Cultivate friendships with other peacemakers. Parents need to seek out other families who believe in peace as a way of life and cultivate friendships with them. As children learn to know and become friends with the children of other peacemakers, these primary group relationships help them to develop their own peacemaking behavior."[5]

While our children were of school age, five families in our church joined together to form an experimental church school class. Our group had a total of fourteen children encompassing a ten-year age span and met on Sunday morning following the worship service in members' homes.

The entire group planned the curriculum. However, each host family planned the lesson and provided a light lunch on the day the group met in their home. To promote biblical understandings and open discussion of current problems, we used a wide variety of activities: moviemaking, dramatization, banner construction, and simulation games. These helped us grasp the meaning of Christ's teachings and to become aware of their implications for contemporary social problems like world hunger, war, racial discrimination, and other ever-present injustices.

Much individual growth and learning occurred through the interaction with caring people in this family church school. The learning extended far beyond the level of factual knowledge into many effective areas including appreciation of self and family.

As our children, now adults, recall their church experiences, they mention the family church group as being the most meaningful.

—Maxine Frey Diller, Adrian, Michigan. Ages 5 to 15

I was the prayer meeting leader for the month and was using a series of articles in the *Gospel Herald* about how to teach children about peace.

There had been no activities planned for the children, so after the devotional they were dismissed and allowed to play outside. About midway through the evening, the children, excited and angry, came running into the Sunday school wing where the adults were meeting. Some neighbor children had come on the church grounds and started doing something our children considered destructive.

One of the women offered to go with the children to see what could be done to remedy the situation. The neighbor children had already left by the time they got outside. So she took the children to the basement assembly room where they talked out their feelings. Then they role-played what had happened and how they could have invited the children to play with them and to come to Sunday school and church.

When our meeting was over, the children invited us to come

downstairs and watch them act out what they could have done instead of what they had done.
—Kathryn Gregory Yoder, Surrey, North Dakota. Ages 7-11

As the six children of a kindergarten class in summer Bible school worked and played together, they experienced some frustrations and impatience with Karen, a moderately learning-disabled child also in class.

As the more able children worked on the projects, Karen always needed help. She started late and finished late. She often preferred the finished product of her neighbor over her own unfinished one. She caused many interruptions. Finally, one of the able classmates became impatient as she observed the task and predicted failure by saying, "Oh, Karen can't do that!"

However, soon various children volunteered to help Karen. Karen insisted on helping hold the scissors even though she couldn't cut. "Karen is helping do it," affirmed a classmate. Everyone was happy along with Karen when she completed the project successfully and on time. This appreciation was not lost on Karen or her classmates, and everyone felt a special togetherness.
—Arlie Hershberger Weaver, Phoenix, Arizona. Kindergarten

Church-sponsored projects that extend concern and love to the global family are welcomed by families serious about peace building. Children become eager participants as they watch their parents' involvement. Many churches sponsor refugee families. Mutual benefits emerge as the children relate to each other in Sunday school. Wise parents will encourage the children to spend more time together in other settings, such as at home, at parties, and at family outings. Differences in culture will be minimized but respected if both parents and children perceive each other as individuals with names, identities, and feelings.

Our house church sponsored a Vietnamese family. Several of the children from our fellowship attend an inner-city school where this Vietnamese family and families of many other nationalities attend. When asked who was his best friend, one of the fellowship children named a Vietnamese child.
—Lorraine Roth, Kitchener, Ontario. Age 7

Children who visited Anatoth, the children's library of the Brussels Mennonite Center, had a global education experience.

A school class of four- to five-year-olds visited the children's library Anatoth for the first time. The library is focused on peace education. We started with an activity using an inflated globe of the world which we lightly tossed around. While we passed it around our circle, we sang the following song written by a Belgian singer:

La terre roule boule,	The world rolls 'round,
La terre boule tourne.	The world, a turning ball.
De quel coté, toi, tu es né?	On which side were you born?
De quel coté tu es tombé?	On which side do you stand?

As the song ended, whoever held the ball shared about one's own place of birth, or the class teacher helped in speaking of that child's nationality. Everyone had a turn. They all enjoyed their chance to end with the "world" in their hands.

Sometimes we looked for a home country on the globe to see how far or close it was in relationship to Belgium. This particular class had children born in Belgium, France, Spain, Italy, Morocco, Algeria, Korea, Turkey, and Iran. Some children did not seem much aware of their nationality. Others were excited and proud to share their place of birth.
—*Jean Gerber Shank, Brussels, Belgium. Ages 4-5*

Resource people can provide vicarious contacts and promote understandings of other cultures. Vacation Bible school children in Archbold, Ohio, learned about the Soviet Union recently through a Mennonite Board of Missions project called "Building Bridges." Special resource person Nancy Grulick of the Interfaith Justice and Peace Center for Northwest Ohio told the Bible schoolers at Zion Mennonite Church that Soviet children are just like American children.

Grulick had visited the Soviet Union in April and was in Kiev on the day of the nuclear plant accident in nearby Chernobyl. The Zion children then wrote letters to children in Kiev and donated money to MBM's Russian-language radio broadcast, "Voice of a Friend."[6]

Children often respond positively to meaningful, well-planned projects in which they are actively involved. Wise Sunday school teachers will capitalize on this and enlist the help of others to encourage such projects.

A circle of friendship was established between a Sunday school class from a Mennonite church in Denver, Colorado, and a small, isolated, one-room, rural Quechua Indian school in Villa Amboró, Bolivia. Children from two different cultures, lifestyles, and religions shared their gifts with each other.

The friendship circle started when the Sunday school children's department in Denver asked how they could best help the school in the small Bolivian village where I taught. Since each Indian child had only one textbook, the Sunday school children sent enough money to purchase 250 library books in Spanish and Quechua plus a locked bookshelf for the entire Bolivian community. The community accepted the library of children's books, religious books, agriculture books, books on knitting and crocheting, and many other topics with an awesome, reverent thanks. Because the people were so overwhelmed at the sight of so many new books, the library was left untouched for a week before people finally felt comfortable enough to use it.

The Sunday school children also created a banner with each child making an individual block representing something typically American. This was sent along with the money to the community of Villa Amboró. The Bolivian children responded by making a banner depicting typical Bolivian scenes. Some of the Quechua children also wrote thank-you letters, while younger ones drew pictures. The American children were so delighted with the banner and slides of their new friends that they made thank-you cards to send to the Bolivian children.

Once a circle starts rolling, it really is hard to stop it. This exchange of gifts across continents opened the eyes of all the children to see that there really is a larger world than their daily life encompasses. Other children are different, yet alike.

As a teacher who strongly desires world peace, I feel this kind of exchange is important. Even an exchange of letters with children of other states is important. If children are to love and desire peace, they must realize that brothers, sisters, and neighbors do not just live with them or next door to them, but that they span the entire world.

—*Geneva Hershberger, Villa Amboró, Bolivia. Grades 1-5*

Special programs given at church can provide a means of helping children realize that they are a part of a global family. Mission and service workers have lived with and related closely to people of other cultures. They can enrich the understanding of those unable to have the same experience. Participating in a drama aids in clarifying the concept of a world family.

> One year we chose to adapt parts of the story *Henry's Red Sea*[7] into a drama for our children's Christmas program. Using direct quotes from the book with simple costumes and staging, it was a memorable retelling of the Christmas story. The unusual setting added a depth of meaning for both participants and audience. We incorporated beautiful hymns actually sung by the refugees to help us "feel" a bit of their experiences and faith. Awareness of a global family, effects of war, relief efforts, and love for enemies were all a part of this celebration.
>
> —*Cara Frey Ulrich, Archbold, Ohio. Grades K-7 plus a few adults*

Children of both church and nonchurch families can be taught ways of peace through church-sponsored activities such as Bible school, clubs for boys and girls, youth groups, and day schools. Because children spend more time in these various settings, conflicts may arise frequently, providing opportunities to develop skills in peace building.

For example, teaching peace in the weekday Christian education classes, an opportunity in some public schools, presents special challenges not encountered in home or Sunday school situations. Children attend in their primary peer group—the public school class. They bring with them their experiences of the day: some have had fights; something has "disappeared"; there are illnesses, excitements, and disappointments to report. The class may be excited about an upcoming field trip or uneasy because they have a substitute teacher.

Thus, they come needing to find ways to make peace with one another, needing the inner peace that the Holy Spirit can bring through a prepared, serene teacher and a special place, the released-time setting. Through appropriate curriculum, impromptu discussion, and modeling godly character, there is freedom to help children discover God's good way to live in the world with one another.

June Thomsen reported an incident from the weekday Christian education class at Bluffton, Ohio:

> J., a third-grade boy, was adept at getting attention through his well-developed verbal skills. He could talk and reason so impressively that most of the other third graders believed anything he said.
>
> Alex, another third-grade boy, was perceived as a chronic troublemaker. Beset with learning difficulties, he was seemingly always in some sort of trouble with the other children or the teacher. Impulsive, immature, down on himself, acting out emotions in aggressive ways, yet not meaning to be bad—that was Alex!
>
> J. brought his new Transformer toy to school after Christmas. Everyone admired it, including Alex. When it disappeared, J. declared loudly and persistently that Alex was the last seen with it, that Alex had stolen it, and that Alex had lied about it to boot! The whole class, and eventually the whole third grade, came to believe that Alex took the Transformer, because every ten days or so J. brought up the issue again and told the story in ever more vivid details—how his father had selected this special Transformer that he had longed for, and how someone had seen Alex recently playing with it somewhere new in town. J. was relentless.
>
> Alex was slowly but surely disintegrating. The principal and parents became involved. Alex's mother searched the house for the toy, as well as their church and other places where J. reported "sightings" of Alex and the Transformer. Throughout, Alex maintained a stubborn but increasingly tearful plea of innocence. No one believed him.
>
> Our last unit of lessons in weekday Christian education had to do with peacemaking. The week that we studied the "building blocks" for peacemakers, students worked in small groups on a real-life problem, deciding which building blocks they could use to help make peace in that situation. These building blocks included learning to know people's names, learning to know people's families, being friendly, forgiving, praying for others,

learning to see others as God sees them, learning the truth, and telling the truth.

One of the assigned problems was the thinly disguised story of J., Alex, and the Transformer. That small group worked through this situation and then shared with the other groups their choices and reasoning. A lot of light bulbs went on. "Hey, that's what happened with J. and Alex!" was the common awareness.

And the light bulbs kept turning on. Had the truth been known? Had the truth been told? If what J. claimed was true, should he have prayed for and forgiven Alex? If Alex was innocent, could or should he pray for and forgive J.? What does it mean to see others (even others who wrong us) as God sees them?

That day many of us left class with more light to use in our relations with one another. J. finally confronted Alex. Alex maintained innocence, and J. apologized to Alex for accusing him of stealing.

We were beginning to learn to be peacemakers.[8]

Children who have poor self-images, often caused by neglect or other abuse, seem to have more difficulty in relating to their peer group and adults as well. As the church reaches out to them in loving concern, some of their hurts can be alleviated. Such persons are likely to acquire the skills of cooperative living, thus promoting peace in their homes and community.

> We became acquainted with one family through our girls' club. The mother was hospitalized several times in the psychiatric ward, the children had been neglected, and the girls had been physically abused by a family member. I was part of a support group that took in meals, furnished child supervision, gave rides to treatment and recreation, and offered a listening ear. We have continued to offer friendship and a chance for the mother to show her rediscovered gifts, such as housekeeping and piano playing. She is ready now to join one of the community study groups sponsored by our church.
> —*Kathryn Gregory Yoder, Minot, North Dakota. Ages 5, 8 and 13*

The church gathered is nourished to be the church scattered. "Go in peace" became a familiar parting reminder for one congregation including the youngest present.

Rituals are an important part of our church life. Even the ritual of receiving the benediction each Sunday morning can add meaning and growth to our peace commitment. Rachel Fisher, minister and frequent worship leader in our congregation, usually ended the benediction by saying, "Go in peace." One Sunday this usual blessing was not given. Young Andrea Milne did not budge from her bench. "It isn't over yet. Rachel hasn't said, 'Go in peace.' "
—*Rosemary Gunden Widmer, Goshen, Indiana. Age 3*

How Can the School Help Children Develop Appreciation of Others Worldwide?

Homes that have little or no relation with the church may be filled with conflict, despair, and even violence. Thus it becomes of utmost importance that the schools help parents and children develop peacemaking skills. Prudent teachers will utilize the routine as well as special activities to build self-esteem and understanding, basic attributes necessary in relating to others. Teachers who are able to discern their pupils' needs and who possess or know where to obtain the resources to supply those needs make a significant contribution to world peace.

Some schools provide camp experiences for their middle graders. This can become an excellent setting for teaching appreciation for others on a twenty-four-hour-a-day basis! Teachers certainly learn to know another side of each child, and that is beneficial. Children learn to know teachers as persons who wear tennis shoes and are human too. Children from our school go to camp with inner-city children, so our affluent children meet some who have only the necessities. There are some problems, but the staff and counselors do a good job of integrating all the children.
—*Colene Aschliman Rich, Toledo, Ohio. Grade 6*

Developing the proper sense of pride in the school family is an important step toward world peace. Older children often are eager to perform plays, read stories, or play games with younger children. Upper-grade children should be encouraged to listen respectfully when younger children perform for them, too! Guided interaction between age groups will then provide for positive spontaneous relationships.

When I was principal of Parkside School, Dr. Mary Royer and Dr. Karl Massanari asked me if I would bring a group of children—a boy and a girl from each school year, K through 6—to their class in developmental psychology. Each child would bring along a favorite book and tell why it was a special one. The college class would see at a glance, with the fourteen children on the platform at the same time, the variation in growth pattern in the seven chronological years and also the range of reading interest.

The experience was not only a help to the college group, but also an enjoyable cross-age contact for the children. They had pride in being representatives from their school and felt a oneness in their group from the youngest to the oldest. Such contacts were daily a part of eight-grade, one-room schools.

More could be done in our closely graded schools to help children accept and appreciate differences in age. Little children often fear "big" children, and older children may disdain "babies." Knowing each other as interesting people has a gentling and broadening influence in a kindergarten-through-grade-six school; it is fundamental in developing, not only a tolerance for diversity, but also a valuing of differences basic to growth toward peaceful interaction.

—*Parke Lantz, Goshen, Indiana. Grades K-6*

Some teachers have had the good fortune of having children from other countries enrolled in their classes. This often requires extra adjustments by both teachers and pupils.

Mary, a little girl from Scotland, moved in. She was a friendly, outgoing child. The other children had a little trouble understanding her speech but immediately made friends. We studied about Scotland and found it on the globe.

Ingrid, from Germany, was a little more shy and at first unable to speak English. She was well-disciplined and bright. Soon she was speaking and reading fluently. Her parents picked up the language from her. We found stories about Germany to share with the children.

Kim was a little Chinese girl, extremely bright and aggressive. She made friends easily. We shared stories about China.

Juan was a boy from Brazil. He was on the shy side. Both his father and mother were medical doctors. After he became more fa-

miliar with the language, his shyness vanished.
                    —*Minnie Sutter, South Bend, Indiana. Grade 1*

A girl from India enrolled in our school after Christmas. We spent much time asking her how they do things there. We discussed holiday celebrations, favorite foods, school subjects, clothes, and family fun times. She also taught us Indian words and sentences. We took turns helping her become more adjusted to our school during the first few weeks.
                    —*Elizabeth Beyeler Jacobs, Goshen, Indiana. Grade 3*

Among our fourth-grade pupils in an American school in India was a charming little girl of Indian-British parentage. She was a brilliant child, and I can still hear her precise English diction when she spoke. One day a fellow British teacher who taught art in the various grades approached me and said, "The children are making it miserable for B. because of her speech, and I think you should do something about it." I hadn't been aware of the problem but decided to work on it.

One day when B. was out of the classroom, I gave the other pupils a little talk on being kind to B., whose speech was different. I asked them to consider how they would feel if they were in her place. Then I concluded, "Her speech is more correct than ours."

Somehow B. learned what happened in the classroom. She came excitedly and said, "Miss Yoder, you know that time you sent me out of the room to get a book? I know every word you said. Thank you, thank you!" Evidently, the situation improved.
                    —*Rhea Yoder, Landour, Mussoorie, U.P., India. Grade 4*

Inviting guests of another race or country to visit the classroom is educational and usually quite interesting. In this TV age, children will remember such visitors as *real* people with whom they can converse. Other classroom guests could be those who lived in another country for a period of time. Returned Mennonite Central Committee workers from Bolivia, Nigeria, the Sudan, and India enriched the classroom experiences of a fifth grade.

We have few people of races other than white in our community. In fifth grade we study U.S. history which, of course, includes the blacks and the American Indians. I invited a young woman

whose mother was a full-blooded Native American to my class. She talked about her background and how different cultures and races need to be respected by all. Then she taught the children how to do bead work, which they thoroughly enjoyed. A black woman also was invited and discussed ways that people of all races should think of themselves as children of God and one large family. She told them that she felt Jesus wanted us all to love and care for each other.
—*M. Irene Slaubaugh, Montgomery, Indiana. Grade 5*

Our daughter, Judith, came home from college with a black girl-friend from the deep South. To surprise me, she came to my fifth-grade class with Hattie. When they appeared, naturally I intro-duced them to the class. "This is my daughter and her friend. . . ." Upon hearing this, one child said, "Which is your daughter?" If only all of us could be so color-blind!
—*Celia Gerber Lehman, Kidron, Ohio. Grade 5*

When studying about a particular group of people and meet-ing people from other places, care must be taken to focus on people as individuals and to minimize stereotypes or exotic dif-ferences.

While teaching fourth grade, I had visitors from each continent. We tasted food and played games from the countries talked about. In some cases we wrote to adults or children in the coun-tries.
—*Elsie Eash Sutter, Goshen, Indiana. Grade 4*

Using literature set in a variety of cultural and socioeconomic groups exposes children to a beginning appreciation of different lifestyles. Samples are *This Is the Way We Go to School, All in a Day, Nine O'Clock Lullaby,* and books by Ann Morris.[9]
—*Carolyn Smith Diener, Tuscaloosa, Alabama. Kindergarten*

Whenever children learn about a lifestyle that differs from their own, they need to understand that environments are closely related to lifestyles.

Living in a university town, we have had many chances to get to know people of other races. My third-grade class was interested in learning about people from other countries. During the spring semester, we set aside a full month to learn about Sierra Leone. The next month featured Japan, and we studied about France the last month.

The children learned about schools, homes, religions, food, and recreation. The emphasis was on our similarities. Differences in language, customs, and music were seen as delightful. They learned songs, dressed in clothing from the countries, ate foods, and tried to step into the life of the country.

On the last day of each unit, we set aside the whole day, and our math, reading, and music were all focused on that country. We invited nationals to come and share native food and give a talk or slide show about their country. "It's a Small World After All" was the theme throughout.

The children learned that they could relax with and enjoy visiting with people who at first seemed so different. We have much to learn from one another.

—*Marilyn Frey Kay, Urbana, Illinois. Grade 3*

An effective method to accomplish positive global awareness is to conduct an intensive study of a particular country. Reading stories, learning songs, eating national foods, wearing national clothes, creating learning centers about other countries—all these capitalize upon the wealth of imagination that children possess. "That imagination can help them identify with other people and what life must be like for them. Other persons are hard to classify as 'enemies' when one is able to put oneself into their shoes."[10]

While teaching first grade at Jefferson Elementary, my class studied about Japan for a month. My intention was to help them discover the similarities and the differences of customs between American and Japanese life. So we read books about Japan, played Japanese games, learned to read some simple kanji, learned to write our names in Japanese, and learned to count to ten. We folded bright-colored origami paper into animals and flowers, wore five-yen coins around our necks, made rubbings of them, and attempted to eat our school lunches with chopsticks. We invited a Japanese exchange student to our class and asked her all kinds of questions.

After a month of Japanese activities, the children were seeing Japan in the world around them. They noticed Japanese cars on the street, names of Japanese computers in magazines, and "Made in Japan" tags on many other products. The children developed a sense of the interdependence between the United States and Japan.

My hope is that by understanding and appreciating other cultures, children will be drawn more closely into our global family and will eventually help bring peace to our world.

—*Karen Kreider Yoder, Goshen, Indiana. Grade 1*

While teaching English to upper elementary and junior high Indo-Chinese students, I have many opportunities to help them understand and interpret the new world around them to which they are adjusting. This is especially challenging at the junior high level. Boy-girl, girl-boy attractions at that age seem to cross all cultural and ethnic boundaries. However, the lack of verbal understandings can cause problems.

The Vietnamese girls who had had a friendly, teasing relationship with a seventh-grade boy were suddenly puzzled and hurt when he began acting upset and made fun of them. After some investigation, I learned that his mother had suddenly taken ill and was in the hospital in a coma with a brain tumor. When the girls understood this, their attitudes changed from fear and humiliation to understanding and concern. It was difficult for them to express this, but they discovered by ignoring him and his comments, they could ease a frustrating situation. Later, they were able to communicate with him in a more casual way.

—*Susan Herr Burkholder, Goshen, Indiana. Junior High*

Learning the language of another person promotes respect for the person and for the culture represented.

During my experience as a primary teacher, I've tried to encourage friendship and peace by using different methods to enhance the uniqueness of each child. I hope thereby to create a spirit of acceptance instead of rejection in my classroom. Our room is named "Friendship Room" throughout each year.

There are usually Spanish-speaking children in our building, so I spend a short period daily presenting the Spanish language and culture. I teach vocabulary, simple phrases, and many songs.

We prepare and sample Spanish foods and handle souvenirs from Spanish countries. We've enjoyed visitors from Spanish countries.

One year we spent an hour with a Goshen College Spanish class. We sang songs for them and with them and talked together in Spanish.

Several years we were invited to participate in the Christmas fiesta, an evening activity sponsored by the bilingual program of our school system. (English was taught as a second language to Spanish speakers and Indo-Chinese students. One year Spanish was taught to Anglo-Americans.) Parents of those in the bilingual program made skirts and vests for the children to wear in Spanish games. Parents also brought ethnic foods to sample. One father read from his book of poems. Our group of second graders sang songs, recited poems, and did finger-plays. The parents of my children were delighted to join their children in this contact with other cultures.

There have been numerous positive attitudes resulting from such exposures. These experiences have a uniting effect and are enjoyed by all types of children: rich, poor, fast learners, slow learners, and the handicapped (emotionally or physically).

Children who are Spanish begin to experience a new feeling of pride in themselves and their backgrounds. This year Jesús is a class member. Initially he was embarrassed to let his friends know that he could speak Spanish. But now he is one of our leaders. He takes pride in teaching us Spanish phrases. I say, "Pick his brain. It's full of that Spanish you want to learn." Jesús, as others before him, shares freely in an atmosphere of friendship and peace.

During each year, a new acceptance and interest in languages and people other than Spanish emerge in our classroom, especially Pennsylvania Dutch, Vietnamese, and Japanese. We learn to count to five in at least four or five different languages during the year, with the teacher learning along with the children.

Here is a most interesting example of true appreciation and acceptance of other cultures by children. One morning Fermin, a refugee from El Salvador living in an area home, came to me and asked, "Wie bist du?" (How are you?) I responded, "Similich gut." (I'm fine.) His foster parents had taught him simple Pennsylvania Dutch phrases, and in our culturally rich environment, he felt a freedom to share.

Each fall I enjoy the unique challenge of leading a new group through the peace-producing experiences encountered in our Friendship Room.

—*Rose Schmucker Fuentes, Goshen, Indiana. Grade 2*

Studying the word "peace" in a variety of languages highlights a value shared by many peoples.[11]

Arabic	سلام	Sah-laáhm
Bengali	শান্তি	Shán-tih
Burmese	၉၆းၛ၆းၛၕ:	Nyehn-chahn-yeh
Chinese	和平	Ho-P'ing
Filipino	See Pilipino	
French	Paix	Peh
German	Friede	Frée-duh
Greek	ειρήνη	Ih-Rée-Nee
Hebrew	שָׁלוֹם	Shah-lóhm
Hindi	शांति	Shan-tee
Hungarian	Béke	Bayh-kuh
Indonesian	Perdamaian	Pear-dah-mý-ahn
Irish	Siocháin	See-uh-káwn
Italian	Pace	Páh-chay
Japanese	平和	Háy-wah
Khmer	សន្តិភាព	San-tee-feé-op
Laotian	ສັນຕິພາບ	San-tee-fat
Nepalese	शान्ति	Shan-tee
Persian	صلح	Sohl'h
Pilipino	Kapayapaan	Kah-pye-yah-pah-ahn

Polish	Pokój	Poh-kóy
Portuguese	Paz	Rhymes with woman's nickname Roz (as in Roz Russell)
Russian	МИР	Mir (rhymes with fear, but with rolled "r" at end)
Spanish	Paz	Pah-th (rhymes with the first syllable of father)
Srilanka (Ceylonese)	සමාදය	Sah-áhm-ah-yuh
Swahili	Amani	Ah-máh-nee
Swedish (same as for Danish and Norwegian)	Fred	Pronounce like man's name in English
Thai	สันติภาพ	Sán-tee-pop
Vietnamese	hoá-binh	Hwa-bean

Holidays can be utilized to encourage special projects through which children become thoughtful of others in the world family. Collecting for UNICEF or other fundraising projects at Halloween time, Save the Children caring and sharing tree or valentine tree (projects to improve the life for over one-quarter of a million children and their families), gathering food items for a needy family at Thanksgiving, and giving presents to children in other countries at Christmas bring joy to both giver and receiver. An abundance of Christmas stories with international settings can be found in most libraries. Discerning teachers will be able to select appropriate literature from settings in countries represented in their classes.

> "Joy to the World" was the title of a bulletin board which led to global experiences. Below the letters was a world map sketched inside a circle with a Palestinian mother and child centered in the Middle East. Each day a child would come to add to the border a large musical note in which "Merry Christmas" was written. These greetings were in Hindi, Swedish, Russian, German, French, Spanish, and others. Each morning we would greet each other in those languages and then sing a carol from one of the countries. Each year the greatest achievement seemed to come from learning a Hindi carol, clapping and fading away as Hindus would.
>
> —*Thelma Miller Groff, Goshen, Indiana. Grade 4*

Special programs which children help plan and present can expand their awareness of a world family. Skits and plays which encourage children to "live" the parts they portray help them recognize that members of the human family are more alike than different. Careful selection of materials by the teacher will also favorably portray the diversity of human experiences.

> When teaching in one-room schools, a number of times I produced an evening program in which we concentrated on appreciation of people of other cultures. I got most of the materials from the Fellowship of Reconciliation and Friendship Press. Parents and friends seemed to enjoy this type of program. I felt it was especially effective when I taught Weldy's School near Nappanee, Indiana, where all the pupils were Amish. Of course, I tried in all my teaching to emphasize through stories and discussions the values of people living in friendship and peace, appreciating and contributing to each other.
> —*Elva May Roth, Nappanee, Indiana. Grades 1-8*

In recent years parochial schools have increased in number. Unrestricted use of the Bible and other Christian materials as a basis for peacemaking is an added dimension in such schools. Family Mission Thanks-Giving[12] kits provide information and meaningful activities for families to become aware of other countries. Recipes to prepare meals which would be enjoyed in that country are included as well as games, songs, stories, prayers, customs, and clothing particulars.

> I used the Family Mission Thanks-Giving kit at my nondenominational school. Seeing the children and people shown in the coloring book and hearing the stories helped to bring awareness of Christian people "over there." Most of my students are from families who travel to the hills of West Virginia and back to Ohio. World awareness and global knowledge is quite limited.
> —*Vietta Cender Nofziger, Barberton, Ohio. Grades K-3*

When adults relate to children in the home, church, and community, they can create an environment which most certainly develops a world awareness in children of all ages. They thereby build for global peace. An atmosphere of wonder, excitement, and joy in learning is created by adults who are effective listeners—genuine, authentic, understanding, respectful, and skilled in interpersonal communication.[13] Children not only gain knowledge, but act upon it tempered by love. They are motivated to grow toward peace. As adults cooperate in various projects and activities, often with considerable cost and effort, they provide positive role models which children imitate.

> While working at a youth hostel in Germany, I became acquainted with an eight-year-old German boy. I spoke no German and he no English. With my eyes, smiles, and arms I expressed friendship. On my birthday he presented me with flowers which he had picked. Love is stronger than a language barrier.
> —*Loretta Zehr Simmons, Bremerhaven, Germany. Age 8*

8. How Can We Help Children Respond to Injustice?

Delores Histand Friesen

As I grew up in Pryor, Oklahoma, I became aware of inequities and injustices. In a farm family of ten, there was plenty of work and lots of fun. But from a child's point of view, there also were many times when things seemed unfair. During our state's celebration of its fiftieth year of statehood, I became aware of some of the injustices Native Americans had endured. Native Americans attended my high school as well as students (including my locker mate) called the Home Kids. Many of these persons had experienced deprivation, institutionalization, and prejudice.

Since my father was a pastor, missionaries were often guests in our home. Their stories of Africa, Japan, and the Argentine Chaco helped to broaden my view of the world and develop an early sense of call and vision.

After college and several years of teaching, my husband and I accepted an assignment with Mennonite Board of Missions, first in Nigeria and several years later in Ghana. We experienced firsthand the hunger, violence, fear, and economic hardships caused by the Biafran War.

During that difficult time, we learned much from our African friends about living with injustice. They freely and courageously chose a deep commitment to community as they encountered injustice and responded to disillusionment with optimistic faith, patience, and hope. Their examples strengthened our resolve to work for justice and shalom.

On a furlough in the United States when our three children were still very young, we were passing yet another gaily lit store. One of the children burst into tears and, wise beyond her years, cried out, "How come they have things falling off the shelves, while in Ghana the shelves are empty?" She gave voice to what we were all feeling as we tried to integrate our life experiences.

Now, however, after a longer block of time back in the United States, our children have become comfortable with the culture and consumerism of the United States. This has happened in spite of the fact that injustices of hunger, violence, prejudice, sexism, poverty, and deprivation continue, and the nuclear threat is mushrooming in our world.

As you read and ponder this chapter on injustice, my hope is that we all may be moved to respond in creative and specific ways to the words of God through the prophet Amos, who said, "Let justice roll down like waters, and righteousness like an everflowing stream" (Amos 5:24, NRSV). Every act of justice flows onward, adding to the stream of grace and hope.

How Can We Help Children Respond to the Injustice of Hunger?

The largest group of hungry persons in the world are the smallest in size and the most vulnerable—the children. According to Arthur Simon, president of Bread for the World, "40,000 children die daily from malnutrition and infection, with virtually no press attention or political discussion."[1] Unequal distribution of food in the world compounds the problem. Up to 50 percent of all young children in the developing countries are inadequately nourished.

It is difficult to imagine the suffering when we have not experienced it. Yet the school curriculum offers many connecting points—nutrition, health, current events, geography, climate, agricultural production, imports, exports, social studies—to name a few. One secret to developing awareness of the problem seems to be to let children experience something of the inequity firsthand. In two classrooms, simulations of world hunger brought learning and deepened awareness of both the problem of hunger and possible solutions to it.

I was teaching a unit on nutrition to fourth-grade students. As we talked about nutritious snacks, the four food groups, vitamins, and minerals, I felt students were beginning to understand what it meant to choose healthy foods.

Yet, the students had little grasp of what it meant not to have enough food or to have only a limited amount. In an attempt to communicate this, I tried a project to stimulate them. When all twenty-four children were out for recess, I put a whole apple on four desks, half an apple on six desks, a fourth of an apple on eight desks, and no apple on the remaining six desks. As the children came in, there were many comments: "Hey, you forgot to give me one. Why do I have a whole apple and Jaime just has half? What are these for? Can we eat them?"

After the children settled in their seats, I talked about the reasons behind the apples. "Here are some of us who have plenty to eat—the whole-apple people. Some of us have smaller amounts, yet we are able to survive and be healthy with that amount—the half-apple people. Some people only have one meal a day and can survive but are not healthy because they don't have enough food—the fourth-apple people. Lastly, there are the people who don't have any food and who do not survive."

I could tell the children were beginning to comprehend how food or the lack of it might affect others. Andy said, "Couldn't we share with the others so we'd all have some?"

It was easy to begin to cut apples and divide sections so everyone had three-eights of an apple. We had not only learned something about the problems of food distribution. We had also begun to work at some solutions!

—*Susan Nyce Stiffney, Goshen, Indiana. Grade 4*

Andy's perceptive response to the solution of world hunger could lead to long-term commitment toward wiping out hunger. If people would share wealth, economic growth, and assistance to produce food where it is scarce, the hungry in the world could be fed. Such action would take international cooperation, but it begins with people like Andy, who encourage the people around them to share.

> In addition to doing a unit on nutrition, I always expanded it to include a short unit on world hunger. During this unit we discussed such things as the average number of calories needed by each person and actually consumed in different countries. For various countries, we checked how much food is produced, average income per person, diseases caused by malnutrition, and causes of hunger and famine.
>
> For a conclusion to the unit, I divided the class randomly (sometimes letting the students choose the country) into the different continents according to their population. I then gave each continent food based on the percentage of food consumed by the average person on that continent. For example, the United States received much more food than Africa.
>
> I divided among the students breakfast rolls, candy, and fruit. North America received more than they were able to consume in the time allotted for eating. I collected the "garbage," threw it in the trash can, and proceeded to talk about the experience. Every time, the "poor continents" would protest throwing away good food when they had little.
>
> Once I had a student sneak on his hands and knees around the room and behind my desk to try to take a bit of the food. When I caught him and sent him back to his seat, he became upset at the inequities of the morning. On another occasion a couple of students tried to raid one of the more "wealthy" continents. One time there was nearly a "war" between two continents. Another time the North Americans decided to give a little "relief" to one of the "poorer" continents and had a few strings attached! This exercise was always an excellent way to end a unit, and it was also a good way to begin a valuable and memorable discussion.
>
> —*David A. Bauman, Millersburg, Indiana. Grades 3-6*

The children discovered food relief as one solution to hunger. Emergency food relief for starving people is essential, but it is a short-term goal and does not solve causes of hunger.

> The theme of our daily vacation Bible school was "We Work with God." At one of our staff meetings, someone suggested that we show we are workers with God in a monetary way. We had read about a group of children who hatched eggs, sold the chicks, and gave the proceeds to Heifer Project International. HPI assists people to help themselves. Those in need around the world are given an animal. They are to care for it, raise it, and share one of its offspring so more families will benefit.
>
> We received additional information and decided to introduce the project to the children. We told them that we could help purchase a calf, lamb, pig, or chickens, but they would vote their choice. The calf was selected, and then they asked questions: "How much does a calf cost? How big would it be? Where would it be sent? How would it be sent? Why do they need animals?"
>
> The enthusiasm continued the entire week. The children drew pictures and used a globe to locate places where it could be sent. The children learned that they could possibly give up an ice cream cone, a can of pop, or something similar so that other children would benefit. An offering was received on the final day of Bible school. When the children shared the Bible school project with our congregation on Sunday morning, some of the adults wanted to give an offering, so an additional amount was contributed to the project.
>
> —*Colene Aschliman Rich, Toledo, Ohio. Age 4 through Grade 6*

International cooperation is dependent on individual response to the problems of injustice.

> Suppose a brother or sister is in rags
>   with not enough food for the day.
> And one of you says, "Good luck to you,
>   keep yourselves warm, and have plenty to eat,"
> but does nothing to supply their bodily needs,
>   what is the good of that?   —*James 2:15, NEB*

Justice often begins with small individual actions of sharing, born of empathy and commitment. Personal strength to practice justice comes through awareness, study, meditation, and prayer.

> One junior-age boy knew his grandfather's experience with tithing. There were no extra pennies to give as debts piled up, but Grandfather happened to read from Malachi one evening before supper. The words seemed plain enough. If he gave his tithe, blessings would pour out from heaven. He and Grandmother started tithing right away, and later on they were able to give twenty percent of their earnings and more.
>
> The boys' parents also tithed, and the boy himself began tithing at the age of ten with earnings from his first paper route. This same boy, a man now, was the first in his class to give a donation to his college after graduation.
>
> Children should have the opportunity to see Christians serving joyfully together to meet the needs of the hungry: helping deliver Meals on Wheels, packing Thanksgiving baskets, and serving in the distribution of garden surplus. They will catch the joy of service, the love in giving. They will want to help in ways they can.
>
> —*Geraldine Gross Harder, Seattle, Washington. Age 10*

Children catch the spirit of giving with joy. Adults can help children participate gladly in all kinds of service and sharing projects. Genuinely caring about the person in need releases joy in giving and sharing money, time, and possessions. Families concerned to make hunger action a daily part of their lives have found many effective ways to do so.[2]

How Can We Help Children Bring Justice to Refugees and to Friends with Other Deprivations?

Always there have been refugees—people who have left their country because of danger such as hurricanes, drought, war, or because of race, religion or nationality. They have left behind their homes, possessions, friends, and sometimes families. Often they are victims of hunger because they are unable to grow food.

As children make contacts with refugees, we need to emphasize the steadfastness of God's understanding love despite the loss of home and friends. Then the children may be less anxious for their own safety. Refugees in our midst provide opportunities for children to show God's love and care in situations which seem hopeless. We can help children appreciate the uneasiness of these strangers, who must adjust to a new culture, language, and foods. With guidance, the children can find ways to lend courage and optimism.

> One fourth-grade teacher pointed out Cambodia on the map and told her pupils of the war there that caused many families to flee. She explained that a refugee family was moving to their community and one child would be in their classroom. The children clapped and cheered! When the frightened girl arrived, the children gathered round and made every effort to welcome her. Even though they didn't speak the same language, they communicated with hands and smiles, and new friendships began.
> —*Nancy Oswald Swartley, Perkasie, Pennsylvania. Grade 4*
> *(via Marie Moyer)*

Can children, who live in stressful conditions with evident unmet personal needs, be expected to give to others in distress? Judy Prieb Harder, director of the Fellowship of Hope neighborhood summer Bible school in Elkhart, Indiana, struggled to determine what might be an appropriate project for their group. These children did not have a swimming pool pass for the summer. They were often left to care for themselves while adults were gone during the day. One family eased the empty-cupboard syndrome through the services of the community food pantry. A little boy's sister was burned in a fire which destroyed their home and took the lives of two other family members. Would these children be interested in or able to contribute to a need outside themselves?

The Bible school leaders decided to try. Since the Bible school emphasis was on Jesus' concern for the homeless, the leaders chose to assist a refugee family from El Salvador living temporarily in a neighboring city. They told their students about this family of seven children; the mother had died, and the father had disappeared. In El Salvador men and boys were taken into the army. The older brothers were afraid they would have to become soldiers, so they left home. They helped their younger brothers and sisters come to the United States.

The Bible school children heard personal details about this refugee family. Then Andrew, who had listened carefully, asked, "Could these be the same people my grandfather is tutoring?" Indeed, they were real people!

As the children became more involved, their empathy level zoomed. They brought money so the refugee children could get bicycles. Although not all of the Bible school children had bikes, they gladly brought nickels, dimes, and quarters to buy bicycles for the homeless children. They were most generous.

Tony's mother worked during the day. The man who lived at their house worked at night. Before he went to sleep during the day, the man locked the door to make sure Tony and his younger brother stayed inside their upstairs apartment.

When Tony came to kindergarten, he found no locked doors. He noticed where I kept the key to the outside door. Tony climbed up onto the counter and got the key from the cupboard. He threw it out into the shrubbery. I never found it.

In time Tony learned to stay where his classmates were. When he ran out of the classroom or climbed the schoolyard fence, no one ran after him, although someone kept an eye on where he was. As he returned to the group, I welcomed him but also told him what he missed. After he learned to stay with the group, he could go along on neighborhood trips walking hand-in-hand with me. Finally he could be trusted to stay with a partner whom he chose.

Tony's mother explained that he began talking during his fourth year. Although television was playing much of the time in his home, it did not supply feedback. It did not respond to what he said. The interaction with his family members was often in short commands. "Stop it! Come here! Be quiet!" During several months, two college students and I made weekly visits in the home. We came with activities for the children and their mother. We acted out stories like *Rosie's Walk*,[3] played games, and made greeting cards. More importantly, we modeled other ways of interacting. The family gradually began to speak positively to each other, acknowledging successes and accomplishments.

In kindergarten, Tony's peers took responsibility to help him follow group procedures. At Halloween time Mr. Bumpkin Pumpkin, a mannequin with a pumpkin head, sat in a corner with the tape recorder. Children recorded their conversations with Mr. Bumpkin.

One day, during the time when everyone was gathering on the rug, Tony remained with the mannequin and sang, "Welcome, welcome my punkin," in a lilting syncopated rhythm. Children were urging Tony to come to the rug. Elaine approached him explaining, "Tony, they're not bossing you. They're just telling you. If they were bossing you, they'd say, 'Turn it off, Tony.' " Elaine shouted this in a commanding way. She continued, "But they're going, 'Turn it off, Tony.' " This Elaine spoke quietly but firmly. Before the tape player was turned off, Tony sang, "Ebreybody come to da rug; Ebreybody come to da rug. . . ."

My goal was that Tony's classmates should see him as a positive person. Toward the end of November, Chris examined a structure Tony had formed out of building materials. Imagine my pleasure when Chris said, "Tony, that's a really fine house!"

Justice for Tony meant expending an unequal amount of time and effort on his behalf. We all benefited.

—*Kathryn Aschliman, Goshen, Indiana. Kindergarten*

Developing a sense of justice and fairness takes time and effort. Sometimes, with a child like Tony, it takes home visits, input from many persons, and specific planning to help make up for the deficits. A key resource is involving others. Thus children can see the solution as more than dependence on the teacher or one special friend. We also need to consider the conditioning from the experienced environment. For five years Tony had known only locked doors!

Perhaps one of the reasons so little attention is given to doing justice for environmentally deprived children is that there are no specific plans for action in mind; therefore, nothing is done. We adults become spectators of life, sitting and watching injustice, but doing nothing to stop it or change it. Courage and creative intervention are imperative. This is shown by cases such as a transitional first grade in a midwest city and a mission school along the banks of the Amazon River.

This class tested low, with IQ's from 54 to a high of 84; most were emotionally disturbed. They didn't want to listen. They were constantly in fights, lacked love and attention, and lived in one-parent homes with no father present. Often three or four families squeezed into a house meant for one family. Franklin School was closed, and the children were transferred to our new addition built around our old Studebaker School.

There were no supplies for us because our principal thought the supervisor had ordered the readiness material for this class, but no one had. I had to improvise games to teach readiness for reading and arithmetic. Because I was on the language arts textbook committee for many years, I had received many free copies of readiness books. In my class I used these with an overhead projector. The children's attention span was so short that the activities had to be varied and changed often.

The main thing these children needed to learn was to play and to live peacefully together. The school's city carpenters made a balance beam, a teeter-totter, steps up to a platform, and steps down the other side. I used Top Value stamps and purchased a set of toy dishes, ceramic food, a Raggedy Ann doll, a black doll with bottle, a white baby doll, and a teddy bear. All of these were in our room. Even the boys loved and cuddled the dolls and the bear. They learned table manners and how to take turns on the equipment. Gradually fighting stopped.

I used stories often, reading, showing pictures, and making up stories using the children's names, usually having the characters doing something nice or heroic. We sang, using teaching records. I always accompanied the children to the restrooms, drinking fountain, and playground. I ate with them in the cafeteria.

Progress was slow, but finally in January we began to read. We had four reading groups. By June some were in the primer, others in the third preprimer, a few in the second preprimer, and one still in the first preprimer. I was fearful that over the summer they would forget. To my joy and surprise, they picked right up where we had left off. By the next June, all were ready for the third grade. I had them only two years rather than the anticipated three years. I couldn't give them enough to read.

—*Minnie Sutter, South Bend, Indiana. Transitional Grade 1*

Most of the children in our mission school live in a community where they see hatred, lying, stealing, murder, and gross immorality. This is the accepted way of life among the tribal peoples unless they come to know the Lord. The parents realize they need to get their children away from these influences and into an environment where love and honesty are the way of life.

As the children interact with each other in the dorm and school, we have many opportunities to share with them the peaceful way to settle differences. Because of the isolation of the tribal posts, many of the children have had little interaction with children other than their own brothers and sisters and the tribal children. Interacting peacefully can be hard for them.

One day near the end of the school year, I observed two seven-year-old girls from the schoolroom window. One was Janet, adopted at three by missionaries. Before the adoption her life was terrible. She had witnessed the murder of her father by her mother, her mother's murder later, and the murder of the caretaker of their farm. After the adoption, she had a sheltered and secluded life. She had never really learned to play with others. The other girl, Leslie, grew up on an isolated post with only two other children.

Janet had lost in a race during field-day events and walked off mad and pouting. Leslie, on the same team, went over and tried to encourage her. Janet shoved her away, but Leslie continued talking to her. After some time, Janet calmed down and joined in the group activities again. This was all done without adult intervention, but had come about through daily counseling, modeling, and encouragement.

—*Jewel Miller Schlatter, Amazonas, Brazil. Age 7*

How Can We Help Children Bring Justice to the Disabled?

Handicapped persons are often discriminated against and even hidden from public view. During the Year of the Disabled, my first-grade class at Penn View Christian School engaged in a two-week study of handicaps and disabilities.

The students interacted with mentally and physically handicapped persons, experimented with equipment used by those persons, and became acquainted with some of the terms applied to such persons. We learned that being mentally handicapped only means one learns very slowly, "dumb" doesn't mean stupid, and persons in wheelchairs have a hard time getting somewhere when stairs are in the way. We also learned about blindness and the use of sign language.

The results of the study were excellent. Throughout the year the students reported interactions with handicapped and disabled persons, as well as sightings of injustices. For example, one boy reported that he had seen a "barrier" the day before at a local department store. "You know, Mr. Klahre, someone in a wheelchair couldn't get in there."

Going beyond facts to empathy is heading toward justice for disabled persons.

—*David Klahre, Souderton, Pennsylvania. Grade 1*

Compassion and pity need to include participation in mutual learning and exchange. Everyone can benefit through the interchange possible through mainstreaming.

To work for justice for the disabled requires more than sitting where they sit (Ezek. 3:15). Administrators, contractors, public officials, and organizations need to be made aware of their responsibilities. They can suggest specific changes to make their services more accessible to those with special needs.

For example, a highlight in our local elementary school was the graduation of Lois, a 22-year-old woman with multiple handicaps and little language. Lois was able to attend public school only a few years, from the time lawmakers passed legislation which provided the facilities she needed. Lois had made profound improvement in motor skills and social skills.

No one but her mother thought Lois should have a graduation ceremony. But after weeks and months of planning, she graduated, complete with cap and gown. Her severely and profoundly handicapped classmates provided the music with their rhythm band. The delight, so evident in her movements and in her face, made every effort worthwhile.

Further illustrations of creative interrelationships follow in the next two school settings.

Seann, a blind child, was a challenge in my classroom. It was necessary to supply many objects for sensory training, especially for touch and hearing. Seann loved music and story time. His singing voice was above average for a five-year-old, and he had an unusual memory. So of course we capitalized on these strengths.

During the time Seann was in my class, there were thirty-eight other children in the room. They were understanding. We tried to make him as independent as possible. The children helped him when it was necessary. They rejoiced when Seann was able to achieve. At times we had to set boundaries. Some things Seann could not do, and the children usually understood.

I have always remembered the many helpful suggestions I received in Mary Royer's classes. She seemed to have a workable solution for every problem which might arise in the classroom.
—*Laura Troyer, Lima, Ohio. Kindergarten*

On the second floor of our school, we had third and fourth grades plus three classrooms of emotionally and mentally handicapped students.

For Reading Is Fun Week, the names of the third- and fourth-grade students were put in a hat. The handicapped students each chose names. Those persons were to be their partners. Each set of partners chose one storybook character. Teachers measured out long sheets of paper for each set of partners. Children could go in any classroom or to the hall (on the floor) and draw the character, color it with crayons or Magic Markers, and cut it out. We posted the storybook characters on the walls of the hall on the second floor along with a large sign, Reading Is Fun.

It was a beautiful experience to observe the caring shown as the children worked on their projects. They seemed to be aware of their differences and yet took great pride when they introduced their new "friend" or partner.
—*Fern Yoder Hostetler, Altoona, Pennsylvania. Grades 3-4*

Alertness led a teacher to an unexpected opportunity to work with emotionally disturbed children in a psychiatric clinic.

In our work in church planting in São Paulo, Brazil, we always looked for activities in the community in which we could be of service and witness. Several unique opportunities opened in our upper-middle-class area. Through them we could show that being a Christian should be manifested in every part of life.

A lady stopped at my gate one day and asked for something to eat because she had left home early to see her ten-year-old son. He had been committed to the new psychiatric clinic for boys near our home. Rice and beans were being kept warm for our two children who had not yet arrived home. She told me her story while she ate the plate of rice, beans, and salad. She said she washed clothes to support her large family and could not control this boy, who constantly ran away from home.

As we talked, I learned that no one at the clinic was working with the boys in their school work nor in religious counseling. I offered to visit her son and take some easy-reading material on the days she could not make the trip across town.

I visited the boy several times and learned to know the director and various attendants and doctors. Then I offered to teach some crafts and Bible stories. The director told me that they could not permit the teaching of "religion" because it was a government hospital. I assured him that I would not teach "religion," but I would not come unless I could be free to talk to the boys about God's love and to tell them Bible stories.

My work began. At times the boys were so heavily medicated that it was impossible to do any formal teaching. I took crayons, magazines, old Portuguese workbooks, Bible story books, toys, and other craft materials. I was given a room which the boys called their *escolinha* (little school). Naturally, all the boys wanted to come, but only the boys recommended by the psychiatrist attended. At first I felt fearful as someone locked and unlocked doors to get to the *escolinha*. The psychiatrist told me that the majority of the boys were interned because their social behavior was not acceptable at home, in the schools, or in their society. They were social problems rather than psychiatric problems.

The boys eagerly looked forward to the days of the *escolinha*. Occasionally a boy came only to sit and talk—usually about spiritual things. If a big boy only learned to add one number combination that hour, he was commended and went away from the class feeling that he had accomplished something.

At Christmas time the psychiatrist asked us to give a religious program. A group sang carols and told the Christmas story using flannelgraph.

—*Alice Leichty Sawatsky, São Paulo, Brazil. Age 10*

Often it is easier to think of injustices in relation to starving, homeless, and disabled people rather than to realize some of the more insidious ways justice is undermined. For example, undue emphasis on competition and achievement may do more than we think to erode the spirit of cooperation and peacemaking.

> Stanley was a large eighth-grade boy sitting in his seat sobbing softly. He was waiting for his mother to pick him up for a dental appointment, and I assumed he was apprehensive.
>
> After he left school, I sensed there was another problem. At the end of the class period, I simply said, "There seems to be something not settled in this group. As you ready to talk about it?"
>
> As it turned out, the class had chosen teams for a softball game with a neighboring school, and Stanley (a hard hitter but slow runner) was not chosen. He was deeply hurt. An honest discussion yielded two major conflicting opinions. The group decided to take a secret vote on whether it is more important to win or to include all those wanting to play. The result? Stanley was included and informed by the captain of the team's decision to add him to the team.
>
> They lost the game, but the captain said, "There are things more important than winning. They had the best players, so we probably would have lost regardless. We feel good about our decision."
>
> —*Esther Eash Yoder, Grantsville, Maryland. Grades 7-8*

How Can We Help Children Respond to the Injustice of Ethnic, Racial, and Sexual Discrimination?

Many times misunderstandings are caused by lack of information. The root meaning of prejudice is to pre-judge. The classroom and the neighborhood are our laboratory in human relations. If children are not given opportunities to interact with other persons who differ from themselves, their perception of justice is thwarted.

> We had two girls in our class from Mexico. When they came, they knew no English. Soon after they arrived, Sheryl said she wanted to ask them to be her friends and to play with her, but she didn't know how to say it in Spanish. Sheryl has turned out to be a true friend—making sure they are always included and letting me know when she feels I have been neglecting them. She has learned some Spanish from them. They have learned some En-

glish from her. And all three have learned a lot about friendship.
—Irene Rhodes, Las Animas, Colorado. Grade 3

Recently there have been more Indian and Indo-Chinese children in my kindergarten classes than in former years. When I ask children to draw self-portraits, they are to look into the mirror to study their features, including color of eyes, hair, and skin. They are asked to match as closely as possible their crayoned drawing to their actual body colors. As children learn that there are differences in the colors of their skins, they also learn to enjoy differences.

Some time ago a disparaging remark was made about a racially different student. I attempted to use the above type of redemptive reasoning to help that child feel a part of the group without belittling the critic.
—Verelda Zook Roth, Glen Ellyn, Illinois. Kindergarten

During my second year of teaching, I was twenty-two years of age and taught in a one-room school with about thirty pupils, grades three through eight. All the children were from Old Order Amish homes.

One family (I will call them the Browns) sent four hapless children to the school. The father was a widower who lacked the usual Amish characteristics of hard work, thrift, and good management. So the children were known in school as the "poor Brown children." As each incident of prejudice occurred, I tried to handle it. Gradually I became aware of the long-standing discrimination and ostracism which this family had experienced. The schoolchildren were reflecting what they had learned from their homes. The problem had developed through the years and would not go away on its own.

After an ugly incident near the end of the school term, I let the Brown children go home early. (They lived within walking distance.) Then I spent the next hour talking with the other children about the Brown family's situation and the meaning of love as Jesus taught it. They listened intently, for this kind of talk was new to them. They had not thought of the Browns being worthy of consideration before. Later I learned from the older children and their parents that they had never heard anyone other than Amish ministers teach about Christ, the Bible, and peace before.

Did these efforts help? I never knew for sure. The climate at school seemed better during the remaining weeks, and my efforts were warmly supported by the father, several parents, and an Amish bishop who came to talk with me.

As I recall that situation, I am sure it was the influence of Mary Royer and her colleagues at Goshen College that made me bold enough to try those steps of reconciliation in that deeply ingrained social problem in the Yoder School and surrounding community.

—*Dorsa J. Mishler, Shipshewana, Indiana. Grades 3-8*

Carlton was a large black eighth grader who had come to live in our community as a result of placement by social services. He knew the city street and its language. When a Vietnamese family enrolled their children in Yoder Public School, Carlton taught some street English to Quang and Sung Thai. The boys did not understand the meanings, but knew the atmosphere in which to use them.

Several days later Quang used the words on Carlton, which resulted in a fistfight while riding the bus home. The next morning, Quang, still trembling with frustration and anger, demonstrated and explained in limited English what had happened.

I called Carlton to the office to hear his side of the incident. The stories coincided. Carlton assured me that he would never apologize—never, even though he acknowledged responsibility. "Carlton," I said, "the problem will need to be resolved before recess. You think about how this can be done."

The forenoon proceeded without incident. Just before recess I called Carlton to the office. "I just thought of something, Carlton," I began. "Quang knows little English, but he does know the meaning of 'I'm sorry.' "

"That's a deal," Carlton responded, apparently ready to be the peacemaker. I asked Quang to join us. Carlton looked Quang in the eye and with mellowed expression said, "I'm sorry, Quang."

Quang rose to his feet, took Carlton's hand between his, bowed politely before him, and said, "I solly too."

The two boys went out for recess.

—*Esther Eash Yoder, Grantsville, Maryland. Grade 8*

My nieces, Tanya and Missy, eight and six years old, lived in Pennsylvania on a hundred-acre farm. During the summer they each spent a week with me in Philadelphia. Traveling on a public bus and walking on crowded streets, they saw abandoned houses, dirty sidewalks, and people of many economic and racial backgrounds.

Tanya and Missy met my friends Yolanda and Crystal, eleven- and eight-year-olds. Missy visited the zoo with Yolanda and three-year-old twins, Johana and Jessica. Missy and Tee, a five-year-old neighbor girl, went to the docks with us to see the Tall Ship which stopped to wish Philadelphia a happy 300th birthday. When my husband's niece, six-year-old Tricia, spent several days with us, Yolanda plaited her hair in cornrows.

I hope these personal relationships with neighborhood children in Philadelphia will work against the racism and prejudice the girls might otherwise develop in their suburban white and rural farm environments.

—*Glenda Detwiler Moyer, Philadelphia, Pennsylvania. Ages 3-11*

As teachers and parents, we need wisdom, patience, courage, vision, and most importantly, a continuing sense of humor and perspective. These will enable us to work through the many dimensions and complications of injustice in our classrooms, homes, neighborhoods, and communities. Sometimes there is no other way than "line upon line, precept upon precept."

Mimi is black, her home is in Ethiopia, and throughout the year, there were some problems with other students using racist labels like *nigger*. We had spent a lot of time talking about name-calling and how privileged we were to have someone from another culture in our room. By February, I was feeling like we had resolved the problem. Then on Valentine's Day, Mimi received an anonymous card addressed "to Blackie"; the same person gave no sucker for Mimi while everyone else got one. She was devastated. We had to start all over.

—*Irene Rhodes, Las Animas, Colorado. Grade 3*

We must have willingness to start over if we want to find ways to help children develop genuine care and concern for all persons, regardless of race, background, or physical appearance. We need to try to find creative solutions to the oft-repeated Valentine box snubbing and status games.

The educational system has an indisputably powerful influence on children, both on their present and future behavior. Often we are unaware of the subtle messages we give both by what is presented as well as by what is omitted. The sports world is heavily masculine and very competitive.

> Our principal had ordered a series of sports books; fourteen of them were about men and only four about women. I expressed my concern to him. Several days later, I offered a list of nonsexist, multicultural books—from *Parenting for Peace and Justice*,[4] which also included books relating to social justice. He said that after I talked to him, he also realized he had not ordered enough books relating to the Spanish culture.
>
> —*Irene Rhodes, Las Animas, Colorado. Grades 3-6*

The chapter on sex-role stereotyping in *Parenting for Peace and Justice* is particularly insightful. It contains several pages of specific applications to school settings, including practical guidelines for evaluating children's books and curriculum.[5]

The task of peace building is so great that every child, every woman, and every man needs to utilize all of their abilities and gifts to work for justice and harmony. Often boys are taught that it is sissy to cry. We need women *and* men who are allowed to express their feelings through crying, if necessary; who are supportive, nurturant, and caring; and whose sensitive qualities are well-developed. Some people insinuate that girls are not as good in math and science as boys. We need men *and* women who grapple with abstract concepts, enjoy beauty, and express their creativity through various channels. When people are denied expression of their emotions or are taught to get what they need by being coy, is it any wonder that we are shorthanded in doing justice and working for peace?

What About the Media?

The images offered by movies and TV are narrow and may close one's eyes to injustice. Ageism, sexism, and racism are regularly portrayed in the media. Advertising promotes consumerism, sports tend to encourage "spectatoritis" and competition, and the news is often slanted or biased with third-world concerns and realities underreported. In monitoring TV, one must be alert to what is omitted as well as to what is included in the presentations and programming.

The following incident tells of several concrete things one teacher did. The children involved learned some things about being selective and discriminating in what they watch and hear.

Over the years more printed and visual materials were made available to schools. Special interest groups, service clubs, and parents occasionally bring materials, requesting that they be shared with classes. Well-meaning parents bring items that are not only unsuitable for certain age groups but that also err by not presenting a complete picture of a situation.

Such was the case when a parent of a pupil brought a film sponsored by the Pan American Union and requested that I show it to my sixth-grade social studies classes. I was then to pass it on to a junior high school where the parent had also made arrangements for its showing.

When I previewed the film, I soon saw that the documentary film footage of atrocities in Central America would not be suitable for my pupils to see. They already saw too much violence on TV. What really disturbed me, however, was not only the violence but what the "documentary" didn't expose.

It didn't mention the great disparity in wealth which exists in Central America—the poverty of peasants in brutal contrast to the lavish wealth of the small percentage of landowners. Nor did it cover the inequities in education—children of the elite sent to United States' schools while education of the masses is virtually ignored.

The film didn't explain that the military presence had been in Central America for decades to protect oppressive economic interests. Large companies export millions of dollars worth of crops without sharing profits with local peasant workers. No mention was made of geological factors such as volcanic and earthquake activity which compound the economic and political problems.

I didn't show the film to my classes. I sent the film to the junior high school and phoned the principal. I asked that he preview it with teachers of classes in which it was to be shown. I mentioned my objection to the film and my concern that the other side of the Central American story was not presented. The result was that the film wasn't shown in the junior high either.

I resolved to involve my pupils in more exercises requiring consideration of different viewpoints. They were later enthusiastically engaged in discussions and writings involving controversial issues such as "Rites and Rights of Native Americans," "Welfare Families," and "Consumer Economy vs. Producer Economy."

In retrospect, the parent who brought the film was helpful. The impetus her act provided, coupled with the Christian college training I received, helped change the humdrum January-March days into a time of growth in language arts, social studies, and understanding of human relationships.

—*Hobert Yoder, Iowa City, Iowa. Grade 6*

Adults need to take responsibility to help children spot and evaluate cultural messages in the light of family values.

Our boys report that *all* the other neighbor children are allowed to listen to hard rock and choose TV shows at will. The main goal in life for many children and adults seems to be "get what *you* can out of life. Don't think about how short life is or what it's all about." Against this background we work to instill Christ's values. We discuss openly the world's views versus ours toward war, abortion, how to spend money, and how to treat enemies.

Though such an approach is often rewarding, it is just as often equally frustrating. A child's desire to be liked and to like the others is terribly strong. And yet, we can already see results with which we're pleased. One small example was a monster show advertised heavily for at least two weeks. To view this, special glasses for the 3-D effect were needed at a dollar a pair. It truly surprised me that *neither* boy asked for them. In fact, one of them commented, "They just want our money, don't they, Mom?"

—*Donna Yordy Grove, Durham, North Carolina. Ages 8 and 11*

TV can be a valuable resource, but it must be used wisely. Group or family discussion is the best way I know to deal with it.

The commercials trouble me as much as the programming. There appear to be few, if any, controls, and often children pay more attention to commercials than to the program itself. Because of this concern, we have now sold our TV.

—*Maribeth Shank Shank, Washington, D.C. Ages 4 and 6*

Concerned parent groups have affected television advertising and programming. *Television Awareness Training*[6] is an eye opener.

Television itself is an injustice to children when it is their only recreational outlet, particularly when so many children watch adult programming and when there are so few child-oriented programs. As parents and teachers, we can offer alternatives to television viewing that are attractive enough to motivate children to do something else.

The fifth grade No TV Week in our local school is gaining in popularity. The first year only a few children earned their T-shirts, which proclaimed that they actually made it through a whole week with no TV! The next year the number of successes doubled; the following year more than half of the class accomplished it.

The teacher plans carefully and uses this as part of the health unit on addiction. The most important part of the activity is helping the children make a list of alternate activities (they must have at least twenty!) that they can do when they get the urge to watch TV. Part of the program's success is that positive images and alternative actions are substituted for television. The children soon realize that one can make a conscious decision to leave the TV off and do something else.

Friends of ours in Des Moines, whose children are four, eight, and ten, have instituted a No TV Week once each month. Their ten-year-old's comment: "It's not so bad; you get a lot of reading and other things done."

A creative mother gave some structure to a long summer day and provided alternatives to television in the process:

> My daughter wanted her friends to come over for the day. I was unable to have them come in the morning because I was tutoring. So I planned an envelope "treasure hunt." Brooke delivered to each friend a book and stack of envelopes with times marked on them. The schedule had a few adjustments for age differences and for more than one child in a family, but basically was as follows:
> 9:30 Read (in the book provided).
> 10:00 Practice your piano pieces each two times.

10:30 Do a job for your mother.

11:00 Make a card (paper provided).

11:30 Listen to your mother tell about *her* school days.

11:45 Find a verse in Psalms. Read it three times. Write it.

12:00 Pick two flowers on the way to Brooke's house for lunch.

After lunch each participant made another card. Then we took cards, flowers, songs, and verses to two shut-ins. After a stop at the Dairy Queen, it was time to go home.

—*Mary Ann Smucker Roth, Goshen, Indiana. Ages 6-12*

How Can We Help Children Respond to the Injustice of Stealing?

Stealing is another form of injustice which children encounter. Each year most classrooms have one or more incidents related to stealing which can become teachable moments. What do you do when money is missing from your desk or someone's treasure is taken?

The third-grade teacher came to my room one day and told me that Pam, one of my second-grade pupils, had stolen the billfold of Lori, one of her pupils.

Since the children were all out on the playground, I checked and found no billfold. I went out on the playground to talk to Pam. Sure enough, she had a billfold, but she firmly claimed that it was hers. So I got both girls together. Each one claimed the billfold.

Knowing the two girls, I was quite sure Lori was telling the truth, but I wanted the guilty one to admit her act. So I talked and questioned without hearing a confession. At last I asked to look at the billfold. In going through the contents, I knew it belonged to Lori, but I still wanted Pam to admit that it wasn't hers. With more talking, she finally did, handed the billfold back to Lori, and told her she was sorry.

I could see in Lori's face how sorry she felt for Pam. Then she did an unusual thing. She opened her billfold, took out two treasured pictures of her brothers, and asked Pam if she would like to have them. Pam was pleased with the gift, and the two little girls went out to the playground with their arms around each other. Such reconciliation! I had never seen such empathy for the of-

fender as demonstrated by Lori, who so graciously forgave.
—*Oleeda Sutter Albrecht, Tiskilwa, Illinois. Grades 2-3*

We must be cautious about wrongly accusing young children of stealing. They are establishing for themselves an understanding of what is personal property and what belongs to others. The following incident shows an occasion that provides opportunities to help children distinguish between private and public property and to teach them respect for public property.

It was a little past 12:00. The telephone rang. It was Robin's teacher at the daycare center where she went following her morning with us in kindergarten.

"Do you have a frog?" the teacher asked.

"No, but we have a toad in our terrarium," I answered.

"Well, Robin brought an animal in her coat pocket for show-and-tell, and we wondered if it might be yours."

Sure enough, when we carefully checked, our toad could not be located. We agreed that Robin should return the toad to the kindergarten when her father came to pick her up and take her home from daycare. When they came, I assured Robin's father, who wanted to punish her, that I did not consider this an act of stealing. Instead, Robin needed to learn to leave things at school no matter how much she enjoyed them. I commended Robin for bringing the toad back to its kindergarten home.

We became conscious that other things were disappearing from the kindergarten room, and, yes, they were appearing at the daycare center. After careful planning with Robin's parents and the daycare staff, we began to tackle the problem. We explained clearly to Robin that kindergarten equipment was to stay in the room so it could be used the next day. Occasionally this was reinforced by checking her pockets before she left the kindergarten.

Additionally, at the end of the morning I wrote a note about something Robin had enjoyed that day. This she took for show-and-tell at the daycare center. Gradually objects which had disappeared began returning, although it took several visits to the home to identify some of them.

—*Kathryn Aschliman, Goshen, Indiana. Kindergarten*

It is important to interpret for peers what an individual child is learning. A child can be unjustly and wrongly accused of stealing because previous tendencies have been evident. Children need to learn that it is important to get factual evidence before making accusations.

> One time when a child's treasure walked away and did not come back, we talked about it in class. I said I had no desire to know who took it. But I stated that anyone who might have taken it could, by taking this treasure, be tempted to go on taking small things and eventually bigger things.
>
> "Since," I said, "we have nice children, surely no one wants to become a thief. The person who took the treasure may return it or put it on my desk. I need not know who it was, but the individual will be cleared."
>
> The next day J. brought the item to me, saying he found it on the playground. The owner, class, teacher, and finder were happy, and I was the only one who knew it was J. who either found or returned the treasure.
>
> —*Mary Zehr, Morton, Illinois. Grade 4*

In the upper grades, shoplifting is often a problem. Our daughter went roller skating with several friends. One of the girls stuffed her pockets with candy that she had not paid for and later distributed it to all the girls. My daughter said, "Mom, I threw mine away because I just could not eat it." When we suggested that she go back to the pizza parlor and tell them what happened and pay for the candy she threw away, it was too much. She began to wish she had never told us what happened. We considered calling the other parents or the school and telling her teacher or the principal what had happened. But these options were eliminated when we realized the broken-home situation of the instigator, and the fact that it was not during schooltime when the incident happened.

After much discussion, we decided to let the matter rest for the time being, since our daughter's conscience had been significantly tendered by the experience. We, as parents, wanted her to continue to be open and able to share such problems with us. In this instance, we understood and responded to injustice by acknowledging the wrongness of what was done and by discussing options and actions that might be taken.

Since this incident, the topic of shoplifting has been discussed further by my daughter and her friends, our family, and the children in her classroom.

How Can We Help Children Respond to the Injustice of Violence?

On November 22, 1963, I was teaching fourth grade at Parkside School in Goshen, Indiana. Suddenly the loudspeaker intercom came on with the horrifying words, "The president has been shot! The president has been shot!" I don't remember all the things the children and I said to each other during those last thirty minutes of school on that Thursday, but I do remember that we shared our shock, our frustrations, our fears, and our questions.

We talked about shooting, dying, and justice. Many of the children were afraid this violence signaled the end of the presidency, and they needed to be assured that the office of the president would continue. As the children gathered more information from the news media, the discussions and questions continued for days and weeks afterward. My own feelings and thinking were greatly eased by the memorial service for John F. Kennedy held at Goshen College. Likewise, the children found opportunities to acknowledge what had happened.

Children need assistance in dealing with violence in the media, both actual and fictional. Within two decades occurred the assassinations of John F. Kennedy, Martin Luther King, Jr., Robert F. Kennedy, Malcolm X, and the attempt on the Pope's life as well as President Reagan's. In addition, news of hijackings and war between nations are commonplace.

The range of children's reactions to such events include fear for personal safety, loss of control, ambivalence, numbness, anger, cynicism, and despair. These responses suggest that when children are frightened, enraged, and without hope, they need to sense some stability and comfort in a world gone mad.

None of us are prepared for such news. Peggy Ruth Cole says,

As teachers in an era of rapid reporting, unable to protect children from the knowledge of such violent events, we are forced to face young people before we have time to absorb our own shock and sort through our own feelings. As educators we have an obligation to help children express their concerns and feelings. Whatever the external chaos, schools should be places where reliable, trustworthy adults can help young people voice their fears, confusion, and despair. But what reassurance can we honestly give in these alarming times?

Probably the only honest stance we can take is to be open to sharing with children our own shock and bewilderment at the event, at the same time reaffirming our own larger value system.[7]

For example, we can remind children of their values which center around nurturing and caring for living things, such as plants, animals, and one another. Barbara Smucker's book *Amish Adventure*[8] dramatically and concretely illustrates for children the value of such ongoing attention to life in the midst of crisis. We can assure children that there are caring and thoughtful people willing to share not only their shock but also their hope. Although some classroom situations preclude open verbal sharing of spiritual experiences and values, there are many ways to share one's faith in the midst of fear; injustice; family; and national, or international crises.

As teachers and parents, we need to give attention to children's experiences of and exposure to violence. For some children this may be of a personal nature, identified as child abuse and neglect, which usually occurs as a result of adult violence and neglect.

One of my five-year-old students came from a particularly destructive family atmosphere. I saw her roaming the streets at 7:30 a.m. as I came to school. In the middle of the winter, she would come to school with tennis shoes, a light jacket, and no mittens. Neighbors had reportedly complained that she was often locked in a dirt-floor cellar for hours at a time as a form of punishment. When I made a home visit, I will never forget the dog manure strewn on the kitchen floor and the coffee table with a sheet on it in the living room which Erica *proudly* showed me was her bed.

Needless to say, Erica proved to be a disruptive and violent child to deal with. We had many struggles the first ten weeks of school. She was frequently outwardly defiant, and when confronted she would scream, bite, scratch, and kick.

Although she was extremely academically deprived, she proved to be intelligent and learned quickly. Therefore, I was able to encourage her and praise her advances in academics. As for social skills, I made her days as structured as possible since structure was one of many things she lacked at home. I expected a lot from her behavior-wise and clearly stated what her choices were and what the consequences would be each time a confrontation arose. Any time she was showing appropriate behavior, I would point her out as an example to follow.

It was a long semester, and I was sure that minimal progress was being made. On the last day of school before Christmas vacation, I always give every child a book. I was handing out the gifts, and a few children remembered to say thank-you. Most were too excited. When I gave Erica her book, she looked at me with tears in her eyes and said, "But Mrs. Schrock, I don't have anything to give you." What deep feeling came from a child who had been mistreated in so many ways!

—*Mary Thomas Schrock, Goshen, Indiana. Kindergarten*

Personal experiences of violence such as fistfights and verbal and physical abuse—these disrupt the classroom and playground. Working through conflict takes time and may require much from the peacemaker. Nonviolence is not passive. It is an active, positive, alternate approach to violence.

In 1969-70, my husband took a leave from the church where he was pastor and we moved to Winston-Salem, North Carolina, for a year. There I taught at Carver School, one of three white teachers in a 3,000-pupil school (kindergarten through twelfth grade).

In the middle of the year, the Federal Court required integration, but Winston-Salem could not integrate because they had no city bus system and no bussing in the schools. So integration was carried out through the teacher ratio. Seventy-five percent of the black teachers were transferred to white schools and white teachers were brought in to take their places.

The climate of the school was volatile. The struggle to maintain even a semblance of order took its toll on the principal, who was unable to work after that year. I taught a combination of North

Carolina history, literature, and social studies to seventh and eighth graders. I committed myself to making my classes a safe place emotionally. I also made up my mind to not be a hero and to go for help when a fight broke out.

In my previous teaching, I seldom raised my voice, depending on a clear, even-projected tone to get attention and keep it. Once I broke that rule badly at Carver.

A girl in social studies class was trying hard to give a report, and hecklers were annoying her in subtle ways. My pity for the injustice of the situation overruled my best intentions. I slammed my hand on the desk and said loudly to the class, "Shut up!" Everything went still, and a girl in the front row looked up and said sadly, "Mrs. Alderfer, you don't say that." I said to her and to the class quietly, "No, I don't say that." The girl resumed her report.

That school was a jungle. Sometimes I thought I could hear the roaring of lions, and a few times I was afraid. But there were also times when I felt a commitment to peace in the atmosphere of the room which tempered the storm.

—Helen Wade Alderfer, Winston-Salem, North Carolina. Grades 7-8

How Do We Help Children Respond to Injustice Brought On by War or the Threat of War?

The violence of war deprives children of peace, security, and often their homes and family. Many children live in the midst of war; others live with the threat of war hovering over them. In either case, living with the fear of war is an injustice to children. What follows is an example of how teachers and children shared courage and hope in the midst of the reality of war.

I can't say that we set out to teach peace, but we all wished for it! During the unsettled years in Uganda, children came to school early in the morning—it seemed like a sort of "haven of rest." I remember them saying, "I couldn't sleep last night. There was so much shooting around our house." On the last day of school before a term break, little first-grade girls came weeping, arm in arm. "We don't want a vacation. We want to come to school."

Did we teach peace? I don't know who taught whom more. We teachers met in the staff room in the morning, shared the experiences of the night before, then entered our classrooms to give our

best for one more day. We felt that in the midst of the uncertainty, an investment of our lives in the children was worthwhile. The children were eager to be together and to be working and studying together. This reinforced our feeling of hope for another day.
—*Lenora Dietzel Sempira, Kampala, Uganda. Grades K-2*

Clearly evident in the Persian Gulf War was how much children absorb the attitudes and beliefs of the society around them. In a Christian elementary school, the principal struggled with how to approach the students and teachers who were openly praying for Saddam Hussein to be destroyed. They took literally Jesus' teaching to pray for one's enemies, but they used prayer as a way to express hatred, revenge, and power rather than love and goodwill.

Pacifist parents and teachers found their children expressing conviction against war even when they had not previously articulated it. A young teen sat down when his teacher asked everyone to stand at attention for a moment of silence in support of "our" troops in the Gulf. He later told his mother, "I didn't know what to do. I sat down because I could not support a war." The teacher did not repeat this request perhaps because of his convictions and courage.

There is a fine line between implanting fear, giving false hope, and creating courage to respond. All of us need to be both sensitive and realistic. The question, "Are we causing more trouble than we are curing?" is always an appropriate check on our input.

Children for Peace is a peace educational group for six to nine-year-olds that met in the Anathoth Children's Library of the Brussels Mennonite Center. During one of their sessions, the group gathered around a large sheet of paper to send their greetings to children in Nicaragua, a country where there was suffering and war. Most of the children chose to draw things they enjoyed or things they considered to be the good parts of Belgian life—playgrounds, beautiful countryside, french fries, ice cream, pastries, and a Mercedez-Benz!

Mennonite Central Committee workers in Managua provided the link to a group of Nicaraguan children in a Mennonite con-

gregation. They made a drawing which arrived in Brussels a few months after they received ours. The Children for Peace group in Brussels were excited about the response from Nicaragua. "Look, the Nicaraguan children sent us a big drawing!" they exclaimed. It included a swimming pool, children going to church, a helicopter, a Nicaraguan boat carrying rice, beans, and oil, and this message: "We desire brotherhood with the children of Belgium."
—*Sylvia Shirk Charles, Brussels, Belgium. Ages 6-9*

Raising children in a climate of fear is a grave injustice. However, today's children are well aware of the possibility of nuclear winter, and many of them think every day about whether or not they will grow up in a world that continues to stockpile nuclear weapons.

But it is an even graver injustice never to speak of fears and threats of war. Children need a chance to voice their opinions, questions, and frustrations; otherwise we invite despair or apathy. We need firmly and concretely to counter comments like "What's the use? It won't make any difference," and "We're all going to blow up tomorrow anyway."

Children need to know that they themselves are a sign of hope. As the Indian poet Tagore put it, "Every child is proof that God is not yet discouraged of man."[9] The very fact that one goes on teaching and working with children is an expression of hope and belief in humankind's ability to learn new and better ways of dealing with problems.

We want to empower children, not overwhelm them with terror. Children need to be helped to a life-affirming stance. If one values life, then one works for life. Work and involvement in concrete tasks are healing. Children find hope and courage as they and their parents and teachers become involved in life-affirming activities which cultivate a sensitivity to all life, to human needs, and to human concerns.

Your own attitudes toward such things as giving, death, and work will be catching as you discuss and learn together.

Teachers can help children to participate in all kinds of sharing and service projects. The goal is genuinely to care about the other person; to find joy in giving; to share money, time, and possessions. We want to learn to be joyful in our work and play and be prepared and willing to serve. Children learn best from involvement, from doing. To hear is helpful; to do is better.[10]

Whenever possible, children need to be helped to take action; otherwise they feel inadequate and give up. The type of action depends on the developmental maturity of the child. Bringing articles for health kits, collecting money for vitamins, and caring for refugees—these are tangible ways children can be involved in life-renewing activity.

> At Christmastime the two Mennonite churches in Scottdale made school kits to be sent to Mennonite Central Committee and then to Cambodia. This helped the children in my Sunday school class become aware of the needs of others far away. It was hard for the children to realize the need for paper, pencils, and crayons when we have so much of these kinds of things. This in turn led to a discussion of war, bombs, the nuclear threat, and our response to it. During the discussion I was able to make the children aware of our belief in peace and nonparticipation in war and the alternatives open to us.
> —*Suzanne Beechy Kauffman, Scottdale, Pennsylvania. Ages 7-8*

For some early adolescents, making a poster, helping with a paper drive, or writing to the president may be appealing. The significance of these acts may lie in the fact that they enable people to verbalize their concerns.

> During Leisa's fifth-grade year, our family lived at Indiana University and learned to know many Iranian students. This was the year of the American-Iranian conflicts with the hostages, and in the depth of Leisa's frustration, she decided to write a letter to President Carter.
> In the sixth grade Leisa wrote a letter to President Reagan. As parents, we are glad that her peace concern not only related to war and world affairs. It also showed in her compassion for a student in her peer group who seemed to be left out. She made special efforts to befriend her.
> —*Sharon Kennell Kauffmann, Bloomington, Indiana. Grades 5-6*

Dear Mr. President,

I, Leisa Kauffmann have been paying close attention to what has been going on in Iran. I thought up a little answer that might be of help.

Why don't you ask the Sha if he would give up a little or some of his money to Iran that they say he took. If he might agree then ask Iran if they'll be satisfied for just some of his money instead.

I feel that the Sha was a pretty bad leader but don't wish for him or any hostages to be killed. Nor do I think there should be a war. (Even though I don't think there will be any.)

I feel your a good president and as it is international year of the child I thought this idea might be of a little help.

Good luck in your campayne! God Bless you and your family.

Leisa Kauffmann

Leisa's letter shows respect, concern, and compassion. The dreams and vision of the young need to be given roots and wings. Children need to know that by recognizing and responding to injustice, we cast a vote for peace. Networks of understanding and goodwill are built piece by piece.

"That's me with a happy face."
Alyssa Johnson, age 4

PEACE IS HAPPINESS, PLAYING JOYFULLY, SHARING, HELPING.

"I shake the rattle to make my baby brother happy."
Kate Hershberger, age 4

"I'm out in the sun with my dog."
Kelly Short, age 5

"We're playing catch."
Crandall Miller, age 4

"Here is me and one of my friends playing."
Kevin Thomas, age 5

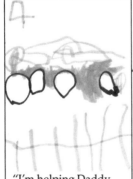

"I'm helping Daddy mow grass."
Casey Yost, age 4

"I'm running and a bird is flying with me."
Nicholas Johnson, age 4

"This is Mommy, and I'm helping her get groceries."
Ashlee McLaughlin, age 4

PEACE IS SOLVING PROBLEMS WITHOUT HURTING ANYONE.

Audrey Schultz, age 9

Matt Honderich, age 9

Rachel Miller, age 8

Philip Swartzendruber, age 8

"I'm stopping a fight between my cousins."
Michelle Santiago, age 8

Cheryl Preheim, age 10
Rebecca Howland, age 10
Bryan Falcón, age 9

One cannot always expect a reply from government officials, but it is still worthwhile to focus and express one's concerns in writing. However, when responses such as the paragraphs excerpted here are forthcoming, they provide yet another opportunity for strengthening the bonds of peace and the will to do one's part in being a peacemaker.

When children express their feelings about war and peace in their art, they often reveal a focus on the more immediate, everyday experiences of family, house, home, and school, and their personal safety and comfort. The following drawings are a glimpse of children's understanding of peace at two age levels.

Children's anxieties about war resemble their other worries about things such as divorce, separation from family, illness, crime, the violence of daily life, or the death of a pet. As they grapple with such experiences of grief and fear, they need a sense of support, community, and stability.

Our involvement in the life of Adriana began one day when the pastor of a Mennonite Brethren Church in a poor area of São Paulo came to the office and began sharing the problems they were experiencing with several young members. Adriana lived with her mother, the breadwinner of the family, and a four-year-old sister. She had not seen her father since her mother moved to São Paulo from Recife.

The *favela* (slum) where they lived was known for the youth gangs involved in drugs and crime. Police were afraid to go into the area. Adriana's mother had reasons to be concerned about her daughter. It appears that the only way the mother knew to discipline Adriana was by beating her. Adriana disobeyed her mother one evening, and instead of coming home to face her punishment, she stayed with a friend. Rumors were that she was living with a young man. The pastor tried to visit her, but was threatened and told to mind his own business.

The Lord spoke to us about sharing our home with this girl. When we went to speak to the pastor, Adriana had returned home to her mother. The mother was grateful for this offer. Adriana was happy to get away from home. She was bitter toward her mother and jealous of her mother's attention and leniency to her younger sister.

When Adriana went home one weekend during the first

month, she had a serious misunderstanding with her mother because of her disobedience. The mother lost control and began beating Adriana until a neighbor intervened. The pastor brought her back and suggested that she not go home for several weeks. One weekend when the mother came to visit, Adriana turned her back and refused to speak to her mother.

We talked about Adriana's responsibility to her mother and the mother's feelings of love, and how she could find help through accepting the Lord as Savior and promising to follow Jesus.

After living with us for six months, she now looks forward to going to spend the weekend with her mother and sister even though the three sleep in a single bed, the wooden shack has no floor nor windows, and there is no running water nor electricity in the house. The Lord is healing Adriana's bitterness. She is showing more love and understanding for her mother, and the little sister thinks her big sister is someone very special. Adriana's mother is also treating her in a more considerate and loving way. With special help in her lessons at school, Adriana is becoming confident that she can do some things well.

—*Alice Leichty Sawatsky, São Paulo, Brazil. Age 12*

How Can We Learn From Injustice in History?

When we recall stories of the past, this strengthens our resolve and gives us courage to deal with the present and future. Much of the biblical message comes through stories of God's faithfulness to his people. History and social studies provide exposure to past injustice and its causes and give opportunities for discussion of what we can learn from the past. It is valuable to read a biography of Martin Luther King, Jr., and classic ethnic stories like *Sounder* and *Amos Fortune, Free Man.*[11] They can inspire others to creative and courageous action against injustice of racism.

Teachers can share their personal perspectives, convictions, and concerns about justice and injustice issues.

Throughout my public teaching career, I read books to the children about people like Mary McLeod Bethune[12] and the Cherokee nation in *The Story of the Trail of Tears.*[13] I gave my slant on them all! One day I suggested that we might have a debate between the North and the South, proslavery and antislavery. I overhead two boys discussing it, and one asked the other, "Which side do you think Mrs. King would be on?" The other emphatically replied, "Why, she'd be against slavery!" One of the boys is now a lawyer in Washington, D.C., working on Brazilian financial concerns.

—*Lois Meyer King, Fisher, Illinois. Grade 5*

Reading another person's life's story is one of the best ways to identify with that person as another human being. One cannot assume that children know the stories of even the immediate past.

I discovered none of my third graders knew who Martin Luther King, Jr., was nor anything about his life. And so, during Black History Month, we spent a lot of time reading and discussing the whole subject of civil rights and the lives of black Americans.

—*Irene Rhodes, Las Animas, Colorado. Grade 3*

When possible, history should be linked to persons. Anne Frank[14] brought the Holocaust into our seventh grader's awareness. Our daughter identified with Anne Frank and puzzled about how and why such horror could have happened.

Likewise, Sadako[15] can provide a link to the Hiroshima experience for older children.

Several years ago on a friendship visit to Japan, I visited Hiroshima, the city where the United States Air Force dropped an atomic bomb in an attempt to end World War II. What I saw exhibited in the museums of the Peace Park of this city was so horrifying that I resolved to do all I could for the cause of peace when I returned home. I had taken many colored slides throughout the country. I decided to write a narration to use with the slides showing glimpses of Japan's country, people, and culture. I included pictures of Hiroshima's Peace Park and the Children's Peace Monument to commemorate the story of Sadako.[16]

This twelve-year-old school girl suffered from radiation sickness as a result of the bomb. A close friend encouraged her to fold 1,000 paper cranes. With a wish to get well, day after day she folded paper cranes in the hospital. After the 644th crane had been folded, leukemia claimed her life.

Following her death, Sadako's friends began dreaming of building a monument to her and all children who were killed by the atom bomb. Young people throughout the country helped collect money for the project. In 1958, the statue was unveiled in Hiroshima Peace Park. Sadako stands on top of a granite mountain. She is holding a golden crane in outstretched hands. A message is engraved on the base of the statue: "This is our cry, this is our prayer, peace in the world." People place thousands of folded paper cranes beneath Sadako's statue on Peace Day, August 6.

As I share this presentation and the story of Sadako with older children, I give each child a folded paper crane as a souvenir to remember that peace comes only through loving.

—Pauline Yoder, Goshen, Indiana. Grades 5-8

In a park in our city stands a tall, stately statue of a Russian Mennonite farmer. His hat is off and his head is bowed in prayer as a reminder of the dignity and courage of these men and their families. They left their wonderful homeland on the steppes of Russia to find a new home where they could be peaceloving people once more. Around the base of the statue are scenes done in small tiles depicting the trek to America.

On a previous Sunday our fifth graders had a lesson on nonresistance, and we felt that a drawing session in the park would help to climax the study on this important subject which is so much a part of our Christian faith.

It was a balmy Sunday morning in September, and it was quiet in the park as our juniors were drawing. Some of the children made sketches of the statue while others spent their time drawing scenes of the exciting journey. There were the Russian Orthodox Church and the homes of the Mennonites in Russia, the ships sailing to America, the train continuing its journey from New York City to Kansas, and finally the bright sun shining over the new homes and churches and wheat fields of the red Turkey wheat farmers on the prairies of Kansas. My co-teacher and I wanted this story to become an integral part of our pupils' lives.

Then came the surprise. Shortly before we left the park, not one hundred yards away, a group of National Guard soldiers marched by, guns held high and feet keeping time in perfect rhythm as the officer barked out orders. Pencils stopped in midair and our hearts almost stood still. The contrast was plain for all of us to see and hear and feel. On a peaceful Sunday morn-

ing in mid-USA, and in the presence of a significant statue depicting Christian belief of peace, the National Guard practiced war.
—*Geraldine Gross Harder, Newton, Kansas. Grade 5*

Stories such as *Days of Terror* and *Coals of Fire* help children trace family roots and genealogy to courageous forebears.[17] One way to do justice is to see religious, national, or racial groups as individuals as in Aliki's biographies of Johnny Appleseed, William Penn, and George Washington Carver.[18] The stories of history can help children to integrate head learning with heart learning. In *The Bronze Bow*, a young Galilean, intent on revenge toward the Romans, is influenced and changed by the friendship of an amazing Teacher.[19] *Twenty and Ten*, a true story of courage and kindness, describes how French children helped protect Jewish children during World War II.[20] Biography and history are two open doors for learning justice and countering injustice. One cannot hate Anne Frank, Sadako, or Martin Luther King, Jr.

How Do We Move from Paralysis to Solutions?

In order to help children recognize and deal with injustices, we ourselves must see past problems to some possible solutions.

> When we have talked about pollution, war, and social justice issues in the classroom, I have always tried to emphasize that the students are going to be making the laws and decisions in the future and that it will be their responsibility to make the world better. After a discussion like this, Curtis said, "You are always talking about how it is up to us to make things better and it is our responsibility. I have been wanting to ask you for a long time, why don't *you* do something about the bad laws? Why do you keep saying it is up to us?"
> —*Irene Rhodes, Las Animas, Colorado. Grade 3*

Sometimes our suggestions and ideas seem like pipe dreams, but without hope and without vision there can be no future. Faith and hope include both clarity of vision and clarity of method. One does not always see the way ahead, but those first steps need to be taken. One's influence and actions may be small, but they are the promise of more to come.

Teachers and parents need to be involved in personal acts of kindness which overcome evil with good. Adults need to listen to children and extend their understanding of the issues and causes of war, assassinations, and the nuclear threat. Children in the nuclear shadow somehow need to have their fires of hope and faith and imagination kindled and kept burning. Children's suggestions need to be taken seriously. Creativity and imagination and a sense of humor are needed gifts in this age.

> One year our church had a balloon launch to promote our Bible day camp. A few weeks later a man at the Fort Dix, New Jersey, army base sent our nine-year-old son the card from his balloon. "Now," commented our son, "maybe that man will think about the Bible and realize that armies don't solve problems."
> —*Nancy Oswald Swartley, Perkasie, Pennsylvania. Age 9*
> *(via Marie Moyer)*

We need to eliminate causes of injustice whether they be in the home, classroom, community, or world. We must question evil and support nonviolent change efforts, whether they be within individual lives or institutions.

Atlee Beechy has devoted his life to justice issues and peace concerns. He identifies seven factors that can generate peace and reconciliation: movement toward (1) meeting basic human needs, (2) providing greater equality and justice, (3) showing greater cooperation and mutuality, (4) individuals and groups having a sense of self-worth and self-respect, (5) sharing power, (6) lowering the fear and threat level, and (7) experiencing the love of God in Jesus and his people. This chapter has illustrated all of these ways of growing toward peace.

There are many levels of involvement in response to injustice ranging from no concern to surface-level concern, to some depth, to a deep concern, and to a total life commitment. At which level are we?

> One of my kindergarten boys crouched with his father (a Ugandan medical doctor) and his younger brothers and sisters under a concrete staircase in their apartment building during one of the

bombings in Kampala, Uganda, in 1979. The kindergartner asked his father, "What if a bomb hits this building?" His Christian father replied, "That would be special and would take us straight to heaven." This incident tells me that it is only when we know the Prince of Peace that we can truly share faith and hope and peace with our children.

—*Lenora Dietzel Sempira, Kampala, Uganda. Preschool-Kindergarten*

9. What About the Future for Children?

Arnold and Wanda Mast Willems

TODAY'S children are tomorrow's politicians, scientists, sociologists, church leaders, parents, educators, philosophers, and psychologists; they will be the future. We are aware of this in our roles as an educator of elementary school teachers and an elementary school librarian, as parents of two children, as a children's Sunday school teacher and an ordained elder in the Presbyterian Church. We interact directly with children and with people who will be working with children. Our experience leads us to believe that children can be prepared to face the unknown future with confidence and competence through the concerted efforts of those who influence their lives.

"Why worry about the future? Won't it happen anyway? I can't control it. I don't have enough power. I'm not smart enough. Besides I have other, more immediate things to worry about. Kids will do what they want to do. They're more concerned about the here and now. They don't listen to me." Attitudes such as these are prevalent, defeatist, and must be overcome. They *can* be overcome.

A kindergarten teacher helped her students imagine a peaceful future.

Several weeks before Christmas I was browsing through a display of books at our church emphasizing peace. One of the books which caught my eye was *The Alphabet Tree*.[1] It is about a tree full of letters. Each letter had its favorite leaf where it sat rocking in the breeze. The letters huddled in the foliage of the lower branches when a storm came.

To avoid being scattered by the strong wind, a word-bug taught the letters to get together in groups of threes or fours and make words.

A purple caterpillar encouraged the letters to get together—to say something important. They agreed that a certain sequence of words was really important. The important words they chose were "Peace on earth and goodwill toward all men."

The caterpillar complimented the letters for forming these really important words. He asked that they climb on his woolly back. When the letters asked where they were going, the caterpillar responded, "To the president."

After reading the book to my kindergarten class, I asked, "What kind of world would we have if there were 'peace on earth?' How would people feel?"

Responses from the children were spontaneous. They spoke with deep feeling. I was encouraged to send the responses from the children to our local newspaper. *The Elkhart Truth* published the responses in an editorial on the Friday before Christmas.

—*Pauline Yoder, Elkhart, Indiana. Kindergarten*

The responses of these young children raise profound questions that head the sections in this chapter.[2]

The Elkhart Truth

Editorials and Opinions

FRIDAY, DECEMBER 22, 1978

Children's Voices

THIS IS a Christmas message from the mouths of children. It was compiled by a kindergarten teacher at Weston school, Pauline Yoder, who offered to share it with Truth readers.

The children's remarks came in a discussion of a story featuring a purple caterpillar with the words "Peace on earth and goodwill toward all men" on its back.

The teacher pursued the discussion by asking, "What kind of a world would we have if there was peace on earth? How would people feel?" The children's answers, she said, were spontaneous and spoken with deep feeling. Here are some of them:

They would be happy.
They wouldn't beat up people.
They would be nice.
They would be good.
They would listen to their mommies and daddies.
They would like each other.
They wouldn't fight.

They would listen to God, preachers, and babysitters.
They would give presents to everyone.
They would listen to their teachers.
They would never be mean to people.
They would play together.
They would share their toys.
They would be nice to each other and let them come to your house to play.
They would sit together.
It would be a different world.

They would have a big picnic table and eat.
The world would be pretty.
There would be no more yelling.
Everyone would be glad.
There would be no more throwing dishes.
Everyone would be happy.
There would be no more stealing and doing bad things.
There would be no more shooting.

You would feel comfortable.
You would feel rich.
There would be some flowers left.
There would be no more stealing other people's stuff.
They would love each other.
Everyone would be kind to one another.
Everyone would be thoughtful.

There would be no more throwing beer bottles.
There would be no more hits and fights.
There would be no more mean stuff.
There would be no more burning churches.
There would be no more burning houses.
There would be no more biting and pinching.
There would be no more fighting with other kids.

Everyone would be happy because Jesus was born.
It would be like Jesus was born again.
Teacher Pauline Yoder then adds these reflections:
"Children live in a world of confusion, restlessness, insecurity and violence. They are often torn as to what is right and what is wrong. Children are honest and uninhibited. They speak what is on their heart.

"Adults set the pattern, the model for children to follow. Which of the above responses best describes your model to the child? Is this model one that you are proud of, or do you feel it is one that needs to be changed so that the words on the back of the purple caterpillar become reality— that they bear out the message of importance: Peace on earth and goodwill toward all men. Peace! Peace! Peace!"

Will It Be a Different World?

"The dove of peace brings an olive branch to put into the guns."
Benjamin Yost, age 9

When contemplating the future, we should ask an initial question, "What will the future not be?" The future will not necessarily be more of the present. The future will not be a linear progression from today's world. There will be deviations, peaks of achievement, and real depressions in the human experience.

A return to the past is not possible or even desirable in many respects. The economic, social, and educational systems of the past cannot be replicated. The economic system has moved beyond agrarian values and cannot be forced backward. No self-respecting black, Hispanic, or woman wants to return to the social inequities of the past. And educationally we can look upon the three Rs with nostalgia and respect, but schools must go far beyond them in their teaching of children.

The future is a vast array of possible tomorrows, many alternative futures. Some of these possible futures are nightmarish in quality and can easily be imagined. Nuclear capability expands, weapons' systems proliferate, and the world becomes an armed camp waiting for an excuse for an explosion. The growing population with overcrowding, unemployment, depletion of the world's resources, and escalating political unrest—these forebode a probable but negative future.

Of course the kindergartners hoped for positive futures. Can you picture a world of international peace, social equality, beneficent and supporting technology, and balance of economy, food, and population? Can you imagine cancer, AIDS, and heart disease being eradicated, and an educational system developed to meet the needs of each child?

For too long people have merely been swept along with powerful forces which created the vast social changes of the last century. People have felt powerless in the face of this change. This sense of inadequacy is not a valid reason for inaction, especially for Christians, who know their ultimate future. They have the promise of a new heaven and a new earth. They should not have feelings of hopelessness or lack of confidence. They live "in the world" but "are not of the world" (John 17:11, 14).

The civil rights movement is a good example of people overcoming feelings of powerlessness and working together toward a common goal.

> The 1960s civil rights struggle in the South was a real part of my life. I was a college student in my home state of Tennessee during the time Martin Luther King, Jr., led the movement. So, years later, on the occasion of the new national holiday honoring Dr. King, I talked with my class about my feelings and experiences. One boy with a good memory learned a portion of Dr. King's "I Have a Dream" speech. He recited it for our class and, using the public address system, shared it with the entire school.
>
> To Kelly, who loves to write poems, I gave the suggestion of writing a poem in honor of this new holiday. She wrote, "My Dream."
>
> MY DREAM
> Kelly Short
>
> My dream is that the world will be full of love,
> My dream is that peace will be in the world like a dove.
> My dream is that there will be peace,
> Peace that will never cease.
> Oh that would be a joy,
> Oh boy!
> My dream is that of war
> There would be no more,
> And the blacks would be free—
> As free as me!
> —*Carolyn Gass Hertzler, Goshen, Indiana. Grade 3*

Dreams like Kelly's need to be encouraged, as well as discussions on what individuals and groups can do to make dreams of the future become reality. Are we wise and brave enough to make the hard decisions needed to plan for the future and to inspire children to meet the future with courage in the face of difficulties? Children must feel that life is worth living.

In reviewing two films on nuclear war, Danny Collum suggests that hope lies in the choice to live with grace and selfless love even amidst the worst possible circumstance. The message, he says, "is that the love of life, family, and neighbor that holds these people together in the aftermath of nuclear war is also the only force that, if extended to the human family, might keep war from happening." [3]

Will We Share?

Geoffrey Janssen, age 6

The gain in knowledge and its rapid dissemination have drawn people together into an essentially social world. It is becoming increasingly difficult for people to live in isolation. Few could function alone.

For those people living in technological societies, science and technology have solved many of the problems connected with providing food, clothing, and shelter. Children can see the contrast between the days of Laura in *The Little House*[4] books and present urbanization. Industry and modern farming produce the necessities in vast quantities. Food surpluses are stored in huge stockpiles but do not reach those in need even in our country. Will our children some day want to pass these technological blessings on to the less fortunate living here and in third-world countries?

Adults must provide ways to help children respond individually to community and global needs. Responding to these needs lays the groundwork for a more peaceful future. Notice how the teachers in the following accounts helped children to become personally involved in each project.

> For a number of years, Mrs. McIntosh and I had our fourth graders bring food donations in December to be distributed by the welfare department to the poor of Decatur. We had somebody from the department come for the food during the school day so the children could see their food being picked up. In this way we experienced sharing with the poor and needy.
>
> We got started in this project when Mrs. McIntosh and I proposed that our pupils give food to the hungry rather than gifts to us teachers.
>
> —*Paul S. Liechty, Decatur, Indiana. Grade 4*

> In my second year of teaching, I was impressed with Peter Spier's book *People*[5] and wanted to use it as a way to encourage reading and to develop awareness of differences and similarities among cultures. In our schoolwide Uninterrupted Sustained Silent Reading (USSR) program we recorded each book read on the auditorium wall. We decided to use *People* as our focus and took an imaginary trip around the world, writing titles of books read on posters of ships, planes, and cars.
>
> Each week we tried to have a speaker give a presentation on a different country. Jerry Weaver, the campus minister at Bethel College, brought slides from India to show us ways children in India are the same as children here. He also pointed out stark contrasts—children without clothes to wear and starving children with no homes.
>
> Our students didn't know how to respond to the pictures of deprivation since we hadn't prepared them in advance. But afterwards we had a serious discussion in my room about poverty and starvation. We talked about various charities and what kind of service or help is best. I think every one of my pupils felt lucky that day and also felt a kind of responsibility for those who aren't as fortunate.
>
> —*Kent Rychener, Newton, Kansas. Grade 4*

The project to bring money for Food for Friends was introduced to grades one through six by telling an illustrated story about a boy who wanted to earn money for a special church offering. But he spent each penny earned for something he wanted instead of saving it, until he felt quite sad that he had no money for the offering. He told his dear grandmother about the "runaway" pennies, and she helped him see that he wanted to give the pennies for the offering with only half his heart. The next penny earned he kept safely in his pocket and happily gave it to the special church offering.

Each child in our Sunday school was given a paper vegetable with slots for coins and also a letter for parents suggesting that the children earn money at home for Food for Friends. The superintendent explained how Mennonite Central Committee would use the money for seeds and for food in countries experiencing the disasters of war, famine, and poverty. When the children returned the coin-filled vegetable to Sunday school, they told how they earned the money.

—*Julia Smucker Penner, Mt. Lake, Minnesota. Grades 1-6*

After hearing of the famine in Ethiopia, I suggested to my class of sixth graders that if every child in our school gave a dollar for Ethiopian relief, we could raise about $300.

The class responded enthusiastically, making posters about the fundraising project during study hall. Soon parents, teachers, and children from all the classes in our school were donating money. The class developed a "moneymeter" to show how much money had been donated.

During the three weeks of the project, the moneymeter had to be extended until it reached halfway across the hallway ceiling. At the end of the project, on the day before Christmas vacation, a school rally was held in the gym. Several students revealed the final total—over $1,200—enough to feed 25 Ethiopian children for a year! The children presented the check to people from the Red Cross.

The children's comments on the project showed a new understanding of the needs of people in our world, the work of such agencies as the Red Cross, and how they as individuals and families can respond in a positive way to needs of which they are aware.

—*Marge Pletcher, Goshen, Indiana. Grade 6*

Older children might be involved in putting on a play or organizing a festival to help raise money for hungry people or those suffering from illnesses like muscular dystrophy.

Will We Be Kind?

The reasons third-world countries "have not" are primarily social, political, and economic. Technology may be able to produce enough food for all the world's hungry, but it cannot overcome the social barriers that lead to misunderstandings. Science and technology cannot solve social problems. Technology someday may be able to solve the problems of food production for the needy millions, but technology cannot solve distribution problems. Technology may be able to harness nuclear power but cannot control the cravings for power in people who have made the nuclear-powered weapon so important. In an increasingly interdependent world, science and technology cannot tell people how to get along.

Joe Smucker, age 11

Ridding the world of nuclear weapons would release money and energy needed for vital programs. Yet basic social problems will still exist, and the desire for nuclear weapons is a dangerous symptom of those problems. Ego, greed, and suspicion between and among nations will remain. The feelings of weakness, frustration, and alienation will yet exist in individuals. These underlying causes of violations of peace must be dealt with in the heart and conscience.

In the increasingly interdependent social world, the acts of the individual take on more significance. The motivations, feelings, and beliefs of the individual are especially noteworthy.

After visiting a number of kindergartens in China, I have become convinced that Chinese children learn early in life the value of peacemaking—perhaps I should say "of keeping peace." They are taught to respect family, school, their community, and country (in that order). Thinking only of one's self is a foreign concept to them.

Because of the current one-child-per-family policy in China, many parents are concerned that their child will become self-centered, arrogant, and rude. I feel that won't happen in most cases because of their great respect for other people.
—*Phyllis Ramseyer Miller, Chengyang, China. Kindergarten*

As principal of Sarasota Christian Elementary School, I encourage interest in others, concern for them, and sharing with them. Last year our daughter and first-grade classmates sent cards and letters to a parent injured in a construction accident. They also prayed for him. He was confined to his home for over six months, but he was able to attend a special party in the classroom during the last month of school. It was great for the children to see how their prayers were answered.
—*Samuel W. Martin, Sarasota, Florida. Grade 1*

The eight-week series of peace education at St. Pius Elementary School in Chicago included sessions centered on the following:
1. Self-esteem. The children made valentines to themselves.
2. Affirming others.
3. Interdependence. We made a book entitled "Some Things You Just Can't Do by Yourself." Each child thought of something one needs others for—to play catch, to run a race, to have a party. They contributed their illustrated pages to a class book.
4. Conflict resolution.
5. Racial awareness. We talked about pigment, and then each child was given a pack of twenty Crayola crayons in skin colors and colored pictures of themselves.
6. International interdependence. I read a book about Sadako Sasaki,[6] and we learned how to make paper cranes, symbolizing our wish for peace rather than atomic warfare.
—*Karen Kreider Yoder, Chicago, Illinois. Grade 4*

Frustration and alienation motivate an assassin to shoot a president or pope, and these attitudes affect the lives of vast numbers of people. A single person can cause chaos by hijacking a plane, holding people hostage, or going crazy with a car on a busy street. Science and technology cannot solve these problems; people, not machines, can solve them. People must decide how to solve not only the problems of nuclear proliferation, hunger, poverty, pollution, and depletion of energy sources. They must also solve the related social problems of alienation, frustration, and anger.

Marina is a special girl. She's an Anglo who moved to Kayenta when she was in sixth grade. Her parents are divorced, and her mother "sent" her here to live with her father. She rarely sees him, as he spends lots of extra time at work. Thus Marina is often left on her own.

Since Marina doesn't get the attention she needs, she seeks it by making up rather racy stories about herself and her friends. That alienates her friends from her and makes her more miserable than ever. Marina is one of the loneliest people I've ever met. I try to spend extra time with her outside the school setting. I pray for her a lot.

I've found Marina to be talented and loving. She was selected to participate in Project Discovery, a program for gifted students. I scheduled Marina with a group of sensitive and respected students. They have grown to care for her and have developed friendships. They've seen Marina's true self.

In Project Discovery, Marina wrote a song which expresses who she really is. In many ways it is a cry—a question deep within her heart: "What Would the World Be Like?"

Marina's song is original. The music is a combination from our two heads. I would hum a few bars, and Marina and I would see if it was what we wanted. I wrote it out because Marina doesn't read music yet. She is learning to play guitar in Project Discovery.

Marina has never experienced the kind of love she sings about. This has also been a good way for Marina to get attention in a positive way. She sang her song at the Middle School spring concert in early May. She got a standing ovation.

—*Nancy Ryan Nussbaum, Kayenta, Arizona. Grade 7*

Parents, educators, and church and community leaders cannot expect social problems to be solved by presidents or national government. Governments can deal with other governments and certainly with worldwide and national problems and priorities. But governments cannot solve social problems of the individual that lead to so much violence on an intensely personal scale. The solution to such problems must come from institutions which deal with the individual: families, churches, schools, social services, and businesses. Peace lies in the feelings, attitudes, beliefs, understandings, and values of the individual.

I started in the fall with a large world map entitled "Our World" posted on the bulletin board. Strings ran from each country to a doll standing on a table below the map. After our morning prayer, "Father, we thank Thee. . . . Help us to do the things we should," we repeated a poem with words and pictures in front of the room. Each month the poem changed. My favorite was this one:

Dear God,
You do not care about the house in which I live,
The cost of clothes or the color of my skin.
You mostly care about the way I feel,
Toward other persons and toward you.[7]

In about three days, the children had memorized it.

Each year during Black History Week, we talked about black heroes (many pictured on our bulletin board) and learned of their great accomplishments. We watched movies and filmstrips about persons such as Sojourner Truth, George Washington Carver, Martin Luther King, Jr., and others. We read stories from library books.

We talked about how brave Dr. King was in his nonviolent marches to plead for justice. One film was about Dr. King speaking to angry blacks and trying to calm them. Suddenly someone reported his home was bombed. The children were impressed that Dr. King insisted that no one shoot or get violent even though he did not know if his wife or baby were alive or dead!

We cried when Dr. King was killed. We learned freedom songs to sing to relieve our hurts a tiny bit.

—*Miriam Brackbill Nissley, Goshen, Indiana. Grade 3*

I have tried to make the children of our Sunday school aware of needs in the world by choosing projects that reflect current needs

What would the world be like?

Tune by Marina Stover
Harmonization by Charles Peachey

to the Mid - dle East, the world would be much bet - ter if

we could have more peace. Peo - ple are peo - ple, no

mat - ter where you are. If we could work to - geth - er, then

we'd go ver - y far.

D.C. al Fine

such as corn for Africa and school kits for Kampuchea. We brought in articles from the paper and showed the pictures.

However, having a Laotian family living in the community has been a vital, firsthand lesson. The children responded to the needs of the family offering them a used sewing machine, boots in the winter, and a gift for the new baby. Somehow, seeing your gifts received and used is an added blessing. We do indeed live in a small world.

—*Twila Hostetler Nafziger, Wadsworth, Ohio. Kindergarten-Primary*

Will We Love Each Other?

Erica Friesen, age 8

Parents, teachers, church leaders, and others must decide what future for a child is most desirable. We must decide what action is needed to nurture that future. We must decide what qualities are vital in the individual of the future and how to best foster those qualities.

With the rapid expansion of knowledge and the increasing variety of occupational options, schools are no longer able to impart all the information and provide all the experiences a child will need. Emphasis must be placed on the skills needed to learn and gather information when necessary. Children must be taught how to learn and to choose to grow toward peace.

An interest of mine has been nature and ecology. I believe that the more knowledge and information children and adults have about nature, the more care and respect they will show for it.

One of the favorite units in second grade incorporated studying birds, insects, wildlife, wild flowers, and ecology. We did this through books, filmstrips, study prints, creative writing, murals, and actual hands-on experiences.

Our study culminated with an all-day field trip to the Merry Lea Nature Center. We felt rewarded by seeing children excited and turned on to observing and participating in nature and preserving it, without the center offering a gift or gimmick. The children returned to school empty-handed but with a new appreciation of nature.

—*Marlys Oesch Stutzman, Goshen, Indiana. Grade 4*

One of our primary-junior department Sunday school offering projects was to buy food for The Pantry, a local group that provides food for people in need in our church area. When the offerings were totaled, we had $50 to spend.

Several children from each department along with the two superintendents met one afternoon to shop. We made our lists, trying to select items we thought were most useful and nutritious. We split our list, took two carts, and had two groups going through the store.

When we got ready to check out, we told the checker what we were doing and asked for a subtotal to be sure we used all the money. The checker was cooperative and kind. He gave us time to get a few additional items.

The children displayed a real sense of responsibility while they shopped. As we were checking out, one of them commented, "Fifty dollars for that! It doesn't look like that much."

What a lesson in economics—and we did have five bags full!

—*Margaret Kauffman Sutter, Lombard, Illinois. Grades 1-8*

Dr. Seuss was a master of fantasy with his contorted creatures and exaggerated rhymes, but many of his books are also quite serious in theme. Children love *How the Grinch Stole Christmas* with its message of peace and goodwill; the *Sneetches*, about prejudice; and *Horton Hatches the Egg*, about responsibility.[8] These books are fun, but the messages come through loudly and clearly.

—*Wanda Mast Willems, Laramie, Wyoming. Grades K to 6*

In competency-based education, children may learn certain facts and skills to be able to pass a test, but go no further. Process also is not enough. Children may know how to think and make choices, but what values and attitudes shape that thinking and guide the choices? Schools, churches, and especially parents need to foster desirable values and attitudes in children.

As we tucked our young child into bed at night, we discussed, "What made us most happy today?" and "What was our least happy time?" Parent and child verbalized what was important to each! It led to sharing through prayer.

—*Cara Frey Ulrich, Archbold, Ohio. Ages 4 and 5*

When Geneva Hershberger taught in a small remote mountain community in Bolivia, she had her students write letters to my class about their homes, school, lifestyle, and country. My class did an excellent job of realizing the situation of the Bolivian children and what would be appropriate to include in our letters to them. They developed an interest in a community quite different from their own experience.

—*Jane Zehr Birky, Wheatridge, Colorado. Grade 3*

Parents, churches, and schools can encourage values which lead to accepting and respecting others by concentrating on a specific child. A lecture to the class about the moral value of nonviolence will not be as effective as guidance based on the needs and background of an individual child.

In social studies the way our textbook dealt with American history made it seem as if the United States never did anything wrong. I couldn't teach an Indiana unit and not show what the settlers did to the Native Americans, so I had to use various books.

In the text I now have, we start out by working with the concept of what culture is. I try to relate that concept to the students' experiences throughout the year. If problems arise, we look at the different ways of solving problems. I remind the students that just as different cultures have different ways of providing their food, shelter, and clothing, so different people can have different viewpoints on the same issue.

I ask quarreling students to sit down to talk over their problem. I ask one to listen while the other tells that side of the story, and then ask the other to listen. After getting both sides of the story, I tell them that often the truth is somewhere in the middle. They each need to look at the problem from the other's viewpoint. It usually works.

—*James A. Martin, Middlebury, Indiana. Grade 5*

One year one of my students came to class filled with unvented feelings. Invariably he would be involved in a fight before the day was over. I talked with him about how those feelings would come out some way, but he could determine the direction. We helped him learn a nondestructive way of relaxing. He would step outdoors and do twenty exercises (jumping jacks). It is hard to be in a tense, fighting mood after vigorous exercise.

—Ardyth Hostetler Steckly, Houston, Texas. Grade 4

Children's attitudes influenced by television are often due to oversimplifications or stereotypes: good guys versus bad guys, winners and losers, bigger is better, and heroes and superheroes. Children need to be guided to understand, for example, that bigger is not necessarily better and that winners are not always right. And, as in *Millions of Cats,*[9] a twentieth-century classic, conflict over who is the prettiest may be fatal.

Children are immersed in a culture of overabundance. They learn what it is they should want long before they can analyze what they need.

Eighteen-month-old Jessica, my great-niece, was riding with us from my father's apartment to our house. She was sitting in her car seat in the back of our car jabbering to herself as we traveled the fast-food strip along U.S. 33. Suddenly we heard her say, "Taco Bell." To our amazement, we noticed we were passing Taco Bell on our right. A little further on when we passed the Kentucky Fried Chicken restaurant, Jessica commented, "Chicken." We heard her repeating, "Rax, Rax," as that restaurant came and went from view.

When my niece came to pick up Jessica, I said, "You must take this child to every fast-food restaurant there is because she recognized Taco Bell, Kentucky Fried Chicken, and Rax."

"She has never eaten in any of those places," declared my niece. Impact of media influence at eighteen months!

—Martha Mishler Bender, Goshen, Indiana. Age 18 months

The family is the first place children learn values. If children feel alienation, frustration, and anger at home, they will carry this over into antisocial acts outside the home.

True peace certainly begins with peace with ourselves and God. Soon after we had adopted our son, I personally was going through some hard times when I did not have peace with myself. There were unresolved conflicts with a person close to me. As a result, I was taking out my frustrations on my son in much too violent a way. He needed calmness and care to help him adjust to his new environment. Instead, he was being punished with spankings and impatience, which made him react in a violent way, hollering, kicking, and hitting.

When I realized what was happening, I asked God to forgive me and give me the patience to deal with our son positively. Already many patterns had been set, but when I then answered him softly and requested something instead of yelling, he reacted calmly. He had far fewer temper tantrums. With God's help, I maintained a calmer, more relaxed atmosphere, so our new son reacted in a more relaxed way.

—*Verla Fae Kauffman Haas, Bluesky, Alberta. Ages 2-3*

Schools and churches can work to overcome negative attitudes by concentrating on the personal and individual, stressing social responsibility, and interacting constructively and peacefully with others. The child must learn processes for solving interpersonal problems as well as how to solve math problems.

Darren was a student who left my class to attend self-contained special education for two hours each morning. He returned in the middle of our independent work sessions. Before entering my classroom, Darren would throw open the door and roar like a lion. My other students would acknowledge Darren's entrance with muffled laughter and giggles.

After a few days, I decided to discuss Darren's behavior with the class. The students talked about their frustrations with Darren as a classmate and offered their ideas as to why Darren needed attention in this way. They were quite willing to help Darren with this particular situation.

We decided to ignore Darren the next time he made his grand entrance. Everyone agreed that it would be a team effort. One giggle or look in Darren's direction would undermine our efforts. Perhaps if Darren did not get attention, his roaring would cease.

Did it work? I wish I had a video of my students' faces as they concentrated on ignoring Darren and his roar! Not only did Darren's roaring cease forever, but this experience paved the way for many student-initiated plans to help Darren and other classmates!

—*Nancy Ryan Nussbaum, Kayenta, Arizona. Grade 3*

Several weeks after reading *The Alphabet Tree* (see the beginning of this chapter), four children were playing in the block-building corner of the room. A dispute arose between two of them about sharing their toys for the building they had constructed. One child nearby witnessed what was taking place. He walked over to the two children, raised his hand, and said in a strong voice, "Peace!" All at once there was silence, the dispute ended, and sharing took place!

—*Pauline Yoder, Elkhart, Indiana. Kindergarten*

During morning devotions at our school for missionary children, boys and girls choose one especially meaningful verse to put on the blackboard. Since they pick out the verse, it is theirs and is helpful to them in times of difficulty.

—*Jewel Miller Schlatter, Amazonas, Brazil. Grades 1-2*

I used "Golden Keys" to encourage children to develop life patterns for peace building. The poem was mounted on the bulletin board.

GOLDEN KEYS

A bunch of golden keys is mine
To make each day with gladness shine.

"Good-morning," that's the golden key
That unlocks every day for me.

When evening comes, "Good-night," I say,
And close the door of each glad day.

When at the table, "If you please,"
I take from off my bunch of keys.

When friends give anything to me,
I use my little "Thank you" key.

"Excuse me," "Beg your pardon," too,

When by mistake some harm I do.

Or if, unkindly, harm I've given,
With "Forgive me" I shall be forgiven.

On a golden ring these keys I'll bind;
This is my motto: "Be ye kind."

—Author unknown

Each day one of the attributes of Christian living was stressed—cheerfulness, courtesy, thankfulness, forgiveness—using a Bible verse and corresponding story. Students made their own copy of the golden key presented that day. They added it to the key ring which bore the words, "Be ye kind." The chain of keys provided review at school and at home. Children reminded each other to use the various keys.

—Lucile Miller Miller, Elkhart, Indiana. Grade 3

To educate our children for a desirable future, emphasis must be on developing thoughtful persons who are willing to make wise decisions in solving problems.

Whenever my students went on a field trip or were the recipients of some special favor by persons outside our classroom, we always wrote thank-you letters to express our appreciation. Sometimes we drew pictures to include with the letters. We took many field trips. We learned to thank the ones who gave their time and services by writing to them.

—C. Kathryn Yoder Shantz, Elkhart, Indiana. Grade 2

Resource persons coming into classrooms can share their decision-making processes. A nurse told how she wanted to cheer and help people, so she decided to become a nurse like her mother. Adults who show a sense of satisfaction for service rendered in what they do to earn a living can influence children in career choices.

Our son, Bob, said several years ago, "Dad, you have always done what you enjoy doing. I want to do that too." Recently he turned down a higher-salary job offer in preference for one that was more in line with his values. He felt he would enjoy it more.

—Geraldine Gross Harder, Seattle, Washington. Ages 22 and 25

The underlying curriculum of social adjustment and encouragement of values must take on greater significance. Children learn values and attitudes from emulating and imitating the examples of adult models as noted in the preceding instances. The teacher who handles a classroom conflict with calmness, reason, and without anger is providing an excellent role model. Children should be taught and shown how peace can be achieved.

> James was an emotionally disturbed youngster. He was free in telling me how awful he felt before he had his loud outbursts. I asked him if he would like to be responsible for keeping a table organized behind the movable bulletin board. That actually worked. When he went back to the table and arranged and rearranged, I knew he was having a bad day. It seemed to take care of his urge to upset everyone in the room including the teacher.
> —*Elsie Eash Sutter, Goshen, Indiana. Grade 4*

Models from the field of literature can motivate children to rise above circumstances and find peace amidst turmoil.

> At six years of age Kevin was already severely labeled. While children were usually not tested and labeled until second grade, Kevin came into first grade with the label "learning disabled" already attached because of his difficulties in learning to read. In addition, Kevin had the label of "speech disability" for his speech impediments and his auditory discrimination difficulties.
>
> Every day Kevin was pulled out of my classroom to attend special classes for his reading and speech difficulties. Kevin's interactions with other children indicated that in addition to his learning difficulties, his level of social and emotional development was below that of the other students. Kevin primarily engaged in parallel play rather than playing cooperatively with others. The other children left him alone to retreat into his own play.
>
> Kevin appeared to be behind in all areas of development and seemed primed for failure in school. He spent most of his time in school off in his own little world. Sometimes, however, what was going on in the classroom seemed to catch his attention and inside him the potential for learning would shine through. He particularly enjoyed listening to stories being read aloud and

learning about the authors and illustrators of those books.

We featured a different author or illustrator each week in our classroom. I would tell a little about the person's life and put up a display of their work as well as read some of their books aloud during the week. My goal was to encourage children to read good literature and to feel that they knew authors personally and could search for their work in the library. We read and talked about authors such as Ezra Jack Keats, Eric Carle, Pat Hutchins, and Robert McCloskey. While Kevin seemed to be attending to these studies of different authors and illustrators, I was not sure how much he was understanding or gaining from these experiences.

One morning as school was about to begin, Kevin trudged into the classroom holding a book carefully under his arm. He proudly held the book aloft as if it were a precious painting, saying, "I have an Ezra Jack Keats!" This picture of Kevin will always remain with me: marked for failure by all the school standards, he was displaying a book as if it were the most precious find in the world.

Despite all his learning difficulties, Kevin valued and recognized good literature and the authors and illustrators who created those books. Keats became Kevin's favorite author and was a person he constantly searched for when he went to the library. Keats's stories about children who find love and supportive relationships in their gloomy environments provided models Kevin needed to give him courage to rise above his difficulties. While learning remained difficult for him, Kevin developed a desire to succeed and to be able to read the books he valued so highly.

—*Kathy Gnagey Short, Millersburg, Indiana. Age 6*

By age twelve only 7 percent of a child's time has been spent in school. This simple fact demonstrates the value of the home, the church, and the community as well the school in the development of the child. Parents should look at the models they present for their children. They need to look at the atmosphere of the home. Is it peaceful, intellectually stimulating, warm and loving, sustaining and encouraging?

When our two oldest children were in grade school, we set aside one evening each week (Thursday for us) to interact separately with them. On Thursday, Dad would take our son out for supper while Mom took our daughter. The next Thursday evening, Dad

would take our daughter while Mom took out son. We had originally set the third Thursday for all four to eat out together and the
fourth Thursday for just Mom and Dad to eat out. But the first and
second Thursdays were much more popular and became a good
time of sharing—so much so that we just alternated those two
Thursdays.

—*Faye Newcomer Litwiller, Goshen, Indiana. Elementary*

Our two sons are three and five years older than our daughter.
Often the brothers provoked their sister to tears by name-calling
or put-downs. As concerned parents, we would intervene and
"admonish" them to love each other.

On one occasion, we sat around the dining table and asked
each one to give a shape and color to each other. With paper and
crayons, we drew the table for a beginning. We made no suggestion to be either positive or negative, but asked that they draw
what reminded them of each of us.

What followed was one of the most significant times of affirmation that we recall after twelve years. It was a turning point toward peaceful relationships as brothers affirmed their sister as
yellow sunshine—one who brought light and cheerfulness. Our
sons beamed as they heard affirmations of true-blue trust and
green refreshing and growing qualities.

For us as parents to hear the love and care coming through to
each other and to us gave us a continued base of peace to build
on, even in the midst of differences.

—*Mary Yutzy Herr, Goshen, Indiana. Ages 9 to 14*

My goal is to teach children to accept and extend forgiveness. To
work toward this, I ask for forgiveness from them if I've gotten
upset or done something I shouldn't have. My children were embarrassed the first several times I asked them to forgive me. But as
they got older, they could accept it more easily. It now appears to
be easier for them to accept it and also ask for forgiveness or at
least say, "I'm sorry for. . . ."

Their grandfather reported that one time he asked their forgiveness for something, and they both responded with a smile,
hug, and "That's okay, Grandpa." We need to ask for forgiveness
ourselves in order to teach it to children.

—*Suzanne Beechy Kauffman, Scottdale, Pennsylvania. Intergenerational*

Will There Be Some Flowers Left?

The future is shaped by the social responsibilities assumed in the present. A Kenyan proverb reminds us, "Treat the earth well; it was not given to you by your parents. It was loaned to you by your children."[10] The American Indians have similar regard for nature as acquaintance with the Paiutes by a Wycliffe translator indicates.

"For me peace is a meadow."
Lisa Koop, age 6

In our work with the Paiutes, we have become aware of their deep respect for nature, for the animals that are hunted, and for the plants that are gathered. None of these are taken for granted. To them, hunting is not a sport, and what they hunt and get, they use for food and for the skins and furs. If they can't use it, they don't hunt or gather it.

We try to teach our daughters a respectful appreciation for animal life. One summer we took a few days' vacation camping with our three girls, ages nine, seven, and three. Near our campsite ran a small creek where the girls enjoyed playing. One day they found a toad to play with and later put it back in the water before returning to the campsite. We had the opportunity to talk with them about animals in their natural habitats and how it can be harmful to animals to remove them from their environments.

Several weeks later, friends of ours went on a weekend trip and asked us to take care of their rabbit, a young wild cottontail they had found out in the field. The tendency of our daughters was to want to hold and cuddle the rabbit. We had the rabbit for only several hours before it died. This was another opportunity for us to talk to our daughters about animals and their natural environments. Captured animals might be fun for a while, but no matter how cute, cuddly, and furry they might be, it is detrimental to the natural life of the animal.

We learned later that another family frequently caught wild rabbits and tried to raise them, but they survived only a short time in captivity.

—Mary Ann Aschliman Eastty, national forest
near Bend, Oregon, and McDermitt, Nevada. Ages 3, 7, 9

An appreciation of the world around us leads to careful use and preservation of its resources.

Each October on one of those bright perfect days, I would get permission from our local college to use its nature preserve. What a glorious afternoon we would have, admiring the colored leaves, watching squirrels getting ready for winter, finding pretty stones and interesting bits of wood, identifying birds, and watching white clouds in the blue sky. We would trudge back to school with pockets and hands and hearts full of the wonder of God's creation.

—Leona Yoder Hostetler, Urbana, Ohio. Grade 3

From Sunday to Sunday, children enjoyed singing an illustrated version of "Each Little Flower that Opens." Some children, on their own at home, made illustrated songs to sing in family worship. We also made an illustrated copy cooperatively in our class worship time.

> He gave us eyes to see them,
> And lips that we might tell
> How great is God almighty,
> Who has made all things well.[11]

Little children want to be good stewards of God's beautiful world.

—Mary K. Nafziger, Goshen, Indiana. Grades 1-3

In our many campouts, we have taught our daughters that garbage and trash should always be disposed of properly. We make a special point of leaving the areas free of debris. On Labor Day, our family and another couple drove into the mountains for a picnic. We found paper plates, disposable diapers, and even food dumped in the bushes around the picnic area. This drew quite a few bees, which made our own picnic less pleasant than we had anticipated. It was a vivid example, especially to our girls, of what can happen when we do not take care of God's creation.

—Mary Ann Aschliman Eastty, mountains, Northern Nevada. Ages 3, 7, 9

One fall an abundance of acorns fell on our school playground. They kept finding their way into the classroom. I thought, There must be a better way to make use of them than by repeated show-and-tell experiences. So I took soil and cups to school. Each student planted an acorn. After several weeks the acorns started to grow. The children were jubilant with their own trees.

At parent-teacher conferences, I used each tree to explain the growth of their children: "This is an oak tree planted by your child. It will continue to grow tall and sturdy as you give it the needed soil, sunshine, and water. Just so, your child will continue to grow as you supply the needed food, clothing, shelter, and loving care." I sent each tree along home with the parents.

—*C. Kathryn Yoder Shantz, Elkhart, Indiana. Grades 1-2*

We are saved by hope, as Job of old said,

> There is hope for a tree,
> if it is cut down, that it will sprout again,
> and that its shoots will not cease.
> Though its root grows old in the earth,
> and its stump dies in the ground,
> yet at the scent of water it will bud
> and put forth branches like a young plant.
> —*Job 14:7-9, NRSV*

Arlin Hunsberger, project director of Pan American Development Foundation, had a dream to work through children to again clothe Haiti's denuded hillsides with hope-bearing trees. Projè Pyebwa (Project on Environmental Education) was approved in 1988.

School children in rural Haiti are being trained to rehabilitate parts of their environment which have become badly degraded. At school they learn how to grow hardwood and fruit-tree seedlings in plastic sacks to transplant later in the students' gardens at home. On field trips to plantations, farmers show how to prune and manage resprouts after trees have been harvested. This provides instruction on how to maintain and harvest trees on a continuing-yield basis. Some schools maintain their own demonstration plot. Future farmers learn the importance of planting trees, of caring for trees, and of respecting trees.

We found it difficult to change the habits and attitudes of farmers who respond to their immediate need for cash by cutting trees. Protecting tender trees from goats and cows is a continual challenge. In working with schools, we recognize that change may come through a new generation of planters. The US Agency for International Development puts 80 percent of its investment in education. Regional team leaders work with teachers, give training sessions, encourage formation of "Friends of the Trees" clubs, and provide highly illustrated reforestation booklets. They hope that the schools will integrate environmental concerns into the curriculum. Learning to conserve, protect, and appreciate the God-given environment can also help to lead the next generation out of a life of poverty.

—*Naomi Derstine Hunsberger, Port-au-Prince, Haiti. School age*

If children are to be faithful stewards of the world and its resources, they need to be guided to think what is within their power to do. In an important growing-up story, *Storm Boy*[12] and his rescued pelican understood the wind and the waves and thus are instrumental in helping to rescue a shipwrecked crew.

Following are examples of budgeting money to support life-giving projects, eating healthy foods, turning off lights for resource conservation, and reusing throwaways:

Matthew has had an allowance since he was five or six. To begin with, we gave him twenty-five cents a week. He had money to spend for things he wanted—usually candy or toys.

In first grade he saved his money for an incredibly long time for a toy advertised on television which cost $8.00. He played with it for several days and then lost interest completely.

When Matthew was in second grade, we raised his allowance to one dollar a week. He gave ten cents for church and put ten cents in savings.

Now Matthew has a paper route. He keeps out $1.00 a week for church, $1.25 for spending, and the rest goes into the savings account in the bank.

Matthew is learning that if he wants something special, he has to save for it. He's learning that part of his money does go to help the work of the church.

—*Marlene Aschliman Bell, Elkhart, Indiana; Sterling, Illinois; Norton, Kansas. Ages 5-9*

Even in preschool, children can be made aware of the fact that the kinds of snacks eaten can have an effect on their bodies—their health. One day at school is Fruit Day; another day is Vegetable Day. We also have weeks when certain colors are emphasized and tie that in with foods. We might have zucchini or cucumber circles during green week, apples during red week, and bananas during yellow week.

We try for as much variety as possible to give the children the opportunity to taste many new foods. Usually they will taste them when they see their peers eating them. I always say, "Give it a try."

I encourage positive comments and usually say, "This is just the way God made it grow for us to enjoy."

—*Twila Hostetler Nafziger, Wadsworth, Ohio. Ages 4-5*

Several faculty members in human development and family life who are laboratory school teachers at the University of Alabama have developed an energy awareness curriculum.[13] It is designed to aid children in understanding the sources and uses of body energy, mechanical energy, fossil fuels, solar energy, and electricity. This curriculum develops the concept of how to use energy wisely (conservation).

Children are introduced to this study through interesting activities, songs, and games. The unit contains activities which help children learn through firsthand experiences, by manipulating materials, by discussing what is happening as it takes place, by noting examples set by adults, and through play.

—*Carolyn Smith Diener, Tuscaloosa, Alabama. Ages 3-5*

I am frequently reminding my children to turn off lights when they leave a room or to close the refrigerator door quickly or to turn off the water while brushing teeth. As many mothers and teachers know, one is not always certain that the teachings are becoming a part of a child's life.

One day, however, our three-year-old son let me know that he had assimilated some of my teaching on energy consumption. I

was vacuuming his bedroom when I discovered I had left the dusting attachment in the other room. I told him where I was going and why and started to leave the room. My son promptly turned off the vacuum (which I had intended to let run). When I questioned as to why he had done this, his reply was, "We mustn't waste electricity, Mom."
—*Suzanne Beechy Kauffman, Scottdale, Pennsylvania. Age 3*

One thing I tried to do, especially in the economically depressed, throwaway-minded Appalachian area (trash piles on every mountainside, junked cars in every stream bed), was to use recycled materials for craft projects. Indian crafts were excellent for that. Brown paper bags are a great substitute for animal skins, rinsed drinking straws can be cut for beads, and feathers can be made from construction paper scraps. Dried seeds are in abundance in the Appalachian fall. In all my craft projects, I tried to stress, "You can do another one at home."
—*Joyce Gingerich Zuercher, Harlan, Kentucky. Grades K-1*

Will We Be Happy?

"A person shaking hands with another person and the sun."
Adam Klaus, age 4

Children are often afraid of the unknown. They are inexperienced and do not know how they will react to new situations. Change is often frightening for children. Moving to a new school, coping with divorce, remarriage of a parent, death, or arrival of new siblings—these are enormous problems for a child. They are problems for adults! Many children and adults are worriers. We worry when we could be engaging in constructive thought, planning, and action. Children worry about problems which are beyond their power to solve.

This powerlessness too often becomes frustration.

A crying nine-year-old said to his teacher, "I'm so afraid. I was so afraid when my dad left, and when my mother married another man. Now that man left, and my mother is going to marry somebody else. I'm so afraid. What will happen to me?" Fortunately, his teacher could give him a new schoolroom experience and many lovely things to think about which helped him feel that life was worth living.

> Bruno, a nine-year-old in our son John's class in school, sometimes drops by our house. He is a likeable, communicative boy, open in a nonaggressive way. His mother works at a nearby grocery, and he often stays there with her while she works. A few months ago he explained that his father couldn't work because he was sick—an alcoholic.
>
> This past Sunday when Bruno came by, I asked him about the store. He said, "Oh, we're going to sell it. That way I can get a new schoolbag. We're separating in our family. We've moved to a room where my mother sleeps on a bed. My brother, the lucky one, sleeps on a mattress, and I sleep in a chair. We're separating because of alcohol. Drinking is one big accident. We're going to move to another house. It's going to be good."
>
> Two days later my husband, Stephen, went into a nearby bank and heard this same Bruno, alone, talking to a cashier, saying, "And if my mother comes in here, please give her the money because we're separating in the family. . . ."
>
> Bruno strikes me as being amazingly resilient. I am amazed by his courage and by the way he verbalizes his situation. There's a Nigerian proverb, "What the child says, he has heard at home." Someone has been helping Bruno to focus his anger on the source of the problem. He said, "Drinking is a big accident," instead of saying, "Drinking (or my dad) is bad." Someone has been helping him leave a bit of room for objectivity and respect for his father.
>
> I am struck by this example of "peace education" in a difficult situation, and by its contrast to thinking of peace education as some formally constructed educational program.
>
> —*Jean Gerber Shank, Brussels, Belgium. Age 9*

In so many cases, children are burdened with adult-size

problems which they are expected to share. Deep depression leads to suicide even among young children, and this is a growing problem in America. Children need new hope in a depressing world.

To be able to cope with the problems of the present and face the unknown future without worry, the child needs to feel confident and secure deep within of being competent, capable, and ready for what might come. This requires love from family and friends, an education that provides the skills needed to cope with future change, and an abiding faith that leads to the realization that there is an eternal future with God.

Families of Chicago Housing Authority's ABLA Project increasingly experience the realities of the drug culture and related crimes. Youths, who otherwise would be in school, are on the streets selling drugs to drive-by customers. A high-rise apartment building without security provides a temporary hideout from police.

The lure of drugs is multifaceted. Take drugs to feel good! Sell drugs to get money and prestige among peers! Caring adults must start early to prepare children for the right responses to these lures.

Children who growing up in this environment experience waves of negative attitudes and behavior. Bethel Day Care Center provides a safe island of positive messages, inviting children to make peace with their inner feelings and undergirding their successes with more opportunities for happy experiences.

Marquail was beginning his second day in the Threes Group. He was overwhelmed by his distress over leaving his mother after a week's vacation from daycare and adjusting to a new classroom and teachers. During a washroom routine after breakfast, Marquail still could not contain his grief.

Concerned over his crying, Ms. Evans suggested, "Marquail, what I want you to do is go to the bathroom and cry as loud as you want. Then wash your face with a paper towel and come back."

Marquail slowly moved into the bathroom. Suddenly there was a two-second outburst, and without another word Marquail came back. When asked "Are you finished?" he said, "Yes."

From that moment on, he was like sunshine after the rain.

There has been a greater buoyancy in his step and lots of smiles.

Marquail may not remember the details of this incident in the future. But the acceptance of his emotional needs by an understanding adult was essential to releasing inner strength for his moment of need. We pray we can follow him in his later needs.

—*Ruth Kehr, Chicago, Illinois. Age 3*

One of our primary boys became terminally ill. As a Sunday school department, we were much concerned about his welfare. We prayed for him and his family. We sent him cards. We prepared a surprise box of gifts, asking that he open one each day. Our friend died. We had our own memorial service on a Sunday morning in his memory. His father spoke about his son's illness and death. The fact that our friend had gone ahead of us to heaven seemed to be of comfort as we thought together about his illness and death.

—*C. Kathryn Yoder Shantz, Goshen, Indiana. Grades 1-2*

When there is a death in the family of kindergarten children with whom I work, I give the family an illuminated and laminated copy of "God's Home in Heaven" by Katherine Royer mounted on bright paper. It has always been well received.

This practice began when Sue Ann had leukemia and was often unable to join her kindergarten classmates at school. We worked out a visitor's schedule so her friends could share their love with her at home. We had frank discussions about the fact that doctors were still looking for the right medicine to help people who have leukemia.

Sue Ann died late one Sunday night. I told the children on Monday morning and read "God's Home in Heaven." We were glad Sue Ann wouldn't be sick any longer. I sent a note home with the children so parents would all be officially informed of Sue Ann's death.

It wasn't long until I began getting calls from parents with similar messages. "Whatever you did was right. Our child was relaxed about the news." I sent a copy of "God's Home in Heaven" to each family for future reference.

This same message of comfort and hope was given on the occasion of the murder of a kindergartner's father. Having read Greg's copy of "God's Home in Heaven," his grandmother said, "It helped me, too," as she dealt with the mysterious shooting death of her son, Greg's father. Adults as well as children need spiritual resources to draw on when they meet the unexpected.

—*Kathryn Aschliman, Goshen, Indiana. Kindergarten*

During my last year in Newfoundland, no teacher could be found for the four students who would be in the special education section, so I offered to take that class. These four children included a thirteen-year-old girl who sat on the floor and couldn't put on her own coat, a five-year-old Down's syndrome girl, a seventeen-year-old mute, and Tommy, the eight-year-old first cousin of the mute. Tommy had cerebral palsy and was in a wheelchair. The first time Tommy's mother brought him to my room, it was time for the opening. I introduced the hymn, "For God So Loved Us" [14] and we sang,

> Love so unending,
> I'll sing thy praises.
> God loves his children,
> loves even me.

I explained to the children that God loves even me with a hearing aid. I took the aid, showed it to each child, and explained how great our God is to have made people smart enough to make hearing aids for people and also people smart enough to make wheelchairs like Tommy has to take him places.

We had been having a devotional each morning. Teachers were selected in Newfoundland by denominational boards, and Bible reading was the rule. We used the hymn "For God So Loved Us" each morning for some time. If we used another one, Tommy would request that we sing this one also. The one- or two-sentence prayers and a verse which followed began our day.

A few weeks before Easter, Tommy announced, "Miss, I have some information for you."

"What's that, Tommy?"

"Oh, I have to go home now, but I'll tell you pretty soon."

The next morning I almost forgot to ask Tommy about the information he wanted to give me the evening before.

"Oh, Miss, I talked to God last night."

"How good. What did you say to him?"

"Well, 'I love you, God.' "

"And then what did he say?"

"I love you, Tommy."

"Oh, that's beautiful. And then what happened?"

GOD'S HOME IN HEAVEN

od has a home for us in heaven which is the best home of all. It is more beautiful than any place we have ever seen. God has many lovely surprises for us in heaven. God's beautiful home in heaven is for you, and Daddy, and Mother, and Sister, and Brother, and Grandfather, and Grandmother, and for all of us who love God and ask him to forgive our sins.

Jesus told his friends about heaven. Jesus said, "I am going to heaven. Someday you can live with me in heaven."

Jesus' friends wanted to know how to get to heaven. Jesus said, "I am the way." When it is time for us to live in the happy home in heaven, Jesus will show us the way.

When we are too sick or too old to live here, we can live in God's home in heaven. In heaven, God will give us new bodies.

We will always be well and happy.
We will never feel sad or cry.
We will never be afraid or get hurt.
We will always be kind and good.

When our friends die and go to heaven, we need not be sad, because they are very happy in God's beautiful home. And we can see them again when we go to live in heaven.

John 14:1-6; Revelation 21:4

My Book About God's Gifts, Katherine Royer[15]

"Oh, then I told him that Miss teaches us about how we can talk to you and I have a bad hand and I'd like for you to touch this bad hand very much. And see, he did!"

Tommy's right hand had always hung limp, and he had to reach over with his left hand to pick it up and put it on the little table that he had on his wheelchair. But this morning he raised that right hand above his head without any aid.

Well, I was excited and also delighted. I said, "Tommy, I want to thank God for this right now." And I did.

Then Tommy said, "I want to thank him, too." And he thanked God for touching his bad hand.

I explained, "But Tommy, that's not your bad hand. That is your right hand."

"Oh yes, that's right," Tommy said.

One morning Tommy announced, "Miss Lehman, I have a song I wrote, and I want you to write it on the chalkboard."

"What kind of a song did you make for us? Is it something that someone taught you?"

"No, I made this up myself." And with his left hand he tapped the rhythmic beat on his wheelchair and said,

I know what it's like to pray with you, my Father,
I know what it's like to pray with you, my Father,
I love you more and more.

"Oh, that's lovely, Tommy. Who taught you to play that? Did your brother? He plays a guitar, doesn't he?"

"Oh yes, but he plays for the club. He wouldn't play this."

In the weeks that followed, Tommy added other verses. By the end of the year he had made up seven. And every time he brought a verse, the five of us would sing it.

One verse was "Thank-you, Lord, for touching my right hand. You help me more each day." Another was "Thank-you, Lord, for helping with my speech. I talk better every day."

Tommy didn't speak clearly and neither did Dorothy, the little five-year-old. When we asked, "Which verse shall we sing today?" Dorothy would request, "Thank-you, Lord, for helping with my speech." She would sing that one over and over.

Tommy's mother brought him some clothing at Christmastime. She always carried him. He was rather heavy for her to carry, but she did it anyway. And so Tommy made a verse for that:

The clothes that you gave me were bought by my mother.
The clothes that you gave me were bought by my mother.

She lugs me around each day.
And then the last verse was
Thank-you, Lord, for helping with this song.
Thank-you, Lord, for helping with this song.
I can praise you every day.
It was a joy indeed to hear those children sing this whole song.
—*Melva Lehman, White Bay, Newfoundland. Age 8*

Will We Listen to God?

The church through the many individuals around the world must take the lead in thinking and planning for a peaceful future for children. The church is uniquely able to deal with the spiritual, social, and material, and with the individual and society. The church has the necessary autonomy, viewpoint, and organization to do constructive future planning. The church is spiritual and optimistic in orientation. Both orientations are fundamental to planning a peaceful tomorrow for children.

Craig Christophel, age 8

Churches are in a position to influence those who affect the lives of children—parents, schoolteachers, social service workers, and children's club leaders.

Our summer Bible school was to be held Sunday through Friday evenings for children four years old through grade eight. The commitment sheet given older persons in the congregation asked for volunteers to serve as teachers, food suppliers for the staff, prayer partners, recreation leaders, participants in drama. . . . I had taught several years and decided this year to check "drama."

Bible school superintendent Jane Leatherman reported to me that a number of high school and college students had also checked "drama." She asked if I would lead the group to present a drama each evening at assembly time. The action would capture the attention of the young as well as the older students.

We chose "peace" as the theme for our Bible school assembly. The dramas we used were adapted to the seven young people for the six- to eight-minute presentations. We used a scene of conflict between two boys, an imaginary international conflict, a dramatization of the *Sneetches*, the life of Menno Simons taken from *Peace Be with You*, and Jacob and Esau from the Old Testament.[16]

The assistant Bible school superintendent, Marian Hostetler, reported that the dramas were quite effective. She also mentioned that the recreation leaders taught games from *New Games Book*[17] emphasizing noncompetitive peaceful play.

"Make Peace" was the theme song of the Bible school. Bookmarks with those words were given to children who came to the superintendents with personal peacemaker stories. One pair reported that they went outside to play so their mother could rest. Another couple argued at the beginning of class, but then decided to draw a picture cooperatively.

The Bible school project emphasized "peacemaking." Gifts were for groceries to be distributed by LaCasa, a local agency providing assistance to low-income and Spanish-speaking people. In every session, each class bought groceries with their offering money from storekeeper Darrel Hostetler, who wore a meatcutter's apron. The purchases were placed in a grocery cart. Before the end of the week, it overflowed into four additional grocery bags.

The message of peace was truly proclaimed to the neighborhood. Our congregation has a small number of children. Some classes were composed entirely of community children. Marian thinks we could continue this peace theme next year.

—*Ron Weirich, Goshen, Indiana. Ages 4 and up*

The church can take a trilevel approach to future planning. Its influence must be a leaven in global, national, and community planning. A congregational approach to future planning must deal with individual adults and children so that responsible adults who guide the lives of children are vitally concerned about the quality of the future.

For 1985 the peace group at Parkview Mennonite Church in Kokomo, Indiana, compiled a calendar with an original drawing for each month. Children created most of them, and a few were done by adults. They were glued together and given to all households in the church as reminders to work and pray for peace throughout the year.

The calendar's monthly themes included Martin Luther King Day (January), Disabilities Awareness Week (March), Peace Pentecost/Mennonite World Fellowship Sunday (May), Independence Day (July), Hiroshima Day (August), and Thanksgiving/Hunger (November).

The small, loosely organized peace group has been functioning for several years. Made up of several families with young children plus a few others, it usually meets monthly and has planned and carried out a number of programs and activities. The group's purpose is to encourage each other in active peacemaking and in teaching the ways of peace to their children.

Other activities have included producing short plays for the congregation, making some bulletin inserts at special times of the year, folding "peace cranes" to be sent to Russian children, and participating in a community gathering to commemorate Hiroshima Day.

—*Margaret Glick Metzler, Kokomo, Indiana. Intergenerational*

On all these levels, from global to individual, our goals must point toward and identify what future is desired. Undesirable futures also should be identified so that time, effort, and money can be expanded to impede undesirable tomorrows.

Linda Liechty helped organize a school in Dublin, Ireland, whose purpose is to "teach" peace.

Basically it's a school run by people who want their children to grow up to love and respect each other. Forgiving and forgetting is a universal problem, but here the need is vital.

Essays by children in sixth class, ages ten to twelve, describe the school. Excerpts follow:

The name of the school is called the North Dublin National School Project. It was set up by a group of parents on the north side and people from the community who want children to have a good education and to learn about the different religions. The school is multidenominational, coeducational, and democratically run. The school gives children freedom to believe. It was set up so girls and boys would mix a lot better. —*Colin Moore*

This school is a multidenominational school, which means that people with different beliefs can be educated together and can learn to respect each other and other people's beliefs. In this school the children learn about different religions and beliefs.

In the two years since the school opened, the number of pupils has risen from 95 to 253. I hope that in years to come all the schools in Ireland shall be like this one. —*Vanessa O'Brien*

In the month of May, a group of children from the Forge School Project Belfast came down on an exchange visit with the fifth and sixth classes of our school, the North Dublin National School Project.

While the children from Belfast were down here, they noticed an awful lot of differences about the streets, the shops, and our homes. When we went up to them, the army vehicles on the streets were real frightening. I think this visit was a good idea because it showed us that not everybody in the North of Ireland was violent and most of them wanted peace. —*Sinéad Libreri*

I believe in peace in all countries in the world, especially Ireland. We have a big problem in the North of Ireland. I think that war in northern Ireland should be stopped but with no force. —*Bruce Ballagh*

A suggestion is to have mixed multidenominational schools in the North. If all religions learned to recognize each other as humans, probably there might be less violence. —*David Jacob*

I think so often of the spirit in which Mary Royer taught her classes, and I wish she were here. I see this school as trying to embody the principles by which she taught every day. I am still grateful for the many, many ways she showed us that it was possible to "teach" love and respect.
—*Linda Bender Liechty, Dublin, Ireland. Ages 10-12*

How can the church help to relieve world hunger and the depletion of energy sources? How can the church influence the use of national resources for peaceful ends and help in the solution of unemployment in economically depressed areas of the country? How can individual children and adults be helped beyond feelings of frustration, alienation, and anger? Illustrative answers have been given throughout this chapter.

The church, with the concerted efforts and energy of its many individual members, internalizes these questions and finds answers for individual action and for working within the group.

> As a deaconess (deacon's wife) I have considered peacemaking a major goal and have worked diligently to live a life of peace. In school I have never been involved in a formal way in planning a peace program, but I have always considered it as important as teaching content material. Even in parent-teacher conferences, I had peace-living as a major inherent function.
> —*Esther Eash Yoder, Grantsville, Maryland. Elementary*

The church's thinking can be guided by ministers who will draw upon and include the best, most knowledgeable, and most respected people from various disciplines, such as sociology, psychology, theology, political science, biology, medicine, physical science, education, and technology. These people must not only be knowledgeable but wise, seeking spiritual guidance. Together these people can prayerfully guide decisions about the future and lead congregations toward actively participating in planning and shaping futures of children.

> The way of love is being taught and lived in Africa today. Chaybah, the first Christian ever of his Senoufo village in Burkina Faso, shared the following experience:
> Once we realized that someone had been stealing from us. Then the women told me that they had seen who it was—that they had seen B. take some sorghum from our granary. I was so angry that I couldn't even sleep that night. Then the Bible made me think that I should do something for B. rather than something against him. So the next day I went to his house with some sorghum and said, "This is a present for you—take it." He took it, but was so ashamed that he wouldn't talk to me.
> My mother was unhappy with what I'd done. She said, "Why didn't you come and give the grain to me if you've got extra?"

But since then, B. has never stolen from me. Sometimes he even comes to buy grain from me!

—*Marian Hostetler, Senoufo, Burkina Faso. Adult*

The future can be a vast unknown to be faced with fear and trepidation—or the church can help people work together toward a future of hope and peace.

This past year and a half, I have been involved in discipling twenty high school students. As we studied God's Word and basic truths of the Christian life, I have seen changes in their lives and in their concern for the world. They have experienced the peace of Christ in their lives and now want to share that with others.

Binshal is a smart student who always scored 100 percent on my math quizzes and exams. He also was involved in my central discipleship group but was often shy and reserved. However, one afternoon we went out witnessing, he and I. Since I didn't speak the local language well enough, Binshal had to do all the sharing since no one understood my English. That afternoon Binshal led twelve adults to find peace with God through Jesus Christ.

Since that time I have seen Binshal's concern for the world's future increase. He realizes that only Jesus can bring peace to our world. During long vacations he works at home in his church, and during school he helps disciple other students in their Christian lives. He even told me once that he thought he had the gift of an evangelist. Through people like Binshal, the world will find answers and peace.

—*Steven Ray Gibson, Langtang, Nigeria. Teenage*

I am part of a house-church fellowship which works consciously at relationships between adults, between parents and children, and between adults and the children in the fellowship.

Recently there was a weekend retreat with sixty to seventy adults and children. The weather was cool and damp, so most of the time we were all indoors. After about forty hours of this close living, I began to realize that the atmosphere was remarkably calm and congenial. The children obviously enjoyed each other.

During the last few hours, two-year-old Rachel was carried from the main room screaming. A few minutes later eight-year-old Michael had three-year-old Raphael by the hand, and I heard Michael tell someone they were looking for Rachel to tell her they

were sorry. Evidently Raphael had pushed Rachel, and friend Michael was helping him make things right.
Michael played a strategic role in rectifying a dispute.
—*Lorraine Roth, Shakespeare, Ontario. Ages 2-3, 8*

For a more peaceful tomorrow, the role of the church is most crucial. Each Christian must accept responsibility for an expanded role in making peace. Only by concerted thinking, planning, and effort can the future be faced with confidence and understanding. "Peace on earth" parallels "good will toward all."

Let us hold on firmly to the hope we profess,
  because we can trust God to keep his promise.
Let us be concerned for one another,
  to help one another to show love and to do good. . . .
Do not lose your courage, then,
  because it brings with it a great reward.
You need to be patient,
  in order to do the will of God
  and receive what he promises. . . .
To have faith is to be sure of the things we hope for,
  to be certain of the things we cannot see.
—*Hebrews 10:23-24, 35-36; 11:1; TEV*

The great reward will come when our growth toward peace brings us into face-to-face relationship with God through Christ, the Prince of Peace.

Then I saw a new heaven and a new earth;
  for the first heaven and the first earth had passed away. . . .
And I heard a loud voice from the throne saying,
  "See, the home of God is among mortals.
He will dwell with them as their God;
  they will be his peoples,
and God himself will be with them;
  he will wipe every tear from their eyes.
Death will be no more;
  mourning and crying and pain will be no more,
for the first things have passed away."
—*Revelation 21:1, 3-4, NRSV*

Mary Royer,
A Messenger
of Peace

Elaine Sommers Rich

MARY Neuhauser Royer was one of my outstanding teachers at Goshen College during the war and postwar years of 1944-47, although I never took a course under her. Each Tuesday and each Thursday afternoon of my last three college years, I climbed the Ad Building stairs to her third-floor office. There I worked for her, or more accurately, I was taught by her. I watered the plants in her office and classroom, returned books to the library, and learned that

> Green things growing and fresh coats of paint
> Make a pretty classroom out of one that ain't.

My specific assignment was to type the manuscript she wrote for Sunday school teachers' and pupils' books published quarterly by Herald Press. For these lessons I also wrote illustrative stories, for which she often supplied the central idea and plot. I became adept at following her beautiful handwriting, even as it curled around the edges of a page.

I also learned a philosophy of writing for children. Mary Royer highly respected the children for whom she wrote. She

considered only the best as good enough for them. She set
rigorous standards and worked "as unto the Lord." Mary carefully thought through the theological implications for children
and expressed gratitude for her courses in Greek and for her
pastor father's library with its aids for Bible study. Her meditation for teachers never failed to inspire me. Here is a sample:

> *Thoughts for the Teacher's Meditation:* "Perfect love casts out fear,"
> John writes to the believers. How clearly we see this promise
> fulfilled in the fearful Peter who became the fearless disciple after
> his restoration by Jesus. The story of the life of Peter is another
> proof of the words, "not by might, nor by power, but by my spirit,
> saith the Lord of hosts." We cannot be brave and courageous in
> our own strength; but through his strength we are made strong to
> face an unknown future. Preparedness for the future consists not
> in a foreknowledge of events to come, but in the assurance that
> the strength of the Lord is our joy and sufficiency no matter what
> the experience may be. (*Primary Teachers' Quarterly*, Dec. 31, 1944)

What influences shaped Mary Neuhauser Royer? Her three
names provide a clue. Mary (what name could be more biblical?) inherited over 200 years of peace-church tradition. Her
father, Isaiah W. Royer, came from a Church of the Brethren
home in Ohio. Her Mennonite mother, Christina Neuhauser,
graduated from a Quaker academy in Tennessee. Outgoing
love flowed from their home in Orrville, Ohio, where Mary and
her sisters Katherine and Elizabeth grew up. In that home gentleness, song, Scripture, and prayer were as much taken for
granted as air to breathe. Favorite verses were Philippians 4:6-
7; Isaiah 26:3; and Psalm 4:8, "Grandpa's verse," which their
grandfather always prayed before sleeping, and so the family
did, too.

The earliest American Royer, Sebastian, a French Huguenot
fleeing religious persecution, came to Penn's Woods in 1718.
His oldest son married a Brethren girl and joined her church.
From this lineage came Mary's father, Isaiah.

As a boy, Isaiah Royer attended Sunday school with his
cousins at the Oak Grove Mennonite Church near Smithville,
Ohio (because his Brethren congregation did not then have a

Sunday school). There he was baptized. As a young man, Isaiah attended the Smithville Academy, Ada Normal School (now Ohio Northern University), Elkhart Institute (now Goshen College), and Bethany Seminary in Chicago. At Smithville he studied with a teacher taught by a student of Pestalozzi, the great Swiss educational reformer and champion of education for children of the poor. Mary Royer's students sometimes call themselves sixth-generation descendants of Pestalozzi.

Meanwhile, in Tennessee, his companion-to-be Christina Neuhauser pursued her education. The wisdom of this remarkable educator is expressed in the teaching ministries of three daughters and a namesake granddaughter (writer of chapter 4). Daughter Katherine says of her mother's youth:

> Her life was filled with music. . . . She learned yet-unrecorded spirituals from freed woman "Aunt Mary" Loomis. . . . At Tina's graduation in 1893 from Friendsville Academy, she sang in a quartet, played a piano solo, and was also organist. Tina confessed Christ as her Savior under the ministry of a Quaker woman preacher and was baptized into the Concord Mennonite Church. . . . At Holbrook Normal School and at the University of Tennessee, she prepared for teaching, then taught primary school for ten years near her home in Tennessee and in the first public school in St. Tammany's Parish, Louisiana.

The young minister Isaiah Royer, on a visit from seminary and pioneer mission work in Chicago, delivered his first sermon in his home church at Oak Grove. Tina Neuhauser (visiting her sister) heard him preach, and a friendship began. On October 16, 1906, they were married at Concord, Tennessee, and began 60 years together. They moved to Goshen, Indiana, where Isaiah was copastor of the College Mennonite congregation. Their firstborn, Mary, arrived on December 26, 1907.

When Mary was three, the Royers moved to Chicago to work at the West 26th Street Mission near Jane Addams' Hull House. Isaiah continued biblical studies at Bethany, where he helped Dean A. C. Wieand develop graded Sunday school lessons for the Church of the Brethren. Later Mary and Katherine carried on their father's early work by helping produce the first Mennonite graded curricula for children. Their conjoint research and teaching continues into the '90s in a unique home-church nursery series designed by Katherine.

In 1912 the family moved to Orrville, Ohio, where I. W. and Tina pastored the congregation for the next 40 years. People called Isaiah "Mr. Sunday School" because of his vigorous promotion of Sunday schools as his denomination's general Sunday school secretary. For 35 years Tina directed the children's department in the Orrville Sunday school, teaching children many memory Scriptures, including the Beatitude "Blessed are the peacemakers: for they shall be called the children of God."

In Mother Tina's teacher-education notes, her daughters found quotations describing her philosophy of teaching:

> Every child is entitled to a happy childhood.
> Throw gentle influences around children.
> Telling is the least part of teaching.
> Education is life, and life is education.
> We need to give children happy memories to tide them over
>   times of trouble.
> The unexpected is the usual.

Mary says, "We had a happy childhood at home, church, and school." She speaks gratefully of the thoughtful courtesy of public school teachers and classmates to them as conscientious objectors during the sad, dark days of World War I.

Mary recalls that before she went to school, her mother read aloud to her *The Five Little Peppers and How they Grew* and *Black Beauty*, establishing lifelong patterns of taste and joy in reading. "Our parents' love of literature, their beautiful oral reading and storytelling, and the experiences they shared with us from their own public school teaching were strong influences in my love for teaching," she affirms.

In 1926, Mary entered Goshen College. She remembers with gratitude that C. Z. Yoder (for whom Goshen's Yoder Hall is named), then minister at the Oak Grove congregation (near her Orrville home), paid the train fare for her freshman trip to college. She treasures a letter in which he wrote, "My prayer is that the Lord may richly bless you in your efforts and that the Holy

Spirit may lead you day by day in fields of usefulness. Yours for Christ and his church. C. Z. Yoder."

Mary never tires of telling of those who helped her financially through college and graduate school. "Dean Noah Oyer paid my first semester tuition from his tithe. . . . E. K. and Mary Greenawalt said, 'If money keeps you from returning, we will pay your tuition and lend you the balance for your college work.' At the end of my senior year, they said, 'We have decided to make it all a gift.' . . . President S. C. Yoder and C. Z. Yoder personally lent me the money for my master's work."

When Mary received a B.A. degree from Goshen College in 1930, she found no teaching position because of the depression. But President Yoder asked her to go to George Peabody College for Teachers for a master's in elementary education, with a view to teaching in Goshen's elementary teacher education program. Of her Peabody experience she says:

> I felt providentially led to Lucy Gage, my adviser, a dauntless pioneer in early childhood education, and a fearless worker for quality education for children which would create continuity between home and school, and make school a place of peace and joy for creative learning in real-life settings.

From first grade through high school and on into college, Mary wanted to become a missionary teacher in India, but her vocation lay elsewhere. Her master's thesis, however, reflects this early interest. Entitled "Education of Village Children in a Central Province Mission, India," it is a study of experimental educational programs of farsighted missionary teachers.

After receiving her M.A. from Peabody, Mary returned to Orrville, Ohio, to teach in the integrated schools there. A family friend lamented, "Isn't it too bad that with all her education, Mary is going to teach second grade!" But Mary commented, "I thought translating Latin and Greek a good deal easier than planning the education of 26 seven-year-olds and the one fourteen-year-old slow learner who was 'mainstreamed' into my second grade that first year."

In 1933, Mary joined the faculty of Goshen College, where she established the first laboratory kindergarten. For several years she received as salary her board and room in Kulp Hall, ten dollars per month cash, and credit on her sisters' college expenses. Over the next years, hundreds of Goshen College students studied with her. She did further graduate studies at Peabody, the University of Chicago, and Teachers College of Columbia University.

Mary received her Ph.D. from Ohio State University in 1950, with a major in elementary education and related fields in philosophy of education, adult and parent education, and teacher education. She calls her Ohio State adviser, Dr. Ruth Streitz, and other professors there, "vigorous educators who valued my Anabaptist belief that life and learning, practice and profession cannot be separated."

During her graduate study, Mary noted similarities between experimental laboratory experience recommended for teacher education, and the kinds of experience available to students at Goshen College through Voluntary Service (VS) under the Mennonite Central Committee. Those first five years of the VS program (1944-49) included center city work with delinquents and service in mental hospitals, deep rural poverty, and European war reconstruction camps and orphanages. Out of these studies grew her doctoral dissertation, "The Implications of a Voluntary Service Program for the Improvement of Teacher Education," and a pioneering, innovative teacher education program for Goshen College, which later became accepted practice in many colleges and universities.

For almost half a century, Mary Royer poured her energy into the education of students at Goshen College. Daily class preparations, assignments, conferences with students, faculty meetings, faculty committee meetings, visits to classrooms to aid student teachers, job placement for graduates, chapel addresses to the entire student body—these made up the warp and woof of her everyday life.

Many activities took her outside the Goshen College classroom. As mentioned earlier, she served as nonresident editor and curriculum writer for Herald Press from 1936 to 1950. During the 1940s she wrote primary vacation Bible school books (later translated into German, French, Spanish, and

Hindi). In addition there were consultations and conferences with parents and teachers locally and churchwide for Goshen College and Herald Press, involving much travel. From 1957 to 1969, she was privileged to spend her Christmas, Easter, and summer vacations helping in the nursing care of her parents in the California home of Dr. and Mrs. Charles A. Neff (sister Elizabeth), her niece Christina, and sister Katherine.

During Dr. Royer's 1964 sabbatical, she conducted teacher education workshops in the Dominican Republic and Puerto Rico. On her 1972 sabbatical, she was language arts consultant at the Navajo Rough Rock Demonstration School directed by Ethelou Yazzie in Chinle, Arizona. When Mary and longtime colleague Dr. Olive Wyse visited our family in Japan in 1972, she followed up former students there and in Australia and Hawaii.

From 1962 to 1974, Dr. Royer visited nine college and university campuses as a member of evaluation teams of the National Council for the Accreditation of Teacher Education. She taught graduate extension courses in developmental reading and children's literature for Ball State University.

Postdoctoral studies at the University of Minnesota, Akron University, and Claremont Graduate School enriched her teaching.

After formal retirement in 1979, Mary taught part-time on campus until 1982. She continues active research and interest in the study of children's literature and has an extensive sharing library of recent and past treasures to help bring joy and peace to children.

Included in this volume are many testimonials from students such as Gerald B. Miller (page 42) and Sharon Schrock Beechy (page 118). At Mary's retirement, Shirley Erb Gingerich wrote:

With Mary every year was "The Year of the Child." Along with her love for children is her deep love for older people, especially her high regard for her parents. When teaching, it seemed right to ask myself not only "What would Jesus do?" but also "What would Mary Royer do?"

In 1980, Mary said to members of the Goshen College Mennonite Church, "I have tried to pass on to my students what *my* teachers in home, church, and school have taught me—that whatever our particular assignment, we are each of us 'ministers of Christ and stewards of the mysteries of God.' Ours is 'the mighty ordination of the nail-pierced hands.' "

You will find her students on every inhabited continent of the globe and the islands of the sea; in inner cities, remote deserts, highlands, and far-north frozen wastes, where they work in home, school, church, and community as preschool, elementary, secondary, college, and university teachers and administrators, parents, counselors, therapists, librarians, preachers, writers, and illustrators.

Today Mary, book in hand, lives in her "little white house on the prairie," surrounded by beautiful family antiques. Above the great-great-grandfather's stand-up writing desk is niece Christina's block print "Tree of Life." Below it are recent family photos which include Katherine; Christina; Christina's parents, Elizabeth and Dr. Charles Neff; Christina's husband, Dr. Jeffrey Okamoto; and their beloved four-year-old son, Stephen, a joy to all the family.

Both Mary Royer and I have traveled far since those war years in the 1940s when as a student I climbed the Ad Building steps to her office to write stories and type manuscripts. But together we and all those participating in the making of this book are *privileged* (one of her favorite words) to be part of Jesus' good news community of peacemakers scattered around the world.

Notes

Chapter 1: *Where Is Peace Born?*

1. Katherine Royer, *Nursery Stories of Jesus* (Scottdale, Pa.: Herald Press, 1957).

2. Royer, *Nursery Stories.*

3. *My Little Bible Picture Book* (Elgin, Ill.: Brethren Press, 1980).

4. Dorothy Nicholson, *Egermeier's Favorite Bible Stories: Selected Stories for Young Children* (Anderson, Ind.: Warner Press, 1965).

5. Dorothy Nicholson, *The Children's Bible* (New York: Golden Press, 1965).

6. Faith McNulty, *The Elephant Who Couldn't Forget* (New York: Harper & Row, 1980).

7. Peggy Parrish, *Amelia Bedelia* (New York: Harper & Row, 1963).

8. Erik H. Erickson, *Insight and Responsibility*, (New York: W.W. North Co., Inc., 1964), 153.

9. Doris Buchanan Smith, *Kelly's Creek* (New York: Thomas Y. Crowell Co., 1975).

10. Leontine Young, *Life Among the Giants* (New York: McGraw-Hill Book Co., 1966), 170, 172.

11. Ira Gordon, *Children's Views of Themselves* (Washington, D.C.: Association for Childhood Education International, 1972), 21.

12. Kathleen and James McGinnis, *Parenting for Peace and Justice* (Maryknoll, N.Y.: Orbis Books, 1981).

13. Miriam Schlein, *The Way Mothers Are* (Chicago: Whitman, 1963).

14. Geraldine Gross Harder, "Visit Your Students at Home," *Christian Herald*, Nov. 13, 1981, 16-17.

15. Edward Reichbach, "A Child's Self-Concept: Accent the Positive," *Parent Cooperative Preschools International Journal: A Magazine of Cooperative Learning,* Summer 1982, 4.

16. Robert Coles, "The Inexplicable Prayers of Ruby Bridges," *Christianity Today,* August 9, 1984, 17-20.

17. *Peacemaking for Children* (Milwaukee Peace Education Resource Center), 2, no. 2 (Spring 1984): 2; used by permission.

Chapter 2: *How Can Children Live Confidently in Spite of Fear and Hostility?*

1. Martin Luther King, Jr., *NEA Today* (Mar. 1983): 10.

2. Eloise Salholz with John Taylor, David Gates, and Susan Klein, "Kids with Nuclear Jitters," *Newsweek*, October 11, 1982.

3. *Weekly Reader.*

4. "K.I.D.S.," *The Goshen News*, June 17, 1986; used by permission.

5. Bill Drake, "Our Children: Nuclear Education and Nuclear Fears," *Families Acting for Peace*, PPJN Newsletter, St. Louis, Mo.

6. *Cease News* 3 (Spring 1983): 1.

7. Jeffrey C. Hindman, "Painful Words," *Physicians for Social Responsibility Newsletter*, Fall 1982.

8. Katherine Royer, *Happy Times With Nursery Children at Home and Church* (Scottdale, Pa.: Herald Press, 1987), 130.

9. "Parenting in the Nuclear Age," *What Shall We Tell the Children?* (Oakland, Calif.: Parenting in the Nuclear Age, 1983), 6.

10. Sibylle K. Escalona, "Children and the Threat of Nuclear War," *Education for Peace: Focus on Mankind* (Yearbook of the Association for Supervision and Curriculum Development) (Washington, D.C.: ASCD, 1973), 160.

11. Patsy Skeen, Charlotte Wallinga, and Ligaya Palang Pagulo, "Review of Research: Nuclear War, Children and Parents," *Dimensions*, July 1985, 27.

12. Jackie Shepard, "Talking to Children About Nuclear War," *Educators for Social Responsibility*, May 1982, 10.

13. Kay Allen, "A Shelter from Fear," *Guideposts*, Nov. 1982, 7ff.; reprinted with permission from *Guideposts* magazine, copyright © 1982 by Guideposts Associates, Inc., Carmel, New York 10512.

14. Pat Fellers, *Peace-ing It Together* (Tigard, Oreg.: Peace-ing It Together, 1982), 1.

15. As reported by Gordon Oliver, "Teaching Peace to Our Children," *National Catholic Reporter*, Dec. 14, 1982, 16.

16. Dr. Robert Coles, "Children Not Afraid of Nuclear Threat," *Harvard Gazette*, Sept. 7, 1984.

17. Barbara Kantrowitz and Connie Leslie, "Teaching Fear," *Newsweek*, March 10, 1986, 63.

18. Ron Jones, *The Acorn People* (New York: Bantam, 1977).

19. "Kids, Toy Guns, and Aggression," *Today's Child*, Feb. 1983, 7.

20. "Kids," 7.

21. Jane E. Brody, "Venting Anger May Do More Harm Than Good," *The New York Times*, Mar. 8, 1983, 13, 15.

22. Charlotte Zolotow, *The Quarreling Book* (New York: Harper, 1963).

23. Clyde Robert Bulla, *The Poppy Seeds* (New York: Crowell, 1955).

24. Julia Sauer, *The Light at Tern Rock* (New York: Viking, 1951).

Chapter 3: *How Do We Help Children Choose to Live the Good News of Peace?*

1. James Metzler, "A Shalom Focus for Christian Education," *Builder*, Nov. 1979, 2-8.

2. Theodore Taylor, *The Cay* (New York: Avon, 1977).

3. Rhea Zakich, "Simple Secrets of Family Communication," *Reader's Digest*, Aug. 1986, 156-160.

4. Stephanie Judson, *A Manual on Nonviolence and Children*, 2d ed. (Philadelphia: New Society Publishers, 1984), 34.

5. Rebecca Caudill, *A Certain Small Shepherd*, (New York: Holt, Rinehart and Winston, 1965).

6. Watty Piper, *The Little Engine That Could* (New York: Platt & Muck, 1954).

7. Celestino Piatti, *The Happy Owls* (New York: Atheneum, 1964); Florence M. Taylor, *Growing Pains* (Philadelphia: Westminster Press, 1948); John Steptoe, *Stevie* (New York: Harper and Row, 1969); Elizabeth Starr Hill, *Evan's Corner* (New York: Holt, Rinehart, and Winston, 1967); Maryke Reesink, *The Two Windmills* (New York: Harcourt, Brace, and World, 1967).

8. Brock Cole, *The King at the Door* (Garden City, N.Y.: Doubleday, 1979).

9. Doris Buchanan Smith, *Kelly's Creek* (New York: Thomas Y. Crowell Co., 1975).

10. Geraldine Gross Harder, "Through Children's Eyes," *Builder*, January 1968, 6.

11. Elizabeth Hershberger Bauman, *Coals of Fire* (Scottdale, Pa.: Herald Press, 1954); Cornelia Lehn, *Peace Be with You* (Newton, Kans.: Faith and Life Press, 1980); Anna Pettit Broomell, ed., *The Friendly Story Caravan* (Philadelphia: J. B. Lippincott Co., 1949).

Chapter 4: *How Will I Make a Place of Peace for Children?*
1. E. B. White, *Charlotte's Web* (New York: Harper, 1952).
2. Honeytree, "Evergreen" (Waco, Tex: Myrrh, Word, Inc., 1975).
3. J. R. R. Tolkien, *The Return of the King* (New York: Ballantine Books, Inc., 1965), 33.
4. Gerald C. Studer, *Christopher Dock, Colonial Schoolmaster* (Scottdale, Pa.: Herald Press, 1967, 1993), 224.
5. C. S. Lewis, *The Lion, the Witch, and the Wardrobe* (New York: Collier Books, 1970).
6. C. S. Lewis, *Surprised by Joy* (New York: Harcourt, Brace and World, Inc., 1955), 66-67.
7. Marguerite L. DeAngeli, *The Door in the Wall* (Garden City, N.Y.: Doubleday, 1949).
8. Anne Holm, *North to Freedom* (New York: Harcourt, Brace, Jovanovich, 1974).
9. Laura I. Wilder, *Little House on the Prairie* (New York: Harper, 1953).
10. Marguerite Henry, *Misty of Chincoteague* (Chicago: Rand McNally, 1947).
11. Meindert DeJong, *The Wheel on the School* (New York: Harper, 1954).
12. Beverly Cleary, *The Mouse and the Motorcycle* (New York: W. Morrow, 1965).
13. John O. Stevens, *Awareness* (Moab, Utah: Real People Press, 1971), 135.
14. George MacDonald, *Lilith* (Grand Rapids, Mich.: William B. Eerdmans Publishing Co., 1981), 25.
15. George Henderson, ed., *Education for Peace: Focus on Mankind* (Yearbook of the Association for Supervision and Curriculum Development) (Washington, D.C.: ASCD, 1973), 189.
16. Studer, 77.

Chapter 5: *How Can We Encourage Empathy and Guide Peaceful Interaction?*
1. Mary Joan Park, *Peacemaking for Little Friends: Tips, Lessons and Resources for Parents and Teachers* (St. Paul: Little Friends for Peace, 1985), dedication page.
2. Dorothy Kobak, "Teaching Children to Care," *Children Today* 8 (March-April 1979), 6-7, 34-35.
3. Charles A. Smith, *Promoting the Social Development of Young Children* (Palo Alto, Calif.: Mayfield Publishing Company, 1982), 82.
4. Russell Hoban, *The Little Brute Family* (New York: Avon Books, 1966).
5. *Sing with Me* (Nappanee, Ind.: Evangel Press; Newton, Kans.: Faith and Life Press; Scottdale, Pa.: Mennonite Publishing House, 1977), 43.
6. Joan Fassler, *Howie Helps Himself* (Chicago: A. Whitman, 1974).
7. Taro Yashimia, *Crow Boy* (New York: Viking, 1955); Eleanor Estes, *The Hundred Dresses* (New York: Harcourt, 1973).
8. Dorothy Corkille Briggs, *Your Child's Self-Esteem* (Garden City, N.Y.: Dolphin Books, 1970), 109.
9. Philip H. Phenix, *Philosophy of Education* (New York: Henry Holt and Company, 1958), 199.
10. Janice Udry, *Let's Be Enemies* (New York: Scholastic Book Services, 1978).
11. Arnold Gesell, et al., *Infant and Child in the Culture of Today* (New York: Harper & Row, 1974).
12. Maya Pines, "Good Samaritan at Age Two," *Annual Editions in Human Development, 1981/82* (Guilford, Conn.: The Dushkin Publishing Group, Inc., 1981), 92-97.
13. Ezra Jack Keats, *The Trip* (New York: Greenwillow Books, 1978); Aliki, *We Are Best Friends* (New York: Greenwillow Books, 1982).
14. Miriam Cohen, *Will I Have a Friend?* (New York: Macmillan, 1967).
15. Paul Henry Mussen and Nancy Eisenberg-Berg, *Roots of Caring, Sharing and Helping: The Development of Prosocial Behavior in Children* (San Francisco: W. H. Freeman and Company, 1977).

Chapter 6: *What Has Celebration to Do with Peace?*
1. Mary Alban Bouchard, C. S. F., "Celebration and World Order: Invitation for a Bimillennium Celebration of Life," *Whole Earth Papers*, no. 15, 2.
2. Jack W. Lundin, *Celebrations for Special Days and Occasions* (New York: Harper & Row, 1971), 3-5.
3. M. Melanie Svoboda, "Best Gifts Anyone Can Afford," WMSC *Voice*, December 1984, 6, 7.
4. Grady Nutt, *Family Time: A Revolutionary Old Idea* (Des Plains, Ill.: Family Time Committee of the Million Dollar Round Table, 1977), 58.
5. Marlene Kropf, Bertha Fast Harder, Linea Geiser, *Upon These Doorposts* (Nappanee, Ind.: Evangel Press; Newton, Kans.: Faith and Life Press; Scottdale, Pa.: Mennonite Publishing House), 55.
6. Katherine Royer, "Easter Day," *Nursery Songbook* (Scottdale, Pa.: Herald Press, 1957), 36.
7. Gerald G. Jampolsky, et al., editors, *Children As Teachers of Peace* (Millbrae, Calif.: Celestial Arts, 1982), 41.
8. Janice May Udry, *A Tree Is Nice* (New York: Harper and Bros., 1956).
9. Jampolsky, 41.
10. Gene Knudsen-Hoffman, US-USSR Reconciliation Program, "Seeds of Hope" (Nyack, N.Y.: Fellowship of Reconciliation); used by permission.
11. Milo Shannon-Thornberry, *The Alternate Celebrations Catalogue* (New York: The Pilgrim Press, 1982), 70.
12. Barbara Rody Cataldo, "Readers Say," *Gospel Herald*, November 6, 1984, 784.
13. Janet Martin, "Readers Say," *Gospel Herald*, November 13, 1984, 800.
14. Leona Weaver Schmucker, "Readers Say," *Gospel Herald*, November 13, 1984, 800.
15. Marcia Brown, *Stone Soup* (New York: Scribner, 1947).
16. Family Mission Thanks-Giving (Elkhart, Ind.: Mennonite Board of Missions).
17. Placemat printed by Franciscan Renewal Center.
18. Royer, 18.
19. Tomie de Paola, *The Christmas Pageant* (Minneapolis, Minn.: Winston Press, 1978).
20. Daniel Hertzler, "Editorial," *Gospel Herald*, July 17, 1984, 512.
21. Jampolsky, 48.

Chapter 7: *How Can Children Develop Awareness of Their Global Family?*
1. J. Lorne Peachey, *How to Teach Peace to Children* (Scottdale, Pa.: Herald Press, 1981), 9.
2. Peachey, 21.
3. Ron Maris, *Is Anyone Home?* (New York: Greenwillow Books, 1985); Judith Caseley, *Grandpa's Garden Lunch* (New York: Scholastic, 1990); Peter Seymour, *What Time Is Grandma Coming?* (Los Angeles: Price Stern Sloan, Inc., 1984); Nancy White Carlstrom, *Grandpappy* (Boston: Little, Brown and Company, 1990); Bill and Kathy Horlacher, *I'm Glad I'm Your Grandma* (Cincinnati, Ohio: Standard Publishing Co., 1987); Ruth Hooker, *At Grandma and Grandpa's House* (Niles, Ill.: Albert Whitman and Co., 1986); Tomie de Paola, *Now One Foot, Now the Other* (New York: G. P. Putnam's Sons, 1981).
4. Katherine Royer, *Nursery Stories of Jesus* (Scottdale, Pa.: Herald Press, 1957), 13.
5. Peachey, 18.
6. Mennoscope, *Gospel Herald*, August 26, 1986, 584.
7. Barbara Claassen Smucker, *Henry's Red Sea* (Scottdale, Pa.: Herald Press, 1955).
8. Letter, June Thomsen, June 2, 1985, Goshen College, Instructional Materials Center, Peace File.
9. Edith Baer, *This Is the Way We Go to School* (New York: Scholastic, 1990); Mitsumasa Anno, et al., *All in a Day* (New York: Philomel Books, 1986); Marilyn Singer,

Nine O'Clock Lullaby (New York: Harper Collins Publishers, 1991); Ann Morris, *Bread, Bread, Bread* (New York: Lothrop, Lee and Shepard Books, 1989); *Hats, Hats, Hats* (New York: Scholastic, Inc., 1989); *Loving* (New York: Lothrop, Lee and Shepard Books, 1990).
10. Peachey, 17.
11. " 'Peace' in Many Languages" (Nyack, N.Y.: Fellowship of Reconciliation); used by permission.
12. Family Mission Thanks-Giving (Elkhart, Ind.: Mennonite Board of Missions).
13. James A. Parker, "Staff Development: Multicultural Education," *Dimensions*, July 1982, 100.

Chapter 8: *How Can We Help Children Respond to Injustice?*
1. "Hunger: The Daily Disaster," *Christianity Today*, Nov. 19, 1990, 49.
2. Patricia Sprinkle, *Hunger: Understanding the Crisis Through Games, Dramas, and Songs* (Atlanta: John Knox Press, 1980), 136.
3. Pat Hutchins, *Rosie's Walk* (New York: Collier Books, 1971).
4. James and Kathleen McGinnis, *Parenting for Peace and Justice* (Maryknoll, N.Y.: Orbis Books, 1990), 65.
5. McGinnis, 86-90.
6. Ben Logan and Kate Moody, ed., *Television Awareness Training: The Viewer's Guide for Family and Community* (Nashville: Abingdon, 1980).
7. Peggy Ruth Cole, "Children, Teachers and the Assassination Attempt," *Childhood Education*, Sept.-Oct. 1981, 33-34.
8. Barbara Claassen Smucker, *Amish Adventure* (Scottdale, Pa.: Herald Press, 1983).
9. Rabindranath Tagore, *Collected Poems and Plays of Rabindranath Tagore* (London: MacMillan Co., Ltd., 1958), 296.
10. Geraldine Gross Harder, "How Children Catch the Faith," *Builder*, Feb. 1980, 15-16.
11. William Armstrong, *Sounder* (New York: Harper & Row, 1960); Elizabeth Yates, *Amos Fortune, Free Man* (New York: Aladdin Books, 1950).
12. Ella Kaiser Carruth, *The Story of Mary McLeod Bethune: She Wanted to Read* (Nashville: Abingdon Press, 1966).
13. R. Conrad Stein, *The Story of the Trail of Tears* (Chicago: Children's Press, 1985).
14. Anne Frank, *Anne Frank: The Diary of a Young Girl*, trans. by B. M. Mooyeart, rev. ed. (New York: Doubleday, 1967).
15. Eleanor B. Coerr, *Sadako and the Thousand Paper Cranes* (New York: Dell Publishing Company, 1979).
16. Pauline Yoder, *Living in Peace*, filmstrip available from Mennonite Central Committee, Box 500, Akron, PA 17501, or Women's Missionary and Service Commission, Box 1245, Elkhart, Ind. 46515-1245.
17. Barbara Claassen Smucker, *Days of Terror* (Scottdale, Pa.: Herald Press, 1979); Elizabeth Hershberger Bauman, *Coals of Fire* (Scottdale, Pa.: Herald Press, 1954).
18. Aliki, *The Story of Johnny Appleseed* (Englewood Cliffs, N.J.: Prentice-Hall, 1963); *The Story of William Penn* (Englewood Cliffs, N.J.: Prentice-Hall, 1964); *A Weed Is a Flower: The Life of George Washington Carver* (Englewood Cliffs, N.J.: Prentice-Hall, 1965).
19. Elizabeth George Speare, *The Bronze Bow* (Boston: Houghton, Mifflin, 1961).
20. Clare Huchet Bishop, *Twenty and Ten* (New York: Viking, 1952).

Chapter 9: *What About the Future for Children?*
1. Lee Lionni, *The Alphabet Tree* (New York: Pantheon, 1968).
2. Editorials and Opinions, *The Elkhart Truth*, December 22, 1978, 4; used by permission.
3. Danny Collum, "Theatrical Aftermath: Two Depictions of Nuclear War," *Sojourners*, January 1984, 39.
4. Laura Ingalls Wilder, *Little House Books*, 9 vols. (New York: Harper & Row, 1973).

5. Peter Spier, *People* (Garden City, N.Y.: Doubleday and Company, Inc., 1980).

6. Eleanor B. Coerr, *Sadako and the Thousand Paper Cranes* (New York: Dell Publishing Co., Inc., 1979).

7. G.C.M., *Highlights for Children*, 2300 West Fifth Ave., P.O. Box 269, Columbus, Ohio 432171-4002.

8. Dr. Seuss, *How the Grinch Stole Christmas* (New York: Random, 1957); *Sneetches and Other Stories* (New York: Random, 1961); *Horton Hatches the Egg* (New York: Random, 1940).

9. Wanda Gag, *Millions of Cats* (New York: Coward-McCann, Inc., 1928).

10. Kate Cloud, et al., *Watermelons Not War!* (Philadelphia: New Society Publishers, 1984), 117.

11. Cecil Frances Alexander, ill. by Leo Politi, *All Things Bright and Beautiful* (New York: Charles Scribners Sons, 1962).

12. Colin Thiele, *Storm Boy* (New York: Harper & Row, 1963).

13. Carolyn S. Diener, et al., *Energy* (Atlanta: Humanics Limited, 1984).

14. August Rische, "For God So Loved Us," in *Hymnal: A Worship Book* (Scottdale, Pa.: Mennonite Publishing House, et al., 1992), 167.

15. Katherine Royer, "God's Home in Heaven," in *My Book About God's Gifts* (Scottdale, Pa.: Herald Press, 1948), 32.

16. Dr. Seuss, *Sneetches and Other Stories*. (New York: Random, 1961); Cornelia Lehn, *Peace Be with You* (Newton, Kans.: Faith and Life, 1981); Gen. 25-33.

17. Andrew Fluegelman, *New Games Book* (Garden City, N.Y.: Dolphin, 1976).

The Editor

In her Mennonite family and church community near Archbold, Ohio, Kathryn Aschliman early experienced the ways of peace and various responses to the fears and pressures of war. A few years after World War II, she visited Europe with a group from Mennonite and affiliated colleges and observed the scars of war. In Leubeck, Germany, she worked with French, German, Danish, and American volunteers rebuilding refugee homes destroyed in the war.

During vacations, Aschliman taught summer Bible school in rural Ohio, in an economically deprived area near Toledo, in the Ozark Mountains of Arkansas, and in London, England. She also volunteered to work with migrants in mid-New York State and with youth groups on the Pacific Coast and in other Western states.

In addition to this firsthand experience with people of varying backgrounds, Aschliman learned much from church leaders, guest lecturers, and Goshen (Ind.) College professors. Through implicit and explicit teaching, Dr. Mary Royer, one of her major professors in the education department, inspired students to share the gospel of peace, as illustrated by the vignettes in this book submitted by her former students.

After graduating from Goshen College, Aschliman wrote primary curriculum materials for the Mennonite Publishing House. She completed a master's degree in religious education at Goshen Biblical Seminary. Her master's program in education at Bank Street College of Education in New York City emphasized the strategic importance of early learnings. Her doctoral program at The Union Institute (Cincinnati) involved field studies of young children and their families in ten countries of North, Central, and South America; Europe, including Poland; and the former USSR.

Aschliman taught in Ohio and Indiana public schools and at Bethel Day Nursery in a Chicago housing project area on the near west side. After seeing a multiplicity of human needs, she accepted an appointment as professor in the education department of Goshen College to help students respond to world needs. In the college classroom and the Goshen College Laboratory Kindergarten, she seeks to demonstrate principles of peaceful living which can be applied in family, school, and church settings around the globe.

Aschliman receives inspiration and encouragement from contacts with her three brothers' families, over eighty persons scattered across the continental United States, Puerto Rico, and Brazil. They are involved in parenting, teaching, assisting refugees and Native Americans, pastoring, farming, trucking, accounting, applying radiology, arranging flowers, and other business-related vocations.

When Aschliman participates in conferences, festivals, presentations, workshops, and interviews, she often uses peace resources from the Goshen College Instructional Materials Center. She considers *growing toward peace* a continuing challenge to share Christ's good news of power for day-to-day living and of hope for the future.

Aschliman is a member of the (Goshen) College Mennonite Church and of many associations that promote education, parenting, and peace teaching. She has published curriculum materials, chapters in books, and periodical articles.